"This book will be an excellent text for a class that addresses sustainability practices. The use of the product development pipeline for jeans is a great way to spotlight key sustainability concepts, and teach terminology and best practices for environmentally green processes and outcomes."

— *Carol J. Salusso, Associate Professor,*
Washington State University, USA

"The sustainability of chemicals and application technologies used to produce fashion garments has become a critical issue for brands and manufacturing industries. This has also started to become a concern at the end consumer level, and Denim, being the King of Fashion, is under scrutiny on eco-tox issues. Paulina Szmydke-Cacciapalle provides deep insight into this increasingly topical matter and describes in a very clear way the current challenges and options for a brighter blue denim."

— *Miguel Sanchez, Head Global Business Development,*
Denim & Casualwear, Archroma

MAKING JEANS GREEN

Consumers spend approximately $93 billion on denim products every year. This consumption comes at a great cost, with thousands of liters of fresh water, hazardous chemicals and energy contributing to just one pair of jeans, leaving the environment and the industry vulnerable to pollution and climate change.

Using facts, figures, case studies and anecdotes, this book investigates why the industry has been so slow to adopt green technologies and offers practical solutions to designers and fashion executives who want to switch to cleaner manufacturing, including those working in the "fast fashion" sector. It also offers advice to the eco-conscious consumer who wants to purchase denim more sustainably. Considering the full lifecycle of a pair of jeans from the cotton crop to disposal, it presents examples of how to go green at different stages.

This book will be of great interest to fashion students and researchers, as well as designers, fashion executives, policy-makers and anyone who comes into contact with the world of denim.

Paulina Szmydke-Cacciapalle is a Freelance Writer based in London, UK. She has gained extensive insight into the makings of fashion through her coverage at *WWD* (aka "the bible"), which serves senior fashion executives, designers, Wall Street analysts and the retail community as an independent and reliable source of information.

MAKING JEANS GREEN

Linking Sustainability, Business and Fashion

Paulina Szmydke-Cacciapalle

LONDON AND NEW YORK

First published 2018
by Routledge
2 Park Square, Milton Park, Abingdon, Oxon OX14 4RN

and by Routledge
711 Third Avenue, New York, NY 10017

Routledge is an imprint of the Taylor & Francis Group, an informa business

© 2018 Paulina Szmydke-Cacciapalle

British Library Cataloguing-in-Publication Data
A catalogue record for this book is available from the British Library

Library of Congress Cataloging-in-Publication Data
Names: Szmydke-Cacciapalle, Paulina, author.
Title: Making jeans green: linking sustainability, business and fashion / Paulina Szmydke-Cacciapalle.
Description: Abingdon, Oxon; New York, NY: Routledge, 2018. | Includes bibliographical references and index.
Identifiers: LCCN 2018003740 (print) | LCCN 2018018444 (ebook) | ISBN 9781351200554 (eBook) | ISBN 9780815391852 (hbk) | ISBN 9780815391876 (pbk) | ISBN 9781351200554 (ebk)
Subjects: LCSH: Denim. | Textile industry–Technological innovations. | Clothing trade–Technological innovations. | Textile industry–Environmental aspects. | Clothing trade–Environmental aspects. | Sustainable engineering.
Classification: LCC TT557 (ebook) | LCC TT557 .S98 2018 (print) | DDC 338.4/7687–dc23
LC record available at https://lccn.loc.gov/2018003740

ISBN: 978-0-8153-9185-2 (hbk)
ISBN: 978-0-8153-9187-6 (pbk)
ISBN: 978-1-351-20055-4 (ebk)

Typeset in Bembo
by Deanta Global Publishing Services, Chennai, India

www.makingjeansgreen.com

I would like to express my gratitude to all people of the Blue World who have so generously shared their experience, knowledge and expertise with me, making this book possible.

CONTENTS

FIGURES

TABLES

FOREWORD

Everybody loves denim. In fact, we love it so much, we spend $92.8 billion[1] on denim products every year. But our consumption comes at a cost. Thousands of liters of fresh water, hazardous chemicals and energy go into the conventional production of a pair of jeans, leaving not only the environment but also businesses vulnerable for the future.

As a fashion journalist, for years my job has been to scout new fashion and business trends. And while usually trends are a volatile affair, in recent years, one topic has emerged as a permanent fixture – and that's sustainability.

No major trade event goes without a seminar on the impact of textiles on the planet and who should pay for it. Each season, game-changing innovations in weaving, dyeing, finishing and recycling enter the scene, promising savings on energy, water and raw materials. And yet the gap between what's available in terms of technology and what actually ends up on the catwalks or the shop floor is somehow getting bigger.

Frustrated, I started to investigate.

A friend of mine, who is dealing with far more complex matters (he is a theoretical physicist), gave me a really great piece of advice once. He listened very attentively to some trivial problem I was boring him with, and he said: "You know, I used to be just like you, asking, 'why this, why that?' all the time, until a professor sat me down and said 'David, don't ask why, ask how.'"

I find this piece of advice very useful because it applies to literally anything, from black holes to the complexity of supply chains, and very often it not only shows the problem, but also suggests a solution. When I asked why the industry was not moving faster towards a sustainable business model, the most popular answer was: "Because it costs more." When I asked how much more, it turned out in some cases it was literally a matter of cents. And it became clear very quickly that the poor math was further complicated by a lack of vision, an unwillingness to do things differently and, finally, the designers' own ignorance of the matter.

Sustainability, of course, means a lot of different things to a lot of different people. But for textiles, it's a fairly simple equation: a fabric needs resources, and these resources are getting scarce. Every year, the economy depends on $72 trillion worth of "free goods,"[2] which are not included in financial statements and are therefore poorly managed. Meanwhile, the environmental impact of doing business amounts to $4.7 trillion a year,[3] a bill that is footed by the economy.

In other words, if the fashion industry wants to stay in business, it cannot afford *not* to be sustainable. New analyst studies show sustainability can pay for itself – and more. For it to work, however, smart design is needed, as most fashion product – its content as well as manufacturing style – is outdated, hailing from an era in which resources were believed to be infinite.

Denim is one of the most popular and resource-thirsty fabrics in the world, yet it's also one of the most innovative ones; its producers have made game-changing advancements in recent years that could serve the rest of the industry. Meanwhile, evidence reveals how much people care about their jeans, which makes this the perfect starting point for addressing issues of sustainability. Nobody gives a jack about a T-shirt; denim, on the other hand, is charged with emotions. Anthropologists are certain: Everybody loves denim. Since jeans first appeared some 150 years ago, they have managed to transcend age, gender and cultural lines; they have withstood every fashion fad and turned into coveted collector's items, fetching up to $46,532 at auctions.[4] It seems denim is the perfect starting point for green talk, because it speaks a language everybody understands, and it is time to talk.

The global fashion industry is at a crossroads. Although it's hard to put a date on it, it is looking at a radically different and uncertain future. By 2025, the global population is expected to reach 8.1 billion people. This means more need for food, water, clothing and energy. By 2030, according to the World Economic Forum, global water demand is projected to exceed sustainable supply by 40 percent. No wonder investment banks are betting their money on water. Water is the new oil.

Meanwhile, it takes up to 11,000 liters[5] to produce a pair of jeans when following conventional methods. Safe to say, when push comes to shove, this precious resource is unlikely to go into fixing indigo or bleaching denim to satisfy the fashion folk.

The apparel industry is aware of these challenges, yet it is divided in its approach. While some brands and retailers have invested and are continuously investing millions into improving their practices by looking to new technologies, switching to green fibers and updating their supply chains, others are not. For denim, this is true on all levels of the price spectrum.

For fashion, 2020 is going to be a crucial date. For one, those brands that have declared their sustainability goals for that year will be held accountable by the public. It is also the year when Greenpeace is slated to publish its next Detox report, the first of which (done in 2011) was considered a wake-up call for the industry, triggering an ongoing movement towards greener manufacturing.

The goal of the book is thus twofold:

First, to show the myriad of green alternatives available on the market, along with the creative and business potential it bears for the brands. This will be done via examples from the industry encouraging brand executives and designers to weigh short-term margin losses against long-term gains and to get busy with new cuts, colors and patterns.

Second, to give consumers the tools to make educated choices when shopping for denim and pressuring brands into action. Companies often fail to reveal the composition of their jeans in general, but also fail to label their green denim accordingly. Yet with a new guard of customers – those much-coveted Millennials – waiting in the starting blocks, it is transparency that will decide a brand's future survival. The truth is, we have more brands than we need, and they produce more than they can sell. It is unlikely, then, that those practicing "business as usual" will last. Change is coming.

Notes

1 *Euromonitor International*, 2016.
2 Fellow, Avery. Environmental Cost of Business Estimated at $4.7T Annually. *Bloomberg*, April 17, 2013.
3 Kering. *Environmental Profit & Loss*. Methodology & 2013 Group Results.
4 Levi's Strauss & Co. *The 501® Jean: Stories of an Original | Full Documentary*. Directed by Harry Israelson. 2016. https://www.youtube.com/watch?v=6R9cAoCyatA
5 National Geographic. *Water Special Issue*. April 2010.

1

HISTORY

Blue blood

The early modern humans, commonly known as the Cro-Magnons, must have been a stunning sight. They had both big brains and big muscles, which allowed them to adapt quickly to their environment and be fierce in combat. They went with spears after mammoths and significantly brought down the number of cave bears, with whom they competed for shelter.[1] They were astute observers of nature, probably knowing more about the social behaviors of animals than any biologist today.[2] And they were artistically inclined, too, as the magnificent artwork they have left behind attests.

Yet, despite all their prowess, they must have experienced at least some level of frustration.

Examining the Stone Age paintings of Lascaux, or the "Sistine Chapel of Prehistoric Art," as the cave in the southwest of France is known, one can't help but marvel at the wide range of colors the Europeans of the Upper Paleolithic had at their disposal. The paintings show rich reds, browns and yellows. There are shades of black, with even a hint of mauve,[3] considered exceptional by researchers – yet, surprisingly, no blue.[4] The prehistoric artists must have scratched their heads over this. Why not blue? Blue, after all, is everywhere – it's the color of the sky and is reflected by water; it shimmers off the backs of beetles and adorns the feathers of blue jays, who draw their name from the elusive hue.

What the Cro-Magnon couldn't have known is that in all these instances blue is a product of optical effects rather than dyes or pigments. These early artists were familiar with powdered metallic oxides from iron and manganese, which delivered all sorts of warm hues, including reds and browns, but for a long time, it turns out, the key to a steadfast blue was hidden in a group of indigo-bearing plants, the most common of which are the *Indigofera tinctoria*, home in the tropics and subtropics, and the *Isatis tinctoria*, or woad, which ironically blooms in yellow and wouldn't be discovered until much later.

Although it is unclear when woad conquered Europe exactly, it reigned as a light-fast blue dyestuff well into the Renaissance and was subject to many myths and rumors. Related to the common cabbage, all that was needed to make it turn blue was a bunch of its spinach-shaped leaves, some water and ammonia, probably in the form of stale urine, rounded off by a pinch of magic. Or, as we know today: a clever chemical reaction, which due to its unpredictable nature is to this day responsible for the dye's rebel reputation in the denim world. Indigo is insoluble in water and must first undergo a reduction, which turns the pigments into a soluble, white form. Only upon exposure to air, within a few moments, the dye gradually turns blue.

British researchers would later discover that it is a group of bacteria that actually reduce the indigo (see Chapter 4). Just imagine how awesome and mystical this color-shift must have looked to humans of the Iron Age, such as the Ancient Britons, who practiced this "magic" extensively. Caesar described how horrified the Roman legions were by the Celtic tribes, which daubed themselves in woad during battle.[5] And they not only painted their bodies blue to scare or confuse their opponents, but also let the woad get under their skin via a volley of flashy tattoos, proof of their courage and a DIY first-aid kit at that. Woad has been shown to have antibacterial properties and, much like urine, can be used to staunch bleeding. "To wear it into battle would be like wearing antiseptic […] it is not surprising that woad was thought to render the wearer invincible by magic,"[6] writes British archaeologist Gilly Carr.

But above all, being blue was seen as an act of rebellion. The body painting and tattooing functioned as "an expression of native identity and resistance to a Roman mode of appearance,"[7] says Carr. At a time when the Romans invaded their lands and imposed their way of life on the Britons, the latter were ostentatiously looking for "a means of distinguishing between 'us' and 'them.'"[8]

Marlon Brando and Jimmy Dean, it appears, were not the first bad boys dressed in blue.

From the Aztecs to the Vikings and from the Touaregs to the Samurai, regardless of whether obtained from woad or *Indigofera*, blue has been a powerful player the world over. It was used for political purposes and figured as a must-have ingredient in tribal rituals. Among the Franks, the blue robe was the mark of a free man, and the plant even served as a currency.[9] In India, indigo was closely associated with "the capricious god Krishna."[10] The Islamic world put it on par with black magic, while Nordic mythology saw in indigo the goddess of death. And while the West had the Blues expressing the dye's moody nature through music, cultures as distant as those of West Africa and Indonesia used indigo-dyed cloth in mourning rituals. Unsurprisingly, the color's alchemical properties were akin to "the spiritually transforming rites of passage of life itself,"[11] which is perhaps why in some parts of the world only natural dyes are accepted for ceremonial textiles. Synthetic substitutes, though readily available, are still a no-go.

The world over, indigo's oddity led to superstitious beliefs. Thought of as being "alive,"[12] in Indonesia, indigo was not to be disturbed, especially not by fertile women. If the process of fermentation went wrong, they would be blamed for having caused the vat's "death." Japanese dyers, meanwhile, have expressed their affection for the dye in the term "ai," which can mean either indigo or love, though spelled with different characters. Preparing the dye was equal to child nurturing.[13]

Similarly, indigo's trade history was adventurous and filled with passion.

Though *Indigofera* and woad are chemically identical, their rivalry fueled centuries of contest. As British researcher Jenny Balfour-Paul accentuates in her stellar account of the dye's history: "The indigo versus woad battle was fierce and prolonged, in some places lasting well into the 18th century."[14] Balfour-Paul notes that although it is not known who first began to cultivate woad, "by the thirteenth century in western Europe the livelihoods of many farmers, merchants and dyers revolved around its production. Governments also gained greatly by imposing heavy taxes at every stage."[15] France, where woad was referred to as pastel or guède, became Europe's largest producer. The trade was so profitable, it gave rise to what Dominique Cardon called the "woad millionaires."[16] Their chic townhouses still adorn the historical centers of cities such as Toulouse in France's Languedoc region, a former woad hub. One such "hotel particulier," which still stands today, belonged to the merchant Jean de Bernuy. He was "so credit-worthy," says Balfour-Paul, "he could stand as the main guarantor of the sum required for the ransom for King Francis I after his capture by Charles V of Spain"[17] following the battle of Pavia in 1525. Across the border in Germany, the "Waidherrn," or "gentlemen of woad," constructed their grand mansions in Thuringia, where at peak times the woad trade accounted for one-third of the region's income, most notably in Erfurt.[18]

In the early Middle Ages Charlemagne issued a decree ordering "every one of his manor estates [to] grow a certain minimum area of woad […] to ensure self-sufficiency."[19] By the mid-1580s in England, "vital grain supplies were threatened by the craze for woad growing – said to be six times more profitable – which had to be restricted by government license."[20] Queen Elizabeth I eventually gave in to the demands of her people and lifted the restriction in 1601, but "on condition that no woad processing would take place close enough to her palaces to offend the royal nose."[21] Woad was also the prime money maker of abbeys, including Glastonbury, where rock stars and their fans gather today sporting their blue jeans. It is believed the town derived its name from Latin "glastum," which translates as woad.[22]

And yet the locally grown woad was not nearly enough to quench the thirst of Europe's flourishing textile industry, particularly in Italy, which was among the early adopters of oriental indigo, imported from the East. Worth twice as much as other luxury goods, the exotic dyestuff was in fact so valuable it was often handed down as property in wills.[23]

Two historical events put the indigo trade on the global map: Vasco da Gama's circumnavigation of the Cape of Good Hope in 1498 and the conquest of America following Christopher Columbus' arrival in 1492. It meant on the one hand that Asian goods could be imported freely, avoiding the heavy taxation imposed by Asian rulers, while on the other hand, more land was available for the cultivation of both local and imported indigo plants.

Naturally, the European woad millionaires would not go down without a fight. Protectionist edicts[24] were issued in France, Germany and Britain, banning the "devil's dye" from the tropics, which was considered "injurious" and "deceitful." And even though, occasionally, using exotic indigo was punishable by death, as ruled by the French king in the early 17th century, *Indigofera* began to outweigh European woad, first arriving from the East (i.e. India), then from the middle of the 17th century from indigo plantations in the New World (i.e. West Indies and Americas). Gradually, European expert dyers realized that more indigo could be extracted from the tropical and subtropical species than woad, and that *Indigofera* was better suited for cellulose fiber such as cotton and flax, whereas woad was more compatible with woolen fibers.[25]

Between 1580 and 1640, "drogas" or spices, which included indigo, made up more than one-fifth of any Portuguese ship's cargo leaving the West Indies. The Dutch were equally industrious. It is reported that at one point in 1631, seven Dutch ships carried between them 333,545 pounds of indigo, worth some five tons of gold.[26]

The trade, however, came at a significant human cost. As E. De-Latour noted: "Not a chest of indigo reached England without being stained with human blood."[27]

Kings would literally kill for it.

In the New World, this meant the slave trade was flourishing. Laborers were needed – four for every five acres of indigo, to be exact. In South Carolina, where indigo almost singlehandedly financed Georgetown, a planter could gruesomely exchange indigo "pound for pound of negro weighed naked."[28]

On the dawn of the French Revolution in 1789, the colonial powers entertained some 3,150 indigo slave plantations in Saint-Domingue (now Haiti), "producing hundreds of tons of dyestuff annually."[29]

In 1791, the slaves fought back, igniting what became the Haitian Revolution, one of history's largest slave uprisings.

Meanwhile in India, the unjust conditions, in which local peasants were forced to cultivate indigo by corrupt European planters, caught the attention of Mahatma Gandhi, who launched an independent inquiry into the exploitations of peasants in Bihar, which, along with Bengal, was the world's main source of indigo in the late 19th century. "Bengal alone exported a staggering 7,650,00 pounds – over 3,500 tons – of indigo (valued at six shillings a pound)" in 1815.[30]

When ordered to leave the area, Gandhi refused to comply and was put on trial. Balfour-Paul writes:

> However, his defiant yet respectful stand caused the case to be withdrawn. His support of the indigo peasants' cause, which in many ways echoed the sympathetic pleas of the more enlightened British administrators and missionaries in Calcutta 1860, was Gandhi's first act of peaceful civil disobedience on Indian soil and made him a national hero.[31]

But eventually, it was science that brought an end to the struggle between European woad and exotic indigo. Today, around 66,000 tons of the dye are produced every year, mainly for the jeans market, though most of it is synthetic, following the discovery of indigo's chemical structure by German chemist Adolf von Baeyer in 1865. Together with BASF (Badische Anilin- und Sodafabrik), in 1897, Von Baeyer brought the first synthetic indigo product, called "Indigo Pure," to the market. It was an expensive and laborious undertaking. The cost of research stood at 18 million gold marks, "more than the capital value of the company at the time."[32]

As Cardon notes:

> The invention meant that for the first time millions of people around the world could wear clothes of a beautiful and colourfast blue, the supply of which could have barely been met by the combined harvests of all the indigo plants of the planet.[33]

Put in figures:

> In 1896, just one year before the discovery of the industrial method for synthesizing indigo, 1,683,328 hectares in India alone were given over to the cultivation of *Indigofera* plantations; 60 years later, in 1956, only 4,289 remained. In 1897, Germany imported annually 1,408,400 kg of natural indigo; in 1904, it was exporting 8,730,000 kg of synthetic indigo.[34]

One thing, however, remains the same. To this day, the desire for the elusive hue is echoed in such terms as "royal blue"; its magical powers are still a firm belief in many cultures the world over.

How the blue got into denim is a bit of a mystery in itself. Recent studies suggest that humans in Latin America were dyeing cotton with indigo as early as 6,000 years ago – that's long before the pyramids were built. An example of a much-faded pair of blue jeans was excavated in northern Peru in 2016, while an indigo-dyed blue wig found on an Inca mummy gave proof: blue has always been a matter of style.

Traditionally, denim is not just defined by color but its distinctive weaving technique – a 3×1 construction, alternating indigo-dyed warp with undyed weft yarn. Both the cities of Nîmes (France) and Genoa (Italy) claim to have invented it, finding support in semantics: "Serge de Nîmes," a woad-dyed twill which was first made of wool, then mixed with cotton, hemp and even silk, became "de-nim," while "Gênes" [ʒɛn], French for Genoa, where a blue weave with a white thread was worn by sailors, lent its name to "jeans." Recent discoveries by Paris-based gallerist Maurizo Canesso and a prolific curator at the Kunsthistorisches Museum in Vienna give Genoa the advantage.[35] It appears an anonymous Italian painter dubbed "The Master of the Blue Jeans" depicted denim as the fabric of choice for the poor (see Figure 1.1). Cue street beggars, barbers, seamstresses sporting the cloth. This would suggest that denim had become a symbol of the working class long before two European immigrants, the tailor Jacob Davis and the dry goods wholesaler Levi Strauss, coined the 5-pocket jeans for the tough miners of California's 19th century Gold Rush, concocting between them the first modern pair of jeans as we know it.

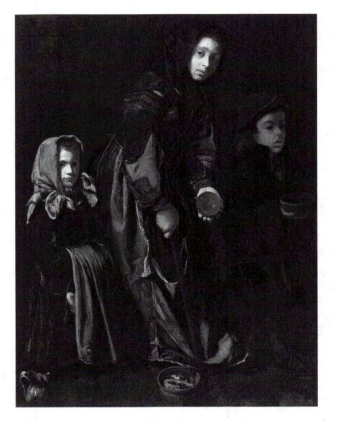

FIGURE 1.1   The Master of the Blue Jeans: *Woman Begging with Two Children*
Source: Paris, Galerie Canesso (@Galerie Canesso, Paris)

Their story kicks off with literally a "riveting tale."[36] "Jacob Davis had a difficult customer," writes Paul Trynka.

> The woman lived close to his tiny tailor's shop in Reno, Nevada, and was in search of a pair of pants for her husband. A woodcutter apparently bloated with dropsy, he was too big for regular pants, and without pants he couldn't work. It was December 1870; she needed those pants by January, when he'd be out cutting wood again. And those pants needed to be strong – workmen's trousers wore out quickly.

With a $3 advance in his pocket from the woodcutter's wife, Davis took a sturdy white cotton duck fabric, which he had purchased from his supplier in San Francisco – Mr. Strauss – and went to work.

> Jacob stitched the pants when his eyes alighted on a pile of rivets that he used for attaching straps to the horse blankets he supplied to a local blacksmith.

"The rivets were lying on the table," he remembered a couple of years later. "The thought struck me to fasten the pockets with those rivets." He hammered the rivets into the corners of the pockets, reckoning they would help the woodcutter's pants hold out that bit longer. "I did not make a big thing of it. I sold those pants and never thought of it for a time."

News of his invention spread quickly. Business was booming – despite the "hefty premium" that came with the trousers for extra durability. Copycats were menacingly close on his heels and so in order to secure the ingenuity of his invention, Davis knew he needed to apply for a patent. But the $68 required for the paperwork were too much for a humble tailor to bear, and so he asked Strauss to pitch in, offering him a 50–50 split on the profits. One of the two pairs he sent him as an example was crafted from white cotton duck; the other was blue, cut from a denim fabric woven at the Amoskeag factory in New Hampshire, the largest textile producer in the US at that time, which Strauss stocked in his shop.

The rest, as they say, is history.

Since it first entered the scene, denim has crossed over class, cultural and political lines, becoming the most *meaning-full* textile in the industry: Following the woodcutter's example, Levi's waist overalls, as the first modern jeans were called, were adopted by gold miners, who spent their days working on their hands and knees surrounded by dust, rocks and mud. They not only appreciated a durable piece of clothing, but once they had no more use for them, they also repurposed their jeans inside the mines. As denim hunter Russ Miller, who dives regularly into abandoned mines to look for hidden treasures, explains: "We found them wrapped around steam pipes and we even think they stemmed dynamite holes with denim also."[37] Lynn Downey, Levi's' former in-house historian, who can tell a pants' previous life just by looking at it, confirms that "occasionally, old pairs of jeans that had outlived their usefulness were stuffed into crevices to stop rockslides or used as ballast when dynamite was needed to open new veins of ore."[38]

These historical examples testify to denim's exceptional durability and its potential for upcycling.

But Levi's needed a new sales pitch. To tickle the mainstream consumer's senses, the brand tapped into the dream and myth of the prairie cowboy. Says Downey:

> Every country romanticizes some part of its history and America has perhaps the most mythic past of all: the period personified by the cowboy, roaming on his horse in the endless hills and plains of the American West. What endured from this symbolic image is the perceived freedom and individuality embodied in the lovely figure of the cowpuncher.[39]

No wonder city slickers from the East wanted a piece of that poetic flair. They found it at the "Dude Ranch," which described a working ranch turned popular holiday destination for Easterners between the 1930s and the 1950s. It was the ideal opportunity for Levi's to launch a collection fitting the occasion. The brand provided the perfect attire, made of satin or cotton shirts, jackets and riding pants in gabardine and the waist overalls, their bestseller.

Downey observes:

> These "dudes" slipped into Levi's overalls and cowboy shirts to experience a week or two as an authentic westerner. Their new clothing and a rusty "howdy, partner" were the souvenir brought back to the East to impress their friends, thus giving Levi's overalls their first national exposure.[40]

Trynka notes it was "the perfect product placement for Levi's" and "signaled the company's unconscious, telepathic ability of being at the center of every new social trend."[41]

The success of the Dude Ranch, which also targeted women, led to the introduction of the first "Lady Levi's" in 1938 – "designed with roomy hips and tapering trousers yet with all the rivets"[42] – heralding a new era of casual dressing and providing a topic of conversation.

The first major fashion publication to endorse blue jeans was American *Vogue*, which ran a piece in its May 15, 1935 issue reading: "True Western chic was invented by cowboys."[43] The caption was accompanied by a drawing of two chic ladies with perfectly coiffed hair, cuffed jeans cinched tightly in the waist, cowboy hats and blouses with pretty scarves. *Vogue's* recommendation:

> Your uniform for a dude ranch or a ranch near Reno is simple-but-severe blue jeans or Levis, turned up at the bottom once, laundered before wearing (to eliminate stiffness), cut straight and tight fitting, worn low on the hips, in the manner of your favorite dude wrangler. With these jeans go a simply tailored flannel or plaid cotton shirt or possibly a Brooks sweater; a plain silk kerchief knotted loosely; a studded leather belt; high-heeled Western boots; a Stetson hat; and a great air of bravado.

All the while Hollywood worked its magic hand. Stars and starlets, including the suave Clark Gable, the eternally seductive Marilyn Monroe, Elvis Presley and Paul Newman, wore their blue jeans on- as well as off-screen, feeding into the growing frenzy for the blue cloth. "Rebel Without a Cause" James Dean (in Lee 101) and Marlon Brando, alias "The Wild One" (in Levi's 501) turned jeans into an item with attitude.

By then Levi's' teenage customers had started calling the waist overalls "jeans." Levi's went with the flow and in 1960 adopted the term in its catalogues as well as advertising.

Denim's increasingly irreverent flair had a flip side too. It was considered a bad influence, which prompted Levi's to market it as "right for school," while Lee suggested camping with the family to take the edge off the image.

In the Sixties, the hippies got hold of it, making it once more political. It was hard to not spot anyone wearing blue in Woodstock. As Downey remembers,

The decade turned the uniform of the working class into a political and fashion statement. Your Levi's jeans said to the world that you belonged, that you were part of the counterculture revolution, part of the Age of Aquarius, one of the Woodstock generation. Young people in jeans spoke a universal shorthand that allowed them to fit in on college campuses all over America, on Haight-Ashbury, in Greenwich Village. In the words of Elton John, you were a "Blue Jean Baby." You wore jeans everywhere because you had arrived.[44]

When a decade later designer jeans emerged, the face of denim would change forever, pushing the old workwear classic into the fashion realm. Jeans suddenly had glamor. Calvin Klein took the lead in 1976, creating what is globally referred to as America's first pair of "celebrity designer jeans." They were "an immediate flop,"[45] writes Lisa Marsh. Designed in-house in the sample room and priced at $50, they were considered too expensive. Also, "customers complained that they didn't fit."[46] In fact, they were so trashy that when Klein launched them at a fashion show at Bloomingdale's, the Calvin Klein label on the back pocket started coming off as the model was strutting down the runway.

Of course, Klein is no quitter. A year later he gave it another go. As James Sullivan writes:

> It was a godforsaken time. The 1970s had little in the way of good news. Inflation, corruption, crime, poverty, nuclear meltdowns, and international terrorism were relentless worries. Faced with such dour circumstances, ordinary citizens did the only rational thing – they went dancing.[47]

Klein was no exception. One night at New York's Studio 54 he was approached with a business offer he could not refuse: $1 million cash upfront for a new denim collection, plus another million each year for the duration of the contract, with a royalty rate of $1 per pair of jeans sold, and with a cost-of-living increase built into the contract. In exchange, he would license his name to Puritan Fashions, who would manufacture the jeans.[48]

This time, the designer looked to the classic 501 for inspiration. "He cut them apart and studied them. He lowered the rise, then trained his gaze on the posterior, accentuating and drawing attention to it."[49] The resulting jeans were made in Puritan's Texas plants, cost $7.50 each to produce, and retailed for $35 in 1978. In only a week, 200,000 pairs were sold, only coming in number two to Gloria Vanderbilt, who had introduced her own line with the Murjani Group after Jackie Onassis, the former US First Lady, refused to put her name on it.

When Klein suggested he come down to Saks Fifth Avenue to witness the shopping frenzy, an executive advised against it. "They'll tear your clothes off," he said. "It'll be like Elvis showing up."[50]

Fashion being the eternal imitation game, despite initial mockery, other designers soon followed suit.

Meanwhile, on the other side of the pond, jeans became synonymous with freedom. Brought over by American G.I.s, they quickly spread across the continent and behind the Iron Curtain. In the former Soviet Union, where jeans were vilified by the Communist regime, wearing a pair could get you fired; selling them meant serious jail time. In one particularly dramatic instance, two young black marketers named Ian Rokotov and Vladislav Faibishenko[51] were sentenced to death by shooting for dealing with foreign currency and western clothing, including stockings and supposedly jeans,[52] which they had discovered their western counterparts wearing at the 1957 World Youth Festival, held in Moscow in 1957. The NY-based denim brand Rokotoff-F., which markets itself as "jeans with an attitude," pays homage to the young victims. No wonder, then, when the first Levi's store opened in Moscow in 1989, it sold out its entire inventory on the first day.[53]

In Western Europe, denim nurtured an aesthetic and a life of its own. "From the beginning there was a desire to make jeans 'not like the Americans,'" notes jeans pioneer François Girbaud.[54] The Frenchman had always wanted to be a cowboy, so he started selling his jeans in 1964. He is credited with giving the five-pocket a new look through stonewashing, setting in motion what he himself described as "an ecological disaster." Girbaud played with new constructions, changed the placements of the pockets and pioneered the baggy jeans, which made him a star among the rap stars. "Commodity jeans didn't fit African-Americans – they were made for cowboys. Too tight, too straight, too traditional,"[55] he acknowledged. The rappers thanked him for it. As Mystikal put it in "Y'all Ain't Ready Yet": "Give a fuck about these raggly ass hoes. Grippin' my nuts as I strut in my baggy ass Girbauds." To Lauryn Hill of the Fugees, a guy with success in 1990s was "A Mister Three Piece Suit. Check the square roots, Girbauds and Timberland boots." And when Jadakiss was rapping opposite Puff Daddy and The Notorious B.I.G. that it was "all about the Benjamins," it was also about the Girbauds: "I'm with Mo' sippers, watched by gold diggers / Rocking Girbaud denims with gold zippers," he proudly proclaimed.

Still, asked about his "favorite denim creation," Girbaud replied: "Inventing the industrialization of fade-washed jeans and subsequently denouncing the mistakes through the use of chemical washing that we had made in all innocence at the beginning."[56]

Meanwhile, Girbaud's Italian counterpart, Adriano Goldschmied, dubbed "the Godfather of Denim," set up a think tank called "the Genius Group," made up of some the industry's most creative minds, such as Katherine Hamnett, who in the mid-1980s put the shredded jeans on the fashion map as a symbol of economic hardship. With his quest for novelty and creative energy, Goldschmied has driven the premium denim market like no other, having helped Diesel, Replay, Evisu, Citizens of Humanity and Gap's 1969 denim line off the ground. As the founder of Denimhunters, Thomas Stege Bojer, notes: "At a time when all denim was dark and raw, his black Labrador retriever had white legs from all of Goldschmied's experimenting with bleach in his back garden."[57] He came up with new treatments, new cuts and new construction, being an early supporter of knit denim, inspiring others. Throughout the 1990s, there was no shortage of ideas on European catwalks, and money was no object. Think Tom Ford's Pocahontas jeans for Gucci, which sold like hot cakes in 1999, despite their £2,000 price tag.[58] Versace launched its Jeans Couture line in 1991, becoming a leader in the top end of the women's market. Jean Paul Gaultier spiced up his jeans with laces and plastic, John Galliano mixed it with leather for Dior and Alexander McQueen, fashion's dark knight, imbued his "bumster" jeans with both sex appeal and rebellion, declaring it a legit fashion item alongside more classic staples. "I don't see the jeans as a diffusion range. They're designed in the same way as the main collection, if you're aware that you are making something cheap, you are never going to come up with the new 501."[59]

Throughout, denim has kept its rebellious air, whether as a trendsetter or a political partner. Today, it is billed as the most progressive and transparent fabric in the industry, heralding a new era of environmentally friendly manufacturing. And with the advent of ath-leisure and tech, its journey seems far from over.

Yesterday's pioneers are becoming today's reformers. To quote Goldschmied:

> Over my lifetime I've probably been responsible for many an ecological disaster, and the idea of someone actually dying as a result of some process – sandblasting, for example – used just to make a pair of jeans, well, the idea is terrible, horrible. It's an industry that has to clean up.[60]

Q&A WITH ADRIANO GOLDSCHMIED, DENIM PIONEER

Q: Where does your fascination with denim stem from?

A: Honestly, I don't even remember [laughs]. But I would say it was politically motivated, because in the 70s, there was a conflict of generations going on – denim represented the new generation, blue tie and blazer was the old guard. And then for me it turned into a love story that is still evolving. There are highs and lows, but mostly highs.

Q: Do you remember your first pair?

A: A Levi's 501, obviously. I was born in Trieste, which at that time was under the rule of the English and American Army. So when I was a kid, we had all these military and American products – from Coca Cola to jeans to chewing gum. It was our dream. I remember a sailor gave me a jean similar to the one you are wearing [a high-rise model with flared legs]. It was what the Navy used to wear, with four patch pockets.

Q: When you think back to the Seventies when denim took off as a category, what was the sentiment in the industry? Where did you think you were heading?

A: I personally had a clear vision – when I started in 1972 my goal was to bring denim to a higher level. I cannot forget when I was going around trying to sell jeans, and a store told me "we don't sell denim, because we don't do low-end products," and I remember how disappointed I was because I thought my denim was amazing [laughs]. But obviously that attitude has changed. When I see the last Dior collection, for me it's mission accomplished! I've been working very, very hard to make it happen.

Q: The industry's new vision for the future is to be sustainable. Where do you see the biggest obstacles on the road to clean denim?

A: In the complexity of the supply chain, because it already starts in the cotton field, and all these processes that follow are extremely complex. If one player does something wrong, you are already out of the game. So for instance if I grow the right cotton but dye it with the wrong technology, my product is not right. Also the coordination is very important. First of all, who is giving [the] authorization to write sustainable on a pair of jeans? And when I ask how sustainable is a product – do you have a number for me from 1 to 10? It has to be readable, like Trip Advisor. I want to see an online filter which allows me to type in a figure, say 4.5 – and below I don't even consider the product.

Q: Having seen it all, what do you think denim will look like in 50 years from now?

A: We are going to be on Mars at that time and I don't think we will wear a traditional 501. The speed of innovation is so fast today. That said, the textiles business is one that has had the least innovation of any other segment in the last 100 years. The concept of making fiber is still the same as in a wool weaving factory in Manchester [100 years ago]. There have been no big changes. We need to create new fibers that we can naturally generate on our planet with a reasonable impact. But that needs a vision.

Q: Who is it up to – the big groups or the small start-ups to foster that vision?

A: There should be room in our business for a start-up. But it's the big ones that will change the game. They have the money for specialists who can dedicate 100 percent of their time to finding solutions. My brand doesn't. If I spend day and night trying to read sustainability reports and understand what they mean, I won't have time to design any more. Also, it is important to find solutions for the mass market. Because if Zara and H&M and Target and Amazon start saying "we won't buy from factories that do this or that, because it's bad," all the others will be forced to play the same game.

Notes

1 Grayson, Donald K. & Delpech, Françoise. Ungulates and the Middle-to-Upper Paleolithic Transition at Grotte XVI (Dordogne, France). *Journal of Archaeological Science*, Vol. 30, No. 12 (2003): 1633–1648, p. 1643.

2 Fagan, Brian. *Cro-Magnon: How the Ice Age Gave Birth to the First Modern Humans*. New York: Bloomsbury Press, 2011, p. 209.

3 Aujoulat, Norbert. *The Splendour of Lascaux*. London: Thames and Hudson, 2005, p. 198.

4 Seefelder, Matthias. *Indigo in Culture, Science and Technology*. Lansberg, Germany: Ecomed, 1994, p. 9.

5 Caesar, Julius. *The Gallic War*. Translated by H. J. Edwards. Mineola, NY: Dover Publications, Inc., 2006, pp. 252–255.

6 Carr, Gilly. Woad, Tattooing, and the Archaeology of Rebellion in Britain. In: Jo Kirby, ed., *Dyes in History and Archaeology*, Vol. 18. London: Archetype, 2012, p. 6.

7 Ibid., p. 1.

8 Ibid., p. 8.

9 Seefelder, p. 25.

10 Balfour-Paul, Jenny. *Indigo: Egyptian mummies to blue jeans*. London: British Museum, 2011. pp. 6ff.

11 Ibid., p. 7.

12 Ibid., p. 126.

13 Ibid., p. 107.

14 Balfour-Paul, p. 55.

15 Ibid., p. 33.

16 Cardon, Dominique. *Natural Dyes*. London: Archetype Books, 2007, p. 376.

17 Balfour-Paul, p. 34.

18 Ibid.

19 Seefelder, p. 25.

20 Balfour-Paul, p. 38.

21 Ibid.

22 Pliny. *Natural History. Volume VI: Books 20–23*. Translated by W. H. S. Jones. Cambridge, MA: Harvard University Press, 1951, p. 295.

23 Balfour-Paul, p. 36.

24 Ibid., p. 56.

25 Ibid., p. 94.

26 Ibid., pp. 44–45.

27 Ibid., p. 41.

28 Ibid., p. 60.

29 Ibid., p. 66.

30 Ibid., p. 71.

31 Ibid., p. 79.

32 Ibid., p. 82.

33 Cardon, p. 336.

34 Ibid.

35 Galerie Canesso, Paris. *The Master of the Blue Jeans: A New Painter of Reality in the Late 17th Century Europe*. Curated by Gerlinde Gruber. Paris: Galerie Canesso, 2010.

36 Marsh, Graham & Trynka, Paul. *Denim: From Cowboys to Catwalks*. London: Aurum, 2005, p. 6.

37 Levi Strauss & Co. The 501® Jean: Stories of an Original | Full Documentary. Directed by Harry Israelson. 2016. https://www.youtube.com/watch?v=6R9cAoCyatA

38 Downey, Lynn, Lynch, Jill Novak & McDonough, Kathleen. *501: This is a Pair of Levi's Jeans … The Official History of the Levi's Brand*. San Francisco: Levi Strauss, 1995, p. 73.

39 Ibid., p. 21.

40 Ibid., p. 25.

41 Marsh & Trynka, p. 56.

42 Ibid., p. 98.

43 *Vogue*, May 15, 1935, p. 73.

44 Downey, Lynch & McDonough, p. 47.

45 Marsh, Lisa. *The House of Klein*. Hoboken, NJ: Wiley, 2003, pp. 41ff.

46 Ibid., p. 41.

47 Sullivan, James. *Jeans: A Cultural History of an American Icon*. New York: Gotham, 2006, p. 148.

48 Ibid., pp. 159ff; Marsh, pp. 41ff.

49 Ibid.

50 Ibid.

51 Barry, Donald & Feofanov, Yuri. *Politics and Justice in Russia*. London: Sharpe, 1996, pp. 22–31.

52 Rudevich, Alexéi & Semyorka, Russkaya. Worth Going to Prison For: Getting Hold of Jeans in the USSR. *Russia Beyond the Headlines*, September 16, 2014. https://www.rbth.com/arts/2014/09/16/worth_going_to_prison_for_getting_hold_of_jeans_in_the_ussr_39833.html

53 Downey, Lynch & McDonough, p. 298.

54 Trotman, Samuel. Marithé et François Girbaud: "From Stone to Light." *WGSN Insider*, December 20, 2012. https://www.wgsn.com/blogs/marithe-et-francois-girbaud-from-stone-to-light/

55 Bojer, Thomas Stege & Sims, Josh. *Blue Blooded: Denim Hunters and Jeans Culture*. Berlin: Gestalten, 2016, p. 94.

56 Trotman.

57 Bojer & Sims, p. 208.

58 Marsh & Trynka, p. 110.

59 Ibid.

60 Bojer & Stege, p. 208.

2

PSYCHOLOGY

Nothing comes between me and my jeans

On a September night in 1944 a man was admitted to a hospital in Klamath Falls, Oregon. He had a broken leg, and it was badly swollen. The man was in pain. A nurse tended to him as he was brought in. She said she would need to cut him out of his jeans so that his leg could be treated. She assured him that this would be the best option, since pulling the pants off his leg would come with a lot more pain than he was already in. But the man would have none of it. "Nothing doing, these pants are Levi's and they are too damn hard to get," he yelled at the nurse. "I don't care how much it hurts, pull them off."[1]

To put it differently, the patient preferred to endure excruciating physical pain rather than suffer through the heartache of losing his blue jeans – giving a new level of intensity to the now-iconic slogan, "Nothing comes between me and my jeans." This was long before 15-year-old Brook Shields coined it in a sassy ad for Calvin Klein in 1980.

But what prompted such behavior?

Perhaps more than any other type of garment, jeans have great emotional value. Clothing in general is inextricably linked to our biographies. As anthropologists Daniel Miller and Sophie Woodward argue, change in our lives and the way we navigate through and locate ourselves in wider social histories is often meditated through music and clothing.[2] Much as a song can transport us back to a significant moment in our lives, a pair of jeans can link the individual to other people, a particular incident or a change of fashion. It also has the ability to provide us with a sense of ourselves, not least in respect to our own bodies.

Clearly, the patient with the broken leg and his jeans had been through thick and thin. Maybe the man had unsuccessfully climbed a tree to impress a girl and could not bear parting with the only tangible evidence of his romantic endeavor, or maybe he had squeezed himself into the only size that was left at his local Levi's store after the government rationed raw materials to help the war efforts abroad and the pair figured as a reminder of his Herculean efforts. In the 1940s all men's jeans were still raw and rigid – they grew with the wearer and adapted to his unique lifestyle, letting the customer "break" them in instead of coming "ready-used," courtesy of a complicated chemical treatment that swept over the industry in the Seventies and would ultimately give jeans their dirty image. What is true today was even more true then: Jeans tell stories, and they can indeed be very personal and intimate.

Curiously, apart from a few nuts – or denimheads, as they are lovingly called – the broader public is not actively aware of the significant role that blue jeans play in their lives. When Miller and Woodward set out to explore the subject through empirical research, stopping passersby on a bustling street in north London, it dawned on them that most participants "had barely given their current jeans a second thought after the initial decisions involved in selecting and purchasing them."[3] Because "jeans are so ordinary and ubiquitous [...] jeans just seem rather uninteresting as if it is self-evident and obvious why people should wear them," they observed.

Things, however, are rarely what they seem at first glance. And so, when the anthropologists dug deeper, enquiring about personal histories rather than denim directly, the subject quickly circled back to jeans. Ordinary by no means equaled meaningless, it turned out.

Suddenly, jeans emerged in the role of weight watchers, functioning as "a reward" for dropping a few pounds;[4] they served as an ersatz-uniform among anxious teenagers, to whom they represented "the uniform that isn't formally a uniform,"[5] or became an instrument of a more subtle flirtation than a mini-skirt. For women especially, jeans resolved "the contradictions of fashion," allowing for a safe place between "conformity and individuality, and that between sameness and difference more generally." "Because jeans have lost their specificity," Miller and Woodward argued, "they can just as easily become casual or dressy depending upon how they are accessorized with other clothing."[6]

Amid all types of garments (skirts, pants, suits, dresses, overalls, etc.), though not necessarily made of denim, jeans are a safe choice in many different social and cultural settings and therefore a global phenomenon, prompting Yves Saint Laurent, undoubtedly one of the most directional fashion designers of the 20th century, to divulge in *New York Magazine*: "I have often said that I wish I had invented blue jeans. They have expression, modesty, sex appeal, simplicity – all I hope for in my clothes."[7]

For over 140 years, jeans have transcended age, gender and cultural code lines; they have been a means to fit in and stand out, imbued with the unique ability to render the wearer fashionable without making him look like a victim. This is perhaps a reason why the fabric has seen a revival on the catwalks these past few seasons.

People not only regard jeans as having a greater capacity than other garments to become intimate and personal as they soften and mold to a particular body but also see wearing this global garment as the best means to present them-selves as citizens of the world.[8]

In fact, Miller and Woodward estimate that on any given day, close to half the world's population is wearing jeans.

Jeans, they argue, can help wearers to a "consistent identity": "People can feel better about themselves and more comfortable in public because denim gives a limited but genuine capacity to feel equal, to feel included through feeling merely ordinary."[9] They called this phenomenon "the art of ordinary." While post-war jeans functioned as a symbol of freedom, especially in Eastern Europe and Japan, their ubiquity today signifies "the freedom from concern" and "freedom from iden-tity," making them the ideal "post-identity clothing."[10] This fact renders denim particularly inclusive as a garment and popular among immigrants, for instance.

Or, as Robert D. Haas – former chairman and chief executive officer of Levi's Strauss & Co and the great-great-grandnephew of the brand's founder – put it:

> I think I know why people feel such strong emotions about their blue jeans. It's because when they wear them, they are their essential selves. Going out in their Levi's jeans, they're not dressed up like doctors, bus drivers, executives or nurses. They aren't playing out a role society expects of them or that they've chosen as a profession. They are simply themselves. Not much different on the outside than anyone else.[11]

More interestingly, it has been found that jeans are something people turn to in moments of crisis.[12] Consider the reports of US soldiers sleeping with their jeans under their pillows while serving abroad.[13] Jeans not only boosted the soldiers' morale, but were also precious enough to function as currency. As Haas noted, this particular garment was highly sought after in Europe and Japan during the war. American G.I.s "could barter their Levi's jeans for stays in hotels, meals in restaurants and a lot of other things I can't talk about on television," he quipped.

But how to create such desire? Some clues can be found in the history of denim itself. We know that the first poster boy for jeans was the cowboy. He exuded such myth and allure that the desire to be like him, to walk like him and to dress like him, caused a seasonal migration from the urban areas of the US East Coast to the so-called Dude Ranches of the west, where city slickers came to vacation and blow off steam (see Chapter 1). The wardrobe Levi's provided for the occasion spread to the streets, helping to sell more tickets to the ranches, which in turn helped to sell more jeans.

The company has used the cowboy in its advertising since the 1920s. In the 1950s, arty coropix posters (pieces of corrugated cardboard designed for retailers' walls)[14] were a hit. Portraying the cowboy as a cartoonish, goofy fella, they signaled: "These boys are having fun, and so will you."

When the ranches went out of fashion, "soap box derbys" stepped in. These races, helped by wheeled, wooden boxes previously used for shipping soap, were popular among boys in the 1950s, and Levi's was again there to dress them for the ride.

Finally, it was the brand's mastery of the moving image that captured a global audience. It was the 1970s, and a new TV generation was looking to be wooed. Levi's didn't disappoint, skillfully walking the line between reality and fiction. Remember the patient with the broken leg who wouldn't give up his pants? It inspired Levi's to create a steamy TV commercial with a flirtatious nurse–patient storyline. And the tearful cowboy burying his jeans as if he were saying goodbye to his best pal? That's also based on a true story.

Drawing from real-life situations is likely one of the reasons the brand boasts such high credibility. Levi's remains the most trusted jeans brand on the planet, especially among men.[15] Consumer trust, in fact, ran so high that the brand would get the benefit of the doubt when it ran into trouble. To wit: In 1942, the manager of a store in Maui, Hawaii, took literally the brand's signature leather patch, which shows two horses trying to pull apart a pair of Levi's, and tested the label's prom-ise per a "two-horse" contest of his own. "Acting under your instruction […] we hitched two Missouri Mules to your pants, and zip."[16] Naturally, the pants did not survive the tussle and the manager demanded a refund. But when Levi's sent the manager a check for $4.50, he sent it back, stating:

> We are returning your check […] the test was hardly fair. Mules are stronger than horses and even at that, the Levi's came near winning. At the end of the tussle, one of the mules dropped from exhaustion and expired a short time later.

The leather patch, which dates back to 1886, was Levi's first exercise in branding and image-making, and it was a home run. Soon the label found another power-ful ally: Hollywood. Since the Golden Age, movie stars and singers had adopted the waist overalls on- as well as off-screen. The jeansmaker reciprocated the favor, helping unknown actors soft-launch their careers – Bruce Willis danced for Levi's, Brad Pitt gave his version of a cheeky outlaw, hot chick by his side, while John Goodman posed as a handyman: "Levi's blue jeans are tools. They fit your body like a good hammer fits your hand. Nice and comfortable," he said, patting his Levi's-clad thighs with his hands.

Levi's was also the first to run a national campaign featuring a physically disabled person, the message being: experience freedom in your 501s despite being bound to a wheelchair.

Lee and Wrangler, close at Levi's' heels, brought ideas of their own. Lee, which was more popular on the US East Coast, targeted the "workers of the newly indus-trialized nation"[17] and originally started off with a design called "Cowboy Pants" in 1924. Two years later it launched the world's first zip-fly jeans for more conveni-ence, prompting Levi's to do the same when it entered the Eastern U.S. market. Lee coined the word Leesures ("Comfort Clothes for Work and Play") long before "ath-leisure" was even a word, while its Buddy Lee collection, which debuted in the

1920s, remains a collector's item to this day. It came about when a business-savvy Lee salesman had the idea of creating little dolls dressed in Lee overalls, expressing the brand's desire to be the best buddy of the working man – from the milk boy to the postman, everybody got their doll.

In the end it was Wrangler who retained the moniker of the professional cowboy's tailor. The company hired a Polish master tailor named Bernard Lichtenstein to collaborate with ranchers on a design of jeans that would cater specifically to their needs. The rancher business was flourishing, buoyed by a rapidly growing post–World War II population with a big appetite for beef and burgers.[18] And so was Wrangler.

However, nothing sold jeans like sex. In the case of Brooke Shields and Calvin Klein, we can put a precise figure on the profitable joint venture. Klein teamed with 15-year-old Brooke, who continued to tease for Klein where she had left off in her subversive role in Louis Malle's *Pretty Baby* two years prior. Her arsenal of sassy lines included "I've got seven Calvins in my closet, and if they could talk, I'd be ruined" and perhaps the most infamous line of all: "Do you know what comes between me and my Calvins? Nothing."

Some TV stations refused to air the ads or, alternatively, ran them during their late-night programs, but that only got more people talking. In the first week after the campaign was unveiled, the designer sold 400,000 pairs of jeans, twice as many as when he first launched the line. Within a month, 2 million pairs had sold over the counter, leaving Klein with $12.5 million in royalties in 1980.[19]

With Guess Jeans breathing heavily down his neck a decade later, the designer pulled another stunt and published a 116-page advertising supplement as part of the October 1991 issue of *Vanity Fair*. It featured the ripped, naked body of male supermodel Marcus Schenkenberg posing under the shower, his private parts concealed by nothing but a bundle of wet jeans. It cost $1 million to poly-bag 250,000 copies of the supplement, but it translated into a 30 percent jump in Calvin Klein jeans sales at Bloomingdale's in the following weeks.[20]

Levi's hit more mainstream notes. There were lots of sweaty models and flirty scenes, but packaged in a more family-friendly frame. Combined with memorable soundtracks, the brand's TV ads remain iconic to this day. To wit: Levi's famous 1985 Laundrette commercial helped the song "I Heard It Through the Grapevine" re-enter the charts, a coup the brand would repeat three more times.[21] The ad shows model Nick Kamen strip to his undies in a Laundromat while his jeans get a stonewash in the machine and ranks among the most successful of all times.

Today, selling jeans is not about lifting morale or selling the concept of industrial washing, but fighting for a greener image. Jeans haven't lost their magic, but voices have grown louder for them to clean up their act. One of Calvin Klein's motivations for the Brooke Shields ads was that everything had been done before and he wanted to try something new. Well, something new is again needed to help jeans up their game – this time, in the sustainability department. Denim is already at the forefront of the green movement, viewing the speed with which novel technologies emerge in this industry and the amounts of water and chemicals they have made possible. But how to convey these complex stories to consumers and make them buy green over conventional? The problem with sustainability is that, unlike fashion and Levi's historical commercials, it just ain't sexy.

Retailers so far have been reluctant to brand their more eco-friendly collections as such in fear of casting their conventional lines, which make up the bulk of their sales, in a bad light. Instead, they focus their communication on novelty and trends. Research suggests that these strategies are counter-productive. In fact, the plethora of styles available on the shop floor today – from skinny to boyfriend, high-rise to baggy – has rendered shoppers weary at best and horrified at worst. Miller and Woodward found that none of the people they interviewed talked about the abundance of denim on the shop floor as something positive.

> Rather, shopping for particular jeans commonly involved anxieties and traumas. The possibility that the perfect pair of jeans is out there seems to have added to the anxiety rather than alleviated it, as the burden is placed on the individual to find it.[22]

This reflects a global market survey by Invista,[23] which found that women on average own eight pairs of jeans; Brazil leads the pack at 9.3 pairs per head, followed by the US and Germany at 8.5 each. With the exception of China, most women describe the experience of jeans shopping as stressful due to difficulty finding a fit that suits them, which suggests that the staggering amount of denim in a woman's closet is perhaps the result of sheer frustration. Moreover, women have signaled that they would actually be willing to pay more for the "perfect pair," though they do not include sustainability among their top criteria.

How tragic, then, that the money spent on marketing these fashion options, which seem to alienate overwhelmed customers, could have been spent on sustainable campaigning instead.

Cue Patagonia's "Don't Buy This Jacket" ad or Stella McCartney's fall 2017 campaign, filmed at a Scottish landfill with models walking mountains of garbage or lounging in trash. These are excellent examples of brands drawing attention to overconsumption and the growing waste problem. Imagine a high street retailer that is traditionally more in touch with the masses asking customers to buy less. Wouldn't that be truly revolutionary?

Essentially, marketing and advertising have the same predicament as the fashion industry itself. They tell people to buy more products they don't need and the content of which they know nothing about. These are missed opportunities to help customers navigate through the muddy waters of today's exasperating retail landscape. Ultimately, putting value over volume is in everybody's interest. And value is not reflected in the price tag. A $39.99 pair of jeans can be socially and environmentally sustainable, while a $300 pair of jeans cannot. A simple way of remedying the situation would be to add transparency to the equation – say what's in it and who did it, similar to Honest By. The Antwerp-based brand offers detailed information about its manufacturing and the materials it uses for every item. Each thread and button is accounted for; even the store's mark-up is included in the description. In fact, the brand is so transparent that its sportswear line has the products' DNA printed on top of the fabric. Where others choose to put their logo, Honest By prints "100% ORGANIC" in big, bright letters, along with the full name and address of the manufacturer (see Figure 2.1).

Transparency is also part of a ten-point guideline developed by former ad man Thomas Kolster, who coined the term "Goodvertising." One of the slogans he created is: "It's time to get naked."[24] In the age of transparency that we live in, we know such invaluable things as the Kardashians' shoe sizes. How come we don't know where that shoe came from, what it's made of and by whom? Mr. Goodvertising, as his LinkedIn profile indicates, pleads with brands not to be afraid to show their weaknesses. It has worked well for companies like Patagonia, which put their garments' detailed ecological footprint on their planet up on their website via the Footprint Chronicles. And who knows, maybe it's those very weak spots that have the power to establish a personal connection with the consumer. After all, he's human too. His story could become the brand's story, as Hiut Denim has demonstrated through its history tag project. The way it works is: Wearers upload their

FIGURE 2.1   Honest By. SPORT

Source: Honest By

experiences and images from their lives with a pair of jeans, which then are passed on to the next consumer, who takes the jeans on new adventures, creating a new set of stories and so on and so forth.

Doing something and doing good, especially, is contagious. Historically, the human brain has been trained to be both greedy and selfless. Greed was useful to pre-historic humans, whose survival depended on them hoarding resources whenever they became available. Today, researchers estimate that around 50 percent of greed is determined by our genes, and that the more value is given to material goods within a society, the greedier its people become. Meanwhile, scientists at the University of Harvard discovered that people who have more time to ponder their actions tend to make more selfish choices.[25] Spontaneous decisions, on the other hand, evoke more altruistic behavior. That's because our intuition tells us to be more cooperative, which comes with advantages in daily life. Together we are stronger. Think back to the days when it came to chasing down a sprightly deer and there would be no shotguns in sight for another few thousand years. Hunters had to work in groups to eat.

In its Nike+ campaign, the sportswear giant understood and used the power of the team spirit by developing products that were digitally linked and allowed people to set their own training goals and compete against others. As we know today, the positive side-effect of greed is ambition, which drives our desire to be better, richer, faster than others. So, why not more ecologically conscious, too?

Where altruism is the trigger, consumers often expect brands to show generosity instead of pure for-profit behavior. As Kolster suggests: "Add value to people's lives."[26] He cites the example of the Cadbury ad that features a gorilla playing Phil Collins' "In the Air Tonight" on the drums. Even if you don't care for a Cadbury chocolate bar, you will instantly feel entertained and hence rewarded by the concept. Perhaps that's the key to making sustainability sexy. As the Danish popular scientist Tor Nørretranders argues, the generous man is the sexiest of them all. Doing good to others makes men attractive.[27]

Or cue GreenXchange was an online marketplace for companies to share intellectual property and collaborate on sustainable innovation across non-competing industries. Though it did not last very long, it was an example of the industry's altruistic behavior. In apparel, a collaborative effort between Patagonia (an outdoor brand) and Walmart (a value retailer) led to the foundation of the Sustainable Apparel Coalition (SAC). This is slated to give us the Higg Index, a single, uniform standard that in the future will (hopefully) provide us with the whole truth of a product's green credentials and, thus, help us choose when shopping for apparel.

Sustainability's greatest challenge from a marketeer's point of view is undoubtedly its gloomy image. We're running out of water, our soil is contaminated, the air is too thick to breathe and the oceans are overflowing with dirty plastic. It couldn't be more depressing.

Consumers, however, value positivity. Kolster notes that positive tweets are three times more likely to be re-tweeted, impacting long-term behavior, while negative messages only work short-term.[28] He suggests using humor as a tool.

Alternatively, marketing could focus on innovation and the creation of green jobs in textiles. According to Business of Fashion, one of the six fashion careers that will be most in demand in the future is that of a sustainability expert.

> When it comes to working in the fashion industry, it might seem like there are only a few pathways in the business, such as becoming an editor, designer, buyer, stylist or photographer. But in reality, these functions represent a small portion of the overall industry. The fashion industry has significantly evolved over the last 10 years and emerging trends, such as the evolving store, changing consumer preferences, a heightened need for radical transparency and more, is shifting companies' priorities and the roles they are hiring for.[29]

And these experts' job descriptions are as diverse as the Pantone color trend report. There are laser designers, ethical trade managers, bio-engineers, denim doctors, green chemists, ethical business analysts, and more. Put differently, sustainability creates profitable jobs *and* is good for the planet.

Whatever you do, telling people to consume less is not going to work. You have to give them something extra. We are all pleasure animals, minus a few Buddhist monks who have attained nirvana through the greatest achievement of all: the renunciation of all earthly desires. For the rest of us, "you have to give some to get some."

Historically, the most successful green campaigns have been those with an added value. Check out *The Scarecrow* campaign by Mexican-food chain Chipotle, which offered an animated short film about the horrors of processed food in a world where robotic crows (or so-called crowbots) stuff chickens with unhealthy fluids that make them grow faster. The ad did not paint a pretty picture, with an impression underscored by an eerie rendition of Willy Wonka's "Pure Imagination" performed by Fiona Apple. So, to counter this, Chipotle came up with an adventure video game in which the main character, an old-school farmer, brings caged animals and fresh veggies into safety, running a gauntlet between menacing machinery in the crowbots factory. Over 650,000 people downloaded the game app for free in the app store. The film itself was viewed over 15 million times and sparked 18.4 million conversations across 17 social media platforms in the first month after its launch alone.[30]

In keeping with the ad's catchy tune, imagine "traveling into the world of [your] creation"[31] and designing a green jean app, the goal of which would be to save denim from harmful PP sprays and toxic dyes. With every level, you get closer to a cleaner planet, boasting clear rivers, zero waste and blue skies.

According to Dan Ariely and Aline Grüneisen, who research behavioral economics at Duke University, the gaming world provides excellent tools for positively influencing consumer behavior. Citing Simple Energy as an example, they write,

> We can encourage sustainable choices by creating competitive games based on point accumulation, and tapping into social motivations such as pride and

shame. We can promote competition between individuals, neighborhoods, schools and towns, rewarding those who save the most energy.[32]

The company has set out to reward customers who save energy during peak times through contests and competitions with their peers, following a tiered prize system. The rule: The more you save, the better your rewards get.

The science duo also suggests that manufacturers and retailers create "smartphone apps that harness peer pressure to influence the decision process": "If a consumer buys an app that tracks shopping expenses and informs his social network about his purchases, social pressure to be green might encourage him to make more sustainable spending decisions."[33]

Perhaps the most obvious path towards greener pastures is through emotion.

While the pleasure of playing games worked for Chipotle, Greenpeace appealed to mushy feelings in its most viral video to date. The environmental activist group forced toy company Lego to break its ties with Royal Dutch Shell in protest of the oil giant's plans to drill in the Arctic. The video depicts a serene arctic landscape bathed in a warm, auroral light, which slowly drowns in a thick, black mass of dirty oil. It's heartbreaking, to say the least. To top that, Greenpeace assembled a group of kids and had them build arctic animals out of giant Lego bricks in front of Shell's London headquarters. The strategy worked. Lego backed away from its partnership with Shell.

As Ariely and Grüneisen note,

> while people may not be motivated to change their behavior for their own sakes, they may do so for their children. As hard as we try to influence other adults, in the end few things will be more effective than the nagging cries of the six-year-old in the back seat.[34]

Educating kids through a green jean app or having them compete against others in achieving green goals could therefore also influence their parents. Imagine their next trip to the high street when it's time to stock up on new clothes. Would they still look for an additional rip on the knee, or would they search for eco-labels?

Despite what recent sales figure might indicate, we are not all mindless consumer junkies. Market researcher Nielsen, which polled 30,000 people in a global online study in 60 countries, concluded that we are indeed seeing the advent of a greener consumer.[35] For one, sales of consumer goods offered by brands with a clear commitment to sustainability grew 4 percent in 2015, while those without advanced less than 1 percent. Across regions and income levels, 66 percent of consumers said they were willing to pay more for sustainable products, compared to 55 percent in 2014 and 50 percent in 2013.

Interestingly, consumers from less developed nations and those with lower incomes (earning $20,000 or less) were 5 percent more likely to buy green, somewhat offsetting the argument that sustainability is unaffordable. By age, Millennials emerged as the greenest generation. Almost three out of four Millennial respondents said they would pay extra, followed by Generation Z (15–20-year-olds) with 72 percent and Baby Boomers (50–64-year-olds) with 51 percent. Main purchase drivers for those willing to pay more were trust in the brand, organic ingredients, company being environmentally friendly and commitment to social values.

But it turns out that communicating those values is key. Before making a purchase, 51 percent of Millennials say they check a company's green credentials. This suggests great potential for brands to up their game. What so many are reluctant to do – communicate their sustainability efforts, however small they may be – can strengthen consumer loyalty. Communication on tags and packaging is helpful, but is a more effective communication tool when used in tandem with traditional marketing strategies to ensure that the message reaches the relevant consumers.

In another study, Nielsen looked at what consumers desire compared to what they end up buying and why. Here, research revealed that people want more innovative products that are affordable, healthy, convenient and environmentally friendly. But they also found a gap between the percentage of consumers wanting more green design (26 percent) and those who said they actually purchased them (10 percent). However, according to Nielsen, "insincerity may not be driving this gap. In fact, product availability, or rather, unavailability may be partly to blame."[36] Viewing that twenty-six percent of polled consumers say they wish more ecologically friendly were available and 16 percent asked for more socially friendly products, "consumers are just not finding the products they desire," therefore buying less.

> In many categories, green or socially responsible options don't exist, are difficult to find or consumers simply don't know about them. Better product labeling, shelf placement and promotion tactics that encourage trial can go a long way in closing the gap between desire and availability. To ensure consumers are not turned off at the shelf, brands must strike the right balance between ecological and effectiveness claims, testing and optimizing claims and packaging before going to market.

This is certainly true for denim.

In a simple field study conducted for this book, 13 brands and retailers on Oxford and Regent Streets, London's two main shopping arteries, were surveyed for their communication strategies with the consumer. All either permanently carried denim in their main lines or specialized in denim entirely.

The field trip involved two steps.

Step one: Ask the shop assistant for "a sustainable pair of jeans" within their offering. Alternatively, the terms "green" and "clean" were used when a salesperson was unsure of what was being asked. Examples to help understanding of what sustainable implied were also provided – for instance, "Do you have something in organic cotton?"

Step two: Look for tags or info-boards indicating a green or socially conscious initiative.

The result: None of the salespeople were able to point out a sustainable product in their stores. When asked "Is it organic?," a shop assistant at a large denim specialist replied: "It's all cotton, just one or two percent elastane," suggesting that since cotton is a natural fiber, it must be organic. Another said he didn't know whether his brand carried any green jeans, but warned about staying clear of buying "the dark colors" (since they must have used more dye) rather than noting the difference between washed and unwashed denim. At another brand, the question "Is it natural or synthetic indigo?" prompted the shopkeeper to answer, "Oh yeah, it's blue."

A failure to respond was most striking among those brands that clearly had a greener version of denim on the shop floor. Two of them redirected the interviewer to their websites. And one of the two said more sustainable options were available online only, while jeans washed with greener technologies were laid out the shop's main sales table.

At four out of 13 stores, the shop assistants called their managers for help, though those individuals were not able to provide any additional information.

In one case, a perky salesperson smiled benevolently, explaining: "It's all sweatshops here. But try Urban Outfitters."

Step two involved some rummaging. Given some brands' extensive offerings and no clear layout, such as a sustainable denim corner, it is possible that some less obvious signs of green branding were overlooked – though if they were, the brands' own salespeople missed them, too.

Here, five out of 13 brands offered written information. At one brand, a label sewn inside a pair of jeans informed the wearer of the brand's commitment to water, though it was not clear from the wording whether the jeans required less water in manufacturing or whether the brand donated part of the proceeds to a water charity. In contrast, another denim specialist put a board up on a table with the name of the more sustainable option, while yet another retailer designated a corner to its recycled collection, which featured mainly jeans. One store accompanied its denim with an organic cotton tag; another attached a tag that said "special indigo dye," though it remained unclear whether it referred to a more eco-friendly dye or simply a shade of color.

The lack of sufficient information is problematic. Depending on the brand's own price strategy, in some cases the sustainable product may be more expensive compared to a non-sustainable option. Retailers often argue that customers won't buy the green product because of its elevated price tag. However, as companies rarely brand their more sustainable products as such, it cannot be surprising that customers opt for the cheaper offering if the price is the only point of difference they see.

Imagine this: You walk into a store in search of a pair of jeans. You know you have the opportunity to save water, help eliminate chemicals, reduce waste and contribute to workers being paid a fair price with your purchase. There is a clearly designated section for clean jeans within the store for your own convenience. No aesthetic tradeoffs. The green options presented before you may indeed come at a higher price than the conventional items from the brand's main collection. At one value retailer the difference between a conventional and a more sustainable pair of jeans was £8.99 versus £39.99. But your gut feeling tells you that growing 1.5 pounds of cotton, spinning the fiber, weaving the fabric, dyeing it, sewing it, giving it a nice washed-out look, shipping it from a farm in India, to a mill in Turkey, to a garment factory in Bangladesh and finally to your local high street retailer in the UK cannot just cost a bit more than an Extra Value Meal Big Mac. What do you do? Unfortunately, we don't know, because no mainstream brand displays a sufficient level of transparency. But how great would it be to be presented with a fair choice like that?

There is no doubt that the lack of adequate information on a shop floor already flooded with products is only one part of the problem. The other part is that we simply like to consume, and as we consume more we of course appreciate a lower price tag to help keep the new stuff coming. But here's the thing: Satisfaction is a fickle friend that tends to elude us the more we seek it. Our brains are like sponges – they soak up knowledge quickly. If the reward switch is turned on too often, the gifting becomes more predictable and loses its appeal. We literally can't get no satisfaction, says neuroscientist Peter Sterling. In his paper, "Why We Consume: Neural Design and Sustainability,"[37] he argues that the concept of action and reward worked well for pre-industrial societies, because rewards were varied. "But capitalism shrinks the diversity of possible rewards, leaving the remainder less satisfying, and making stronger doses, i.e. more consumption, necessary. The path toward sustainability must therefore include re-expanding the diversity of satisfactions."

This is an interesting proposal. Consumption of material goods has become a national sport in industrialized societies and is eagerly watched by those in underdeveloped geographies who aspire to the same standards. But like a bad drug, it comes with severe side effects for the planet and no proven benefits for the consumer. Because the brain is too hard to trick, consuming endlessly just doesn't make us happy. On the contrary, as the reward–satisfaction circuit runs hot, our brains adapt and ask for more, eventually becoming addicted.

So, what if we substituted consumption with other sources of satisfaction that do not create the same level of destruction? Sterling suggests more nature, exercise, crafts, art and music. He does note that this would take a joint effort, including targeted social policies that should ideally start in the classroom, which he judges too authoritarian to allow a diverse reward–satisfaction scenario to play itself out and train children's brains for the future. In fact, "to 'de-lineate' on a large scale would require reorganizing economies and altering patterns of investment."

This is precisely what Tim Jackson is calling for when he speaks of "prosperity without growth" (see Chapter 6). "A limited form of flourishing through material success has kept our economies going for half a century or more," he says. "But it is completely unsustainable and now threatens to undermine the conditions for a shared prosperity. This materialistic vision of prosperity has to be dismantled.[38] Psychologists such as Tim Kasser and Helga Dittmar have argued that materialistic values like popularity, image, possession and financial success are cause for anxiety, depression and low self-esteem, while true prosperity, i.e. someone's well-being, is driven by intrinsic values like self-acceptance and belonging to the community.

> There is a kind of double and triple dividend in a less materialist life: People are both happier and live more sustainably when they favour intrinsic goals that embed them in family and community. Flourishing within limits is a real possibility.[39]

Ergo, in Jackson's opinion the economy of tomorrow has to be based on a combination of "care, craft and creativity." "We can't live entirely from these sectors. But they hold the key to expanding the quality of our lives. And we can usefully import the principles we find there into other economic sectors."[40]

Craft and creativity – if these are not a specialty of fashion, what is? Repair and customization of existing items, as practiced by many denim specialists such as Nudie, Notify and Levi's, may indeed create new business opportunities in a system that has gone into overload. These models also work because they create an added value for the consumer. Giving is sexy, as we know, so how about giving something that is sustainable? Creating a vocabulary around these positive add-ons is certainly a strategy worth exploring by advertisers and the media. Imagine if fashion show reviews – written by the hundreds during the course of one fashion week, of which there are 18 a year just in the main locations of New York, London, Milan and Paris – took into consideration not only the purely aesthetic components of a collection, but also its design ingenuity with reference to sustainability. Most designers do not know where their fabrics came from or what went into making them, as countless backstage interviews have indicated. Yet, in the age of quickly depleting resources and mindless overconsumption, "smart design" (see Chapter 5) is not a criterion the reviewer uses to form an opinion. It is clear that the rules of judging a collection's relevancy got stuck in a time when visual impact was all that mattered. This is no longer the case.

For millennia people have been expressing themselves through clothes and looking for meaning in material goods. This may still be fashion's main driver – because, let's face it, no one needs a new sweater per season to survive – but it's a concept that in itself is démodé. Not only is it based on a malfunction in the circuit formed in pre-historic times, but it is also not at all "on trend," which should ring a true fashionista's alarm bells. Being trendy today would involve consuming sustainably with the acquired knowledge that this entails.

How to get that knowledge across to the consumer is a different question. As we have seen, content driven by emotion, generosity, fun and competition has proven useful. Much has been said recently about the channels that carry such information. Consumers in developed markets, where consumption is highest, are most skeptical about green messages due to having been exposed to greenwashing in the past – a marketing strategy designed to make consumers believe a company is environmentally friendly, when in fact its green offering constitutes a fraction of its business and does not go deep enough.

While Kloster argues that greenwashing is better than green nothing,[41] consumers have grown weary of the word sustainability, as it could essentially mean everything or nothing, depending on individual interpretation.

Green campaigns, therefore, need consistency, tangible figures and ruthless transparency. One day in a very distant future, our brains will probably all be wired through a giant computer. It will be easy to upload information and stimulate people's behavior. Until then, we will have to rely on old-fashioned communication – through personal messages and advertising.

A new group of messengers, called influencers, has emerged in the last few years. Influencers can often be spotted sitting front row at fashion shows. Their power is determined by the number of followers they have on social media. The larger the number, the closer they get to sit to the catwalk and the more likely they will share a seat at the honor table during a lavish PR event, be paid for wearing an item from the designer's latest collection and be given luxurious VIP treatment. In 2017, there were 2.6 billion active social media users in the world. No doubt, online engagement is important. According to the fashion industry's trade journal WWD, 2016 saw a 400 percent increase in the Instagram posts of fashion brands compared to the previous year. "Designers are focused on giving Instagram influencers special treatment and access to their shows and collections. They are trying to make them fall in love," wrote Gabrielle Rein, cofounder and creative director of Viceroy Creative, a boutique creative, design and marketing agency.[42]

> Power Millennials like Cara Delevingne and Gigi Hadid are on top of the pop culture world and making a huge splash in fashion. They are style icons featured in all the hottest runway shows and campaigns. These women have influence over Millennials, and they are drawing them into luxury brands.[43]

Of course, it's not that simple. A fat Instagram account is not enough to get a done deal. As WWD notes: "It's about the *type* of followers one has, not necessarily *how many* followers one has."[44] The trade publication has identified two different types of influencers:

> those who convert and those who don't. And both are equally important. Reaching the coveted million follower milestone is what once legitimized an influencer, giving them the cache, star power and ability to write their own tickets when it came to securing projects with brands that could elicit six, and sometimes even seven, figure fees. But a new divide upon entry into this coveted club is taking shape. Once a blogger attains a certain status they're able to successfully drive sales *or* brand awareness—but rarely both.[45]

In other words, doing your homework as a brand can save you a lot of time and money.

Such influencers need not be (expensive) celebrities at all. RYPL, a new customer acquisition solution by digital marketing company GlobalWide Media, has made it its business to focus on "everyday influencers" instead. "Increasingly, you are looking toward everyday people [such as colleagues and friends] to give a more authentic review," says Zack Cantor, director of decision science at GlobalWide Media.[46] The tool explores influencer versus influence relationships via algorithms and co-location data, essentially tapping into a word-of-mouth environment, but in a more automated and targeted way. Where customers are overwhelmed by choice, word of mouth can cut through the noise and generate twice the sales of paid advertising, says McKinsey.[47] According to influencer marketing platform MuseFind, 92 percent of Millennials trust influencers more than celebrities or traditional advertisement.[48]

Nevertheless, the overuse of social media influencers – i.e. someone with at least 10,000 followers – can be ineffective, despite initial impressions. A study concluded by Launchmetrics, which represents 1,700 brands as clients, with a combined total annual marketing spend over €200 billion, concludes there is often a disconnect between who follows influencers and who buys the products they promote. As Michael Jais, chief executive officer of Launchmetrics and a professor of Fashion Luxury Business at French university Sciences Po, told Fashion Network:

> There's a growing importance in fashion, luxury and beauty for influencers. Brands tell us they will invest 70% more next year – probably double – on social media influencers. They all claim it is cheaper even though they are not sure of the effect! […] If one overlaps the social media fan base and the customer base of most luxury brands, the overlap is 0.016 percent. Which means online fans buy practically nothing. The customers are generally people who are not on Facebook. Obviously brands believe that in the future these fans will be their customers – but today the ROI is tiny![49]

He added: "Surprisingly, the way that brands best use influencers is in real life events. It is not about just sharing imagery. It is inviting them to product exchanges and launches. Real life is still very important."

And don't write off the traditional ad poster just yet. Contrary to common belief, those digitally savvy Millennials and Generation Z consumers can still be effectively reached through traditional, paid advertising. "The youngest respondents are relying more heavily on digital and mobile tools to learn about new products than their older counterparts. But they also say they're using several types of traditional advertising at comparable—or even greater—levels," a study by Nielsen concluded.

> Generation Z and Millennial respondents use TV and radio to learn about new products at similar rates to Generation X and Baby Boomer respondents, and their reliance on outdoor billboards/posters, public transport ads and ads at public events exceeds their older counterparts'.[50]

As far as the message goes, historically the one thing that always sells is sex; denim is proof of that when we look at the history of its advertising. The question is now how to translate the talk of sexy aesthetic into a talk of sexy sustainability.

One idea was offered by Vanessa Friedman, fashion director and chief fashion critic of the *New York Times*, at the Copenhagen Fashion Summit.[51] Frustrated with her fellow colleagues, who kept banishing her story pitches on green fashion to the coverage reserved for Earth Day, which is celebrated annually on April 22, she called up director Adam McKay. He was faced with a similar dilemma – i.e. not having half of the audience walk out on his movie while he was trying to get across a similarly dry and abstract topic: the perils of collateralized debt obligations and private label securitizations in his movie, *The Big Short*. McKay used a trick: He put a pretty, naked girl in a hot bubble bath. That girl was Margot Robbie, sipping on some bubbly in a penthouse suite, the vast blue of the ocean framing the picture behind her sinuous figure. The one line that everyone surely remembers from that scene is Robbie saying: "Whenever you hear subprime, think shit." And boom, just like that: tons of technical material reduced to one universally comprehendible sentence. It could be so simple. McKay's advice to Friedman:

> Get a supermodel and then maybe dress her in some elaborate clothes and maybe have her effectively do a striptease as she describes the potential problems we might all face if we don't start thinking really hard about what we are about to buy.[52]

Friedman noted that McKay's vision ends with the supermodel naked, which he said "would shock people into paying attention."

Friedman herself rejects the term sustainability. She prefers to speak of "responsible fashion" instead. When it comes to consumers, she says, the talk needs a little work. She observed,

> We have to innovate not just in what we do, but in how we communicate in what we do. Stories are really important, they are the currency of communication in this world. Because stories create emotions. That's why Rana Plaza is still mentioned today. Because it put a human face on a generic supply chain.

"Just think about the possibilities in the Green Hornet for you guys," she offered.

How cool would it be to get an influential rapper like A$AP Rocky to rap about sustainability instead of LSD? Or what impact would it have if Kanye West suddenly decided to wear responsible fashion only? Wouldn't that start a movement? Consider, for instance, where the style for rolled-up cuffs comes from. Cowboys used the space as an ashtray and to store their cigarettes so they could reach them while riding without reaching into their pockets. Or how jeans became a symbol of political outcry? Protesting against the Vietnam War involved moving around a lot and running away from police, which made jeans the perfect attire and helped denim transition into the leisure category.

The truth is, no one has figured out how to do sustainability marketing on a product level, notes Jason Kibbey, chief executive officer of the Sustainable Apparel Coalition (SAC). His organization is looking to launch a digital tag for consumers called the Higg Index, which is supposed to grade products according to their environmental footprint. Kibbey confirms that talking about sustainability on the retail level is a double-edged sword.

> I remember when Julie Gilhart, fashion director at Barneys, decided to market product as Barneys Green. They sold worse. It was a big detractor, because it made people question the quality and exclusivity of the product. Levi's too has tried hard with Water<Less, but no one has really cracked the code yet. I think down the road it will not come through some cool campaign but innovation. I don't know what that will look like yet, but when all you have to do is point your phone at someone to know it was made by slaves that will be a pretty strong, enforcing factor, bigger than making sustainability sexy.

Notes

1 Downey, p. 110.
2 Miller, Daniel & Woodward, Sophie. *Blue Jeans: The Art of the Ordinary*, Berkley: University of California Press, 2012, p. 28.
3 Ibid., p. 16f.
4 Ibid., p. 36.
5 Ibid., pp. 84ff., p. 97.
6 Ibid., p. 93.
7 Saint Laurent, Yves. YSL on YSL. As told to G.Y. Dryansky. *New York Magazine*, November 28, 1983, p. 53.
8 Miller & Woodward, p. 6.
9 Ibid., p. 119.
10 Ibid., p. 87.
11 Downey, p. 311.
12 Miller & Woodward, p. 28.
13 Marsh & Trynka, p. 60.
14 Downey, p. 253.
15 Miller & Woodward, p. 94.
16 Downey, p. 140.
17 Bojer & Sims, p. 185.
18 Ibid.
19 Marsh, pp. 45ff.
20 Ibid., p. 97.
21 Trotman, Samuel. Levi's Laundrette Advert (1985). *WGSN Insider*, December 19, 2014. https://www.wgsn.com/blogs/levis-laundrette-advert-1985/
22 Miller & Woodward, p. 48.
23 Pavarini, Maria Cristina. Invista's Survey: Every Woman Owns 8 Jeans, But Shopping Them Is Stressful. *Sportswear International*, November 14, 2016.
24 Kolster, Thomas. *Goodvertising: Creative Advertising That Cares*. London: Thames & Hudson, 2012, p. 19.

25 Rand, David & Cone, Jeremy. Time Pressure Increases Cooperation in Competitively Framed Social Dilemmas. *Plos One* Vol. 9, No. 12(2013, December 31): e115756.

26 Kolster, p. 175.

27 Nørretranders, Tor. *The generous Man: how helping others is the sexiest thing you can do.* Thunder's Mouth Press: New York, 2006.

28 Ibid., p. 218.

29 Chitrakon, Kati. Six Fashion Careers of the Future. *Business of Fashion*, November 14, 2016 https://www.businessoffashion.com/articles/careers/six-fashion-careers-of-the-future

30 Chipotle. *The Scarecrow.* Directed by Limbert Fabian & Brandon Oldenburg. n.d. http://www.welovead.com/en/works/details/fa2wntxAk

31 Fiona Apple. *Pure Imagination.* 2013.

32 Ariely, Dan & Grüneisen, Aline. *How to Turn Consumers Green.* McKinsey & Company. 2017. http://voices.mckinseyonsociety.com/how-to-turn-consumers-green/

33 Ibid.

34 Ibid.

35 Nielsen. *Consumer-Goods' Brands That Demonstrate Commitment to Sustainability Outperform Those That Don't.* December 10, 2015. http://www.nielsen.com/eu/en/press-room/2015/consumer-goods-brands-that-demonstrate-commitment-to-sustainability-outperform.html

36 Nielsen. *Closing the Gap Between Products That Appeal to Our Heart and Health.* June 29, 2015. http://www.nielsen.com/bd/en/insights/news/2015/closing-the-gap-between-products-that-appeal-to-our-heart-and-health.print.html

37 Sterling, Peter. *Why We Consume: Neural Design and Sustainability.* Great Transition Initiative. February 2016. http://www.greattransition.org/publication/why-we-consume

38 Jackson, Tim. *Prosperity Without Growth.* London: Routledge, 2009, p. 137.

39 Ibid., p. 126.

40 Ibid., p. 158.

41 Kolster, p. 9.

42 Rein, Gabrielle. Think Tank: Why Millennials Are the Future of Luxury. *WWD*, April 25, 2016. http://wwd.com/fashion-news/designer-luxury/millennials-luxury-spending-10417737/

43 Ibid.

44 Strugatz, Rachel. The Blogger Divide: Converters or Brand-Builders? *WWD*, July 31, 2017. http://wwd.com/business-news/technology/bloggers-converters-or-brand-builders-chiara-ferragni-kristina-bazan-10952451/

45 Kolster, p. 9.

46 Olsen, Lauren. Everyday Influencers Key to Winning Today's Consumers. *WWD*, October 12, 2017. http://wwd.com/business-news/marketing-promotion/everyday-influencers-11026347/

47 Bughin, Jacques, Doogan, Jonathan & Vetvik, Ole Jørgen. A New Way to Measure Word-Of-Mouth Marketing. *McKinsey Quarterly.* April 2010.

48 Weinswig, Deborah. Influencers Are the New Brands. *Forbes*, October 5, 2016. https://www.forbes.com/sites/deborahweinswig/2016/10/05/influencers-are-the-new-brands/#47d285657919

49 Deeny, Godfrey. A Launchmetrics Study Suggests Social Media Influencers' Impact Will Mainly Be Felt in the Future. *Fashion Network*, April 25, 2017.

50 Nielsen. *How Shoppers Look, Watch, and Listen for New Products.* 2015. http://www.nielsen.com/eu/en/insights/news/2015/how-shoppers-look-watch-and-listen-for-new-products.html

51 Copenhagen Fashion Summit. *Vanessa Friedman, Fashion director and chief fashion critic, New York Times.* On Vimeo. 2017. https://vimeo.com/167737239

52 Ibid.

3

FIBER

Picking the cherries from the crop

A moment of sloppiness, a bump on the road or simple forgetfulness – some of the most life-changing scientific inventions can be traced back to accidents. Think penicillin, dynamite, the microwave, Vitamin C or even our daily bowl of corn flakes.

It shouldn't be a surprise, then, that the one invention that altered the course of fashion forever occurred one day in 1764 when a bunch of kids were playing around the house of a handloom weaver in Lancashire. The weaver's name was James Hargreaves. He was "a plain, industrious, but illiterate man with little or no mechanical talent"[1] who lived with his wife and many children.

According to Aspin and Chapman, who provide a detailed account of what most likely transpired,

> life in the isolated community in which Hargreaves grew up was hard and often harsh [...] Porridge and oatcake made up the usual diet of the large families who inhabited the small stone cottages, and a few plain pieces of furniture were the only possessions to which most villagers could lay claim.[2]

Farming had been replaced by the cotton trade, which "after nearly two centuries of growth in Lancashire, had become highly organised on capitalist lines."[3] This was the case in Blackburn in particular, which boasted a population 4,000, of whom roughly 3,000 were employed as spinners and weavers. Hargreaves was likely one of them. He worked from home and walked to his master's warehouse once a week to exchange the cloth he had made for new raw materials and some cash. His annual income could not have been higher than £50 per year.[4] Anything that could make him spin and weave faster would have made his day lot easier.

Aspin and Chapman suggest that the Lancashire textile workers "at least enjoyed a degree of independence and control over their time,"[5] despite the long hours needed to earn a living, "and by improving their methods and their simple machinery, the more intelligent among them sought to extend their freedom further. Ironically," they note, "their efforts unwittingly hastened the factory system under which much of their liberty disappeared."[6]

Equipped with a simple pocketknife, Hargreaves played his part in this evolution, as depicts the following anecdote:

> A number of young people were one day assembled at play in Hargreaves's house during the hour generally allotted for dinner, and the wheel which he or some of his family were spinning, was by accident overturned. The thread still remained in the hand of the spinner, and as the arms and the periphery of the wheel were prevented by the framing from any contact with the floor, the velocity it had acquired still gave motion to the spindle which continued to revolve as before. Hargreaves surveyed this with mingled curiosity and attention [...] he had before attempted to spin with two or three spindles affixed to the ordinary wheel, holding the several threads between the fingers of his left hand, but the horizontal position of the spindles rendered this attempt ineffectual.[7]

Hargreaves, indeed, somewhat reinvented the "wheel" or, as it became known: the spinning jenny. It wasn't perfect. In fact, it inspired Samuel Crompton to invent the mule in 1779 by combining elements of the jenny (which produced weft yarn) and the water frame, designed by Richard Arkwright a few years prior (which spun warp yarn). The mule made a tremendous difference, as it was suitable for higher quality yarn. For the first time, the Brits were able to compete against the Indians and their finest muslins and assert their global dominance in cotton goods in the 19th century[8] – which would only be toppled by even more efficient methods and, more importantly, cheaper labor from Asia 150 years later.

As the historian Robert C. Allen argues, Britain was the perfect budding ground for industrial expansion, since wages were high, but energy, which came from coal, was cheap. By 1836, the cost of yarn made in British mills had been slashed in half compared to the hand methods of 1760; overall production doubled, making British cotton cloth competitive on a global scale.[9] Ultimately, Allen notes, "the spinning jenny, water frame and mule were key inventions in the mechanization of cotton spinning."[10] They set in motion further innovations and heralded the Industrial Revolution, which planted the seed for much faster fashion.

Nothing would ever be the same.

"Cotton was the wonder industry of the Industrial Revolution," states Allen.[11] In the mid-18th century, European leaders Britain and France spun about 3 million pounds of yarn each.[12]

Today, a modern-day loom can weave some 460 meters of fabric a day. Billions of meters of denim are woven around the world each year, resulting in 3.1 billion "units" – that is, jeans and other denim pants such as shorts – every year, according to Euromonitor. That's a lot of fiber.

Considering that global production of fiber surpassed the historic mark of 100 million tons in 2016[13] and that synthetics such as polyester, which we know today are non-renewable and non-biodegradable, have taken the lead, picking the right yarn can make or break an item's ecological footprint. (See Table 3.1.)

But how to choose?

Designers say they are utterly confused about the choices presented to them. Which is better, they ask: organic or BCI cotton? Should the durability of polyester be valued over the biodegradability of cotton, viewing the latter's water consumption? What alternative fiber options are possible for denim? How can they be sourced to ensure the collections' timely delivery? And does the price tag really reflect the benefits?

Fortunately, denim is a docile fabric. It tolerates blends and experiments and still looks like denim when it's not woven as a 3x1 twill, which is its original structure (see Chapter 4).

Cotton

Despite the advent of synthetics, cotton is still denim's favorite fiber, and denim accounts for some 35 percent of global cotton consumption.[14] But it comes with an array of challenges. Conventional farming consumes large amounts of water and chemicals to make cotton grow on land that is becoming scarce and is needed to feed a growing population. At the same time, it does not provide farmers with enough profit to make a decent living. Soil erosion, water and soil contamination and the loss of biodiversity, as well as severe health risks for farmers, are associated with cotton farming.

Water

Cotton has a reputation as a thirsty crop.

According to WWF, it takes between 7,000 and 29,000 liters[15] of water to produce one kilogram of cotton, depending on the geography and weather conditions in a given season. However, cotton is also both a salinity- and drought-tolerant plant; it doesn't use all the water it is given, some of which passes through the soil and goes back into the water streams. This is why it's imperative to keep the production clean.

On average, agriculture swallows an incredible 70 percent of the water withdrawn from rivers, lakes and aquifers for human use. In contrast, industries and households consume 20 percent and 10 percent, respectively, making agriculture the biggest user. Growing crops, and cotton especially, where incompatible with the local climate adds to the challenge, particularly as the land is getting drier, which makes the harvest more susceptible to pests.

To be fair, data indicates that cotton only soaks up 3 percent of agricultural water, compared to 21 percent and 12 percent for rice and wheat, respectively.[16] But as more food and clothing are needed for a growing population, water withdrawal for irrigation is expected to increase further, expanding irrigated areas to 242 million ha by 2030. [17]

Part of that water – 20–50 percent, according to WWF – never reaches the farm due to evaporation and inefficient irrigation methods, while chemical runoff from pesticides and fertilizers finds its way back into rivers, destroying downstream ecosystems or, as they remain in the soil, increasing salinity and making the soil infertile. According to a study by the University of Sheffield and the Grantham Center for Sustainable Futures, in the last 40 years we have lost 33 percent of arable land around the globe due to erosion and pollution. Overall, the research notes, it takes around 500 years to form 2.5 centimeters of topsoil. Meanwhile, erosion progresses ten to one hundred times faster than soil formation, deprives the soil of nutrients and releases CO_2.[18]

Agriculture also affects the natural circulation of water, which has consequences for entire ecosystems.

On the positive side, irrigation technology and farming practices have improved dramatically. In the US, which is the third largest cotton producer behind India and China, farmers have been able to slash water consumption by 80 percent in the last 20 years, while their chemical input has fallen by 50 percent compared to the generation before them.[19]

There are three major types of irrigation:

- sprinkler irrigation, which works like what you use on your lawn but may cause significant water loss through evaporation in arid regions;
- surface irrigation, which makes water travel along the field, essentially flooding it; this requires optimal design and inclination angles in order to prevent water from being wasted and chemical runoff from reaching water streams; and
- drip irrigation, which delivers water directly to the root of the plant through subsurface tubes – an expensive technology and therefore employed mostly on highly industrialized farms.

Cotton's biggest challenge is that it is grown in more than 80 countries, which not only differ by region but probably also at farm-level; this makes the collection of comparable data difficult, especially with reference to yields.

According to Cotton Inc., "being short an inch of water at the wrong time can easily result in the loss of 75 pounds of seed and 50 pounds of fiber."[20] Keeping irrigation consistent, therefore, contributes to more consistent yields, which is also why rain-fed crops are sometimes helped by additional irrigation. Generally, only about half of the area under cotton cultivation is artificially irrigated, but this accounts for 73 percent of the global cotton production because of higher yields.[21] Fairtrade notes that where inefficient systems are in place they deplete local water resources for communities that are already struggling.

Ultimately, it would be wise to educate each farmer individually on the best practices germane to his specific soil quality and climatic conditions, but this would be a tremendous undertaking. Proper education and training, also on a governmental level, are undoubtedly needed to help avoid disastrous malfunctions, such as that around the Aral Sea. Once the world's fourth-largest lake, its water was diverted per governmental plans to feed plantations built on arid land, depleting the lake, causing local fishing communities to collapse and polluting soil with chemical residue for years to come.

This all shows that cotton per se is not an evil crop. It is a question of water management rather than an inherent flaw in cotton's DNA that determines its sustainability factor. Rather than being a *water-thirsty* industry, cotton is *water-wasting*. And wasting water is not an option, given that by 2030 global water demand is projected to exceed sustainable supply by 40 percent, shutting down entire regions.

Chemicals

Humans have cultivated cotton for millennia without harming the environment, ensuring prosperity for future generations. Protecting cotton from pests is necessary, but it has spun out of control. Excessive consumption and the price volatility of a publicly traded commodity have resulted in an excessive use of synthetic chemicals.

In the last 80 years, yields have tripled thanks to the use of pesticides, herbicides, fungicides and fertilizers as well as increased irrigation, the mechanization of farming and the advent of genetically modified (GM) seeds.[22] At the same time, the percentage of land has remained relatively stable at approximately 3 percent.

In the US alone, cotton production grew by 35 percent between 1980 and 2015; total planted acres fell by 2 percent, while yield increased by 42 percent.

The use of both pesticides and insecticides has dropped since the 1990s. Cotton now accounts for 5 percent of the world's pesticides use and 16 to 18 percent of insecticide use, yet in some countries it is on the rise again as pests are becoming resistant.[23]

French researchers at the Institut National de Recherches Agricole (INRA) have shown that "pesticide use can be significantly reduced without lowering yields or economic performance at farm level if substantial changes in farming practices are adopted."[24] They estimated that an average reduction of 37 percent, 47 percent and 60 percent of herbicide, fungicide and insecticide, respectively, was possible. Moreover, they argued that the hidden costs of synthetic chemicals outweigh their benefits. This is because health impacts in the U.S. resulting from the use of pesticides, fungicides and insecticides have been underestimated; previous studies did not take into account fatal cases following chronic exposure, which would have resulted in health costs ten times greater, or a total of $15 billion in costs. Regulatory costs, meanwhile, should be valued at $22 billion instead of $4 billion if all regulations are to be respected.[25]

The data coincides with a UN report published in 2017 that debunked the myths surrounding the positive impacts of pesticides advertised by the chemical industry, saying: "Pesticides, which have been aggressively promoted, are a global human rights concern and responsible for an estimated 200,000 acute poisoning deaths each year, 99 per cent of which occur in developing countries."[26]

The report refutes the chemical industry's claims that heavy use of pesticides is needed to feed a growing population and calls the reliance on hazardous chemicals merely "a short-term solution."[27] It further notes that the challenge to present scientific proof of the chemicals' toxicity to human life and nature – which the UN links to cancer, Alzheimer's and Parkinson's diseases, hormone disruption, developmental disorders and sterility, neurological health effects such as memory loss and reduced motor skills – "has been exacerbated by systematic denial, fuelled by the pesticide and agroindustry, of the magnitude of the damage inflicted by these chemicals, and aggressive, unethical marketing tactics remain unchallenged."[28]

The UN pointed out that 65 percent of global pesticide sales and almost 61 percent of commercial seed sales are now controlled by only three corporations, posing "serious conflicts of interest."

> The pesticide industry's efforts to influence policymakers and regulators have obstructed reforms and paralysed global pesticide restrictions globally. When challenged, justifications for lobbying efforts include claims that companies comply with their own codes of conduct, or that they follow local laws.[29]

Meanwhile, the price of chemicals is going up, posing a perennial cost to farmers. According to the WHO (World Health Organization), chemical pesticides used in cotton production account for $2 billion annually, of which $819 million are classified as hazardous.[30]

For millennia, humans did without synthetic chemicals, though both consumption levels (volume) and consumption cycles (speed) were significantly lower.

A possible substitute for petrochemical inputs is genetically modified (GM) cotton. It is one of the reasons cotton growers in the US managed to slash their pesticide applications by 50 percent vis-à-vis the previous generation, following the introduction of *Bt* cotton in 1996.

Bt is cotton derived from the bacterium *Bacillus thuringiensis*, which kills certain insects when they eat the plant. *Bt* used to be topically applied by organic farmers in the 1920s. But because it was easily washed away by rain and affected by the sun, it was soon replaced by synthetics – until Texan scientists encoded the *Bt* protein directly into the plant. Although *Bt* helps reduce yield losses due to damage from bollworms, it is not effective against other pests. In areas with no heavy bollworm infestations, the impact on yield of *Bt* cotton is believed to be negligible.

Bio-engineering is controversial. It is hailed as the ultimate solution by some and questioned by others for its unpredictable long-term consequences. In the case of *Bt* cotton, which is considered safe for humans, genetic resistance may evolve, though initial fears have not materialized. While in 2005, the ICAC (International Cotton Advisory Committee) warned "that it is only a matter of time before cotton pests evolve resistance to the Bt toxin,"[31] in 2015 it downgraded the warning, stating: "In time it became apparent that the resistance problem had not emerged to the degree that was generally feared in the beginning." ICAC later added cautiously:

"No seriously alarming situation has emerged in any country, although claims of the development of resistance cannot be dismissed outright."[32]

The danger was largely avoided "or at least largely delayed" by incorporating so-called resistance management strategies in the form of refuge crops and gene pyramiding, following "lessons learned from the intensive use of insecticides,"[33] the ICAC noted.

Fairtrade, on the other hand, observes that "farmers are planting more GM cotton in the hope of increasing yields and incomes. In reality they are tied into buying expensive seeds and pesticides each year from multinational companies amid concerns that yields actually decline after initial gains." The organization points to "an epidemic of farmer suicides" in India that

> ha[ve] been blamed on high levels of indebtedness controversially linked to the rising costs of GM cotton seeds, fertilisers and insecticides and declining yields, while question marks remain over the long-term effect of genetically modified organisms on the environment, biodiversity and human health.[34]

A report released by the Soil Association[35] in 2017 suggests similar skepticism. The promise of performance of GM cotton, which lured farmers into implementing it, proved short-lived. Only four years after its introduction, the dreaded pink bollworm became resistant, also lowering the quality of previously high-quality cotton. As the report notes, this increased the costs of production threefold, as farmers were forced to deal with new pest outbreaks and pump more pesticides to control the damage – driving some of them into ruin and sadly suicide. The Soil Association sees a solution in organic cotton production, especially in India, which accounts for around 70 percent of global organic output.

> In India, before GM ran into difficulties, organic cotton yields were just 14% lower than GM cotton, and the associated costs of organic were 38% lower, which puts organic at least on a par with conventional cotton in terms of profitability.[36]

But it notes that

> to allow farmers to continue to switch from the failing GM technology, consumers need to buy organic cotton products and ask their favourite brands and retailers to stock them, and brands need to include or increase organic cotton in their sourcing portfolio.[37]

Bt makes up roughly 50 percent of global GM cotton. In total, 81 percent of global cotton is genetically modified one way or another. It remains a delicate balance, since the handling of GM crops requires professional training and monitoring, especially in poor regions with little understanding of the intricacies of biotechnology.

Bio-engineers are now working on injecting two new traits into the plant: a drought-tolerant and a nitrogen-use-efficient gene, which would reduce the need for irrigation and chemical fertilizers, respectively. Cotton is already able to absorb 27 times its own weight in water, which makes it quite efficient.

An alternative to planting transgenic seeds is integrated pesticide management (IPM), as promoted by BCI (Better Cotton Initiative) among others, which encourages natural pest control through enhanced biodiversity and the presence of natural enemies of pests. This long-term and cost-efficient prevention of pests includes inter-planting cotton with alfalfa, corn, sunflowers, black-eyed peas and sorghum, for instance. Crop rotations protect soil from pathogens and increase organic matter, while more resistant crop varieties, instead of just high-yielding varieties "that respond well to chemical inputs but are more susceptible to pests,"[38] lower risk of disease. IPM systems normally allow softer chemicals to be used where absolutely necessary, but they also facilitate the transition to organic systems.

People

Around 100 million farmers grow 28.5 million metric tons of cotton on 35 million hectares around the world. Of these, 90 percent live in developing countries, raising the crop on fewer than two hectares. Few of these small-holder farmers have the knowledge, flexibility or resources to employ more sustainable practices, as they are trying to compete with large mechanized farms in developed countries.

As Fairtrade notes, these farmers are "especially vulnerable to market shifts and climate flux, and the performance of a single growing season can make or break a household."[39]

Many farmers lease the land and acquire loans at the beginning of the season to pay for tools, seed, chemicals, rent and labor, hoping to pay the loans back once the crop has been harvested. But since cotton is an internationally traded commodity, its price is subject to market fluctuations, which have been experiencing a downward trend. To wit: The price of cotton has fallen from more than $3.00/kg in the 1960s to $1.73 in 2014.[40]

This puts pressure on the farmers to maximize yield per acre. They do so by resorting to cheaper and more toxic chemicals in hope of short-term gains, risking their own health, instead of investing in technology with long-term prospects of sustainability, both environmental and economical.

Cheap cotton is essential to produce cheap goods as found en masse on the high street. Low prices in turn fuel consumption, placing greater pressure on farmers to produce more and faster. It is a vicious circle. In the UK, the value of the budget clothing market grew 45 percent from 2003–2008, twice the rate as the normal clothing market.[41] Meanwhile, average farm revenue per hectare fell by one-sixth between 1998 and 2008, driven by the rising cost of fertilisers, which makes up 20 percent of production costs. While the value of cotton stands at $37 billion, the resulting textile value amounts to $353 billion. In other words, cotton as a raw commodity feeds a multi-billion-dollar apparel and textile industry, but fails to provide millions of households in developing countries with a profitable living.[42] Independent cotton researcher Simon Ferrigno notes that "250 million jobs depend on the wider cotton lint sector and perhaps as many as a billion people gain their livelihoods in some way from cotton textiles, when retail and services are included."[43] Cotton is a pawn in a complex game of selling, hedging and buying, exposing it to risks and speculation. Government subsidies and stockpiling further distort the market, making it tough for farmers to control their businesses.

As Mark Sumner – cotton expert and professor of sustainability, retail and fashion at the School of Design, University of Leeds – confirms: "The biggest issue that came across from talking to farmers wasn't water or fertilizers or GMOs, but 'Am I gonna get paid on time for my cotton production and provide for my family?'"

Farming cotton the conventional way is therefore environmentally as well as socially unsustainable. Paying more for cotton seems almost inevitable. Traders, brands and consumers must share the cost through the adoption of standards that will provide premiums and help farmers invest in their businesses wisely. Though voluntary cotton standards are a new phenomenon, responsibly grown cotton has never been as easily available as it is today.

Organic

Organic cotton is the strictest among the sustainable cotton standards as it prohibits the use of synthetic pesticides and fertilizers as well as genetically modified seeds. To manage risks on the field, organic farmers resort to a variety of natural practices, including crop rotation (e.g. maize, peanuts, soybeans, wheat, alfalfa or rice), which helps to reduce soil erosion and increase yield. They also plant trap crops to attract pests away from the cotton; employ minimum tillage to improve soil structure and water retention; use animal and green manure in lieu of fertilizers; and manage insects by spraying pheromones to disrupt mating. These methods are harmless to both the farmer and the environment, but they are demanding. It takes three years for a conventional farmer to convert to organic and receive a certificate, which is how long it takes for the land to recover from chemically intensive farming.

Organic cotton comes with a premium to compensate for the extra effort.

Currently only 0.43 percent of the global cotton market is organic. This translates into 112,488 metric tons of fiber grown by 193,840 farmers on 350,033 hectares of land in 19 countries. India alone produces 67 percent of organic cotton, followed by China, Turkey, Kyrgyzstan and the US. According to Textile Exchange, organic is slated to grow between 20 percent and 25 percent year-on-year, provided that those brands that committed to increase their uptake by 2025 meet their objectives. Both the Soil Association report and Greenpeace[44] argue that organic is in a good position to grow, if brands and retailers increase their commitment.

The largest users of organic cotton by volume are currently C&A, H&M, Tschibo, Inditex, Nike, Decathlon, Carrefour, Lindex, Williams-Sonoma, Inc. and Stanley Stella.

In denim, Patagonia and Nudie use 100 percent organic cotton.

BCI – Better Cotton Initiative

BCI cotton is the largest among the sustainable cotton standards and also the most inclusive. It is technology-neutral with respect to genetically modified seeds, which enables it to reach the three-quarters of cotton farmers around the world who use it. It permits the use of petrochemicals, though it strives to minimize its impact through training, helping farmers to adopt more sustainable practices, such as IPM. BCI cotton does not fix a premium for its better cotton, but has been associated with quality "surcharges" in the range of 6 to 8 percent, according to Simon Ferrigno.[45]

BCI's market share currently stands at 12 percent, or 2.5 million metric tons, which are grown by 1.6 million farmers on 3.5 million hectares of land in 23 countries. This is enough to make 2.5 billion pairs of jeans (the world's annual denim production currently stands at 3.1 billion pairs). BCI cotton is physically traced from farm to gin level but from there employs the so-called mass balance system. The way it works is: Mills and retailers purchase credits for each kilogram of reported BCI cotton, which is mixed with conventional cotton from the same country as it moves up in the supply chain through the hands of traders, spinners, mills and manufacturers. At each stage the mass of reported BCI cotton is equal. This means that what ends up in a pair of jeans is not 100 percent BCI cotton, but contains a guaranteed percentage of BCI. BCI collaborates with other standards, including myBMP in Australia, ABR in Brazil and CmiA in Africa. Its target is to account for 30 percent of total cotton by 2020.

The largest users by volume are H&M, IKEA, adidas, Nike, Levi Strauss & Co, C&A, Marks and Spencer, JACK & JONES, VF Corp and Tommy Hilfiger.

Fairtrade

Fairtrade is the standard with a special focus on economic sustainability and women, offering a fair and stable price through a guaranteed minimum and an additional Fairtrade premium. While the minimum price secures income for the farmers and their families and protects them against market volatility, the premium is invested back into the community to build schools or buy tools.

Set by region and variety, the minimum price ranges between €0.66/kg in Kyrgyzstan to €0.39/kg in South Asia, which covers the average costs of production, while the Fairtrade premium stands at €0.05/kg.

Fairtrade also promotes sustainable farming practices such as IPM to minimize the use of agrochemicals. It maintains buffer zones around bodies of water and conservation areas where pesticides and hazardous chemicals must not be used and prohibits GM seeds. Female farmers are paid directly rather than through the hands of their husbands or other male family members, which has resulted in equal pay and a higher participation of women in the production of cotton.

Fairtrade unites small-scale farmers in farmer-owned organizations to strengthen their negotiating power vis-à-vis traders and ginners. There are currently 26 farmers organizations comprising 60,000 farmers in nine countries, including Benin, Brazil, Burkina Faso, Egypt, India, Kyrgyzstan, Mali, Nicaragua and Senegal. Together, they produce 15,900 tons of Fairtrade seed cotton, generating €644,000 in Fairtrade premiums. This compares to $10.35 billion in subsidies paid by governments between 2014 and 2015. These subsidies create artificially low prices that farmers in developing countries are unable to compete with, but allows countries like China and the U.S. to export their cotton at a lower price than cotton produced in West Africa or India.

Research shows that

> the cost of raw cotton as a share of the retail value is estimated to not exceed 10%. As a result, a 10% increase in the seed cotton price may translate into an increase in the retail price of only 1% or less, although there may be some compounding of costs through the value chain.[46]

Given that "the retail segment often receives over half of the final retail value of the various cotton finished products," adjustment to the price structure should indeed be possible.[47]

Cost, however, is relative. As Textile Exchange argues:

> It's not that organic cotton "costs more." It's that conventional cotton "costs too little," because it does not cover all its true costs. Health and environmental costs are often externalized meaning neither the consumer nor the retailer "pays" for them, the farmer and the environment does. When a fair price is paid, it makes a huge difference to producers and only a small difference to the consumer.[48]

In addition, 66 percent of Fairtrade cotton is also organic, accounting for 0.06 percent of the total market.

CmiA – Cotton made in Africa

CmiA's most outstanding feature is that it is 100 percent water-fed, with no artificial irrigation. Its blue water consumption (water withdrawn from groundwater or surface water bodies) only amounts to 1m³ per 1,000 kg of lint cotton. CmiA encourages IPM methods, including mandatory crop rotations, for more robust results and follows the threshold spraying principle. In other words: Only once a field has exceeded a certain level of pest infestation is a pesticide used, one that is specifically designed to eliminate the pest. No GMOs are permitted. CmíA, which helps 780,000 small-hold farmers in ten countries – including Côte d'Ivoire, Ghana, Cameroon, Zambia, Zimbabwe, Mozambique, Malawi, Tanzania, Uganda and Ethiopia – sustain themselves, accounts for 1.31 percent of the global market share, or 341,536 metric tons of fiber. CmiA is integrated into the BCI system and can be sold as BCI, but not vice versa. Brands and retailers that use CmiA include JACK & JONES, Aldi, Otto, Tschibo, ASOS and H.I.S Jeans.

Other sustainable cotton initiatives that are recommended by either Textile Exchange's *Preferred Cotton Matrix* or Cotton 2040 include Bayer e3, Cleaner Cotton and REEL/Cotton Connect.

Which standard to choose

Choosing a standard depends on what matters most to a brand or retailer, as each standard has a different focus. All promote a more sustainable system of producing cotton, however, which remains the most important fiber for denim.

Impact data are tough to compare due to climatic differences as well as differences in soil quality of those geographies where cotton is grown. The standards don't necessarily use the same matrix, either. BCI, for instance, doesn't produce life cycle analyses (LCAs). Organic cotton only compares itself against the benchmark of conventional cotton as documented by Cotton, Inc., which indicates significant benefits, especially with reference to water consumption.

According to Textile Exchange (see Figure 3.1), which promotes organic practices, organically grown cotton boasts 91 percent reduced blue water consumption

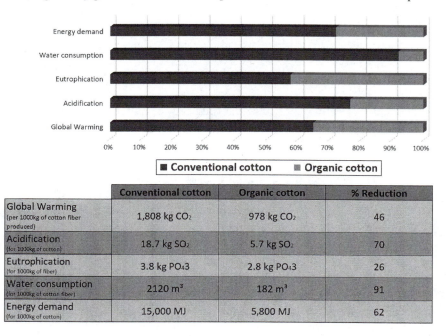

	Conventional cotton	Organic cotton	% Reduction
Global Warming (per 1000kg of cotton fiber produced)	1,808 kg CO_2	978 kg CO_2	46
Acidification (for 1000kg of cotton)	18.7 kg SO_2	5.7 kg SO_2	70
Eutrophication (for 1000kg of fiber)	3.8 kg PO_43	2.8 kg PO_43	26
Water consumption (for 1000kg of cotton fiber)	2120 m³	182 m³	91
Energy demand (for 1000kg of cotton)	15,000 MJ	5,800 MJ	62

FIGURE 3.1   Organic vs. conventional cotton

Source: Textile Exchange

(i.e. water withdrawn from groundwater or surface water bodies for irrigation), as 95 percent of water used in organic production is green water (rain water and moisture stored in soil), while the regions investigated by Cotton Inc. for its LCA were at least partially irrigated. Further, organic production logged 46 percent lower global warming levels through reduced greenhouse gas emissions; 70 percent lower acidification levels, which are mostly caused by ammonia; 26 percent reduced eutrophication (or over-fertilization, which is caused by chemical runoffs and soil erosion); and 62 percent reduced primary energy demand from non-renewable resources. The reductions are calculated per 1,000 kilogram of cotton fiber.[49]

That said, LCAs pose a number of limitations and figures can vary greatly.

As Mark Sumner explains:

> It takes somewhere between 7,000 and 27,000 liters of water to produce one kg of cotton. Not only is the amount of water consumption dependent on whether it's irrigated or rain-fed, on where it's grown or what type of cotton project you are on, but it can vary season to season. We sponsored a project in South India and for the first three years we saw year-on-year reduction of water and pesticides. In the fourth year, we saw a peak in water consumption and pesticide use. The farmers did not all of the sudden become bad farmers, but the weather conditions changed. The rain came at the wrong time, they had to irrigate when it was too dry, and because the rain came at the wrong time they saw a sudden spike in infestation, so they had to use more pesticides to counteract that. The challenge with LCAs is they will give you a feel of what is going on in a particular field in a particular project in a particular season, they won't give you any idea about variability season to season. And comparing one LCA to another is difficult because they depend on whether water use or water consumption is measured.

Rather than comparing sustainable standards, brands and retailers are best advised to pick one or several that speak most to their priorities. At this point, any small change in the sourcing of cotton can make a big difference. Sumner says,

> a brand once said to me it can't do sustainable cotton on the scale that it needed viewing how much it consumed. But if there is a 10 percent improvement, then across 26 million tons of cotton consumed each year, that is quite an impact. That would be spectacular and mean real market transformation.

Alternatively, the cotton expert advises brands to do their own research to scout good farmers, or work with mills that have their own production, such as Arvind. Arvind, one of the world's largest manufacturers of denim fabric, is currently working with over 4,000 farms, both organic and BCI, in an effort to enhance their productivity and reduce their financial risk. The data Arvind collects confirms that both BCI and organic are substantially less polluting than conventional cotton, with organic scoring best except in the water category.

Some brands and NGOs take a more rigorous stance. While Patagonia rejects BCI cotton for its tolerance of petrochemicals, Greenpeace argues:

> Instead of settling for half measures such as Better Cotton, more brands, in particular global brands which hold a significant share of the market, should be prepared to source Organic and Fairtrade cotton and pay a higher price. This is the only way to make a significant positive impact on the environmental and human costs of conventional cotton. However, cotton grown with minimum impact on the environment will limit its availability, which is likely to be at a lower output than is currently squeezed out of the crop. This emphasizes the importance of reducing our consumption of clothing and slowing the flow.[50]

It adds further that the argument against organic cotton and alternative fibers like hemp or nettle is that there isn't enough land to grow it, but who says we need these enormous quantities. We produce more than we can sell and buy more than we need. Why not reverse the system – and produce less with higher quality and longer lifespans, buy less at higher price points and keep longer. Surely, that should take the weight off farming of fibers for textile production.

Contrary to common belief, buying sustainable cotton has never been as easy as it is in today's market. It is uptake that is lagging behind. The *Mind the Gap* report, published by Pesticides Action Network UK, Solidaridad and WWF in 2016, painted a disappointing picture of international brands and retailers. It stated that while the production of more sustainable cotton has never been higher, reaching 2,173,000 metric tons in 2014, only 17 percent – that's 360,000 metric tons – was bought by retailers as sustainable cotton. The remaining 83 percent was sold on the conventional market. Among the four big standards the study took into account, organic logged the largest share of uptake with 70 to 80 percent, while BCI was able to sell only 13 percent of its farmers' harvests.[51]

The study warned that low uptake discourages farmers from adopting more sustainable practices. "If greater demand is not reflected in increased orders from retailers, there is a danger that farmers will abandon sustainable production altogether and the opportunity to improve global standards will be missed."[52] This concerns environmental but also social and economic aspects, as more sustainable cotton initiatives aim to lift farmers from poverty and improve their health and labor conditions. The research further notes:

> When lack of demand forces Organic or Fairtrade cotton farmers to sell part of their harvest on the conventional cotton market, it means they are not fully compensated for the extra effort and expense involved in producing standard compliant crops, resulting in lower incomes. For BCI and CmiA low uptake means low investments in growing the supply. For all standards lack of uptake weakens not only the business case for farmers, but also of cotton gins, traders, yarn and fabric manufacturers.

The report, based on research by cotton maverick Simon Ferragno, identified several reasons for sluggish sales: lack of awareness on the consumer side; an opaque supply chain forbidding brands and retailers from engaging directly with those suppliers who are greasing the wheels of uptake (e.g. spinners); additional costs associated with more sustainable cotton (e.g. premiums with organic and Fairtrade cotton, licensing fees with CmiA, farmer support contribution with BCI); existence of too many standards and initiatives, which confuse brands and retailers; lack of clear sourcing strategies and marketing initiatives among brands and retailers, possibly due to a shift towards issues involving safety and working conditions, which have dominated the media in recent years.

Meanwhile, the researchers argue, these challenges also bear opportunities for both the brands and the market. Protecting one's reputation and securing the long-term supply of cotton should be of concern to any fashion executive. Getting to the bottom of the supply chain would not only make it cleaner but essentially nimbler in securing the supply of preferred qualities of cotton. In addition, the more sustainable cotton is in the market, the less will it cost, which is true for all green initiatives.

Engaging directly with the various standard organizations would also ensure brands have a leadership role at the table as the details of future cotton supply chains are being worked out. Finally, communicating on more sustainable cotton options through targeted storytelling on the shop floor would help brands engage directly with consumers and strengthen their loyalty.

In the end, communication is key to any successful relationship. Cotton 2040, a new initiative by Forum for the Future, which reunites all big sustainable cotton standards in one place, therefore starts with the basic: finding a common language.

Q&A WITH CHARLENE COLLISON, HEAD OF COTTON 2040

Q: What is the purpose of Cotton 2040?

A: To help create a space in which these different standards and organisations can come together and deal with some of the issues that affect all of them.

Standards like the Organic, Fairtrade, BCI or Cotton Made in Africa have done really good work. At the same time when you look at the amount of effort that has been put into these initiatives over the last ten years and the amount of money, outreach and energy that has been dedicated to shifting just one commodity, is quite staggering. Yet the impact is still so small. What would fall into a broad bucket of what is called sustainability is still only about 13 to 15 percent of the market. Organic alone is less than 1 percent. So we needed to create a space in which we accepted the differences and did not try to reach a consensus on key issues. BCI and organic are just going to disagree on GM, but there are areas where there is a lot of mutual benefit from working together.

Q: What are the key areas you are tackling?

A: We want to create a systemic shift to mainstream sustainable cotton through building demand, scaling up cotton recycling and circularity. We are also developing a road map for greater traceability across the supply chain – a common language format and possibly a common lint portal would be an option later on. And we are working around issues of smallholder resilience.

Q: Why do you think is the market not responding faster?

A: There are system challenges that are part of a wider supply chain. Part of the issue is all these standards are telling different stories, each has a different message. If you are a retailer or a brand and you say "OK, I want to increase my uptake of sustainable cotton" you need to knock on three or more doors to explore what your options are, and each has a different set of matrix [sic]. You can't easily compare apples to apples. What is one unit of organic cotton going to cost me compared to BCI? You can't answer that because they don't [work] the same way. So how do you begin to shift some of those barriers, how do you even use the same words within your different reporting systems to make it easier for brands to navigate? An interesting trend our partners have seen is a real increase of brands wanting to source *across* standards. They don't just want to source BCI or organic, but they want a portfolio approach, because there are different types of cotton that are suitable for different types of product. They say: "for some of our upscale items we would like organic, because that's a premium, and we would want to put it into our baby and child products, but we also want to have cotton that we can sell at a lower price point, which is on a par with conventional and yet know that it is not causing damage to the environment or to people, so we might want BCI for our more standard range. Or our policy is also to support women, so we might choose to go with Fairtrade that has a specific program focusing on women empowerment."

Q: So the goal is to create a one-stop shop?

A: Ideally we would like one source to go to. What some of the middlemen have said is: Every time you want to source a different standard, it's a whole other work stream to embed within your organization, because you have to work with a whole new set of criteria and reporting systems.

Q: The Mind the Gap Report shows that brands and retailers are reluctant to pick up more sustainable cotton that is already in the market. Is there a killer argument for them to be more reactive?

A: The killer argument is that if you don't address these problems you will run out of water and there won't be a cotton industry in 2040. I actually tried that and it didn't really work for the CEOs. It worked for the sustainability folks. To be honest, unless you are one of those really pioneering brands that has a clear commitment to being part of the change, the questions that the CEOs will ask and the sourcing teams will have to go back to is: "how is this going to increase sales and improve my bottom line?"

But cotton is a massive global commodity, just by shifting to sustainable cotton you will tick an awful lot of boxes on your sustainability agenda, impacting 300 million people's livelihoods around the world, reduce massively your water and chemicals use. Cotton should be top of your list. For those companies that are not yet sourcing sustainable cotton, cotton is risky. We live in an environment where water is one of the most critical issues, and it will continue be an issue. Do you really want to expose yourself to the reputational risk of sourcing cotton that you just don't know whether it's polluting or using water very irresponsibly or involving very questionable labor practices? There has been a strong response from producers, now there needs to be a pull from brands to buy it. Some brands come in and increase their uptake really quickly like ASOS, which has only been sourcing sustainable cotton for a couple years, but increased its percentage dramatically and wants to be 100 percent sustainable by 2025. But there are also so many who are just starting to think about.

Q: Is there a reason why are you aiming at the year 2040?

A: 2040 is when a lot of the climate change impacts will really hit. According to IPCC, in 2040 you will see even more changes in rainfall patterns, and desertification of large areas of land that are currently used to grow food, and more dramatic disruption. Of course, these are projections and we don't know what the reality will actually be – some of these changes will come sooner, others will take longer. But the issues that are impacting farmers now, through the lens of 2040 will become massive. A lot of the smallholder farmers who supply 60 percent of [the] world's cotton can't make a living. Cotton farmers in India commit suicide simply [because] their seeds don't yield, or they deal with difficulties of high input prices particularly related to GM varieties, or because the market is so volatile, they don't get enough of a return for their prices. And there is pressure on available land to prioritize growing food. A lot of cotton production has been shifted to almonds and other food crops that guarantee farmers an income in the U.S., but also in Asia and other developing countries.

Q: One of the main problems with sustainable cotton is that it costs more. Will brands and retailers eventually need to rethink the way they look at margins?

A: The problem with the current business model is that the value gets shared really unequally across the supply chain, so it's the brands, but it's also the middlemen and women – it's a supply chain problem, and if we want to keep having cotton and farmers that farm it, we need to do a better job at making it worthwhile to farm. It's a question of not if but when the industry wakes up to that.

Polyester

Although cotton is denim's preferred fiber, polyester is the most popular fiber in the world. It is employed across the industry, largely for its performance characteristics and low pricing. Polyester makes up well over 60 percent of the global fiber market, together with other manmade synthetic fibers such as nylon or acrylic. By comparison, cotton stands at about 28 percent and viscose and other cellulosic fibers at 6 percent.

Polyester has seen a stellar performance since it was discovered in an English lab in the 1940s. To wit, in 1980 global demand stood at 5.2 million tons; by 2000 it had reached 19.2 million tons, surpassing cotton in 2002, and only 14 years later it shot up to 41.1 million tons.[53]

Its heyday is far from over. Polyester is slated to grow to between 73 million and 76 million tons by 2030 – that's the combined weight of between 200 and 230 Empire State Buildings.[54] And this is scheduled to happen at the expense of cotton. The "Pulse of the Fashion" report, put together by the Global Fashion Agenda and the Boston Consulting Group, has issued a recommendation to the apparel industry to replace 30 percent of cotton with polyester by 2030, in an attempt to save 22.6 billion m³ of water.[55]

It notes that polyester is not "perfect," but could add to a "sustainable material mix" based on its low water intake, especially when processed via renewable energies.

However, the idea was promptly dismissed by Greenpeace and the International Wool Textile Organisation (IWTO) for missing out on "some critical problems."[56] Greenpeace pointed to synthetic fibers' "reliance on fossil fuels and their contribution to microplastic or microfibre pollution," while the IWTO noted how the report bases its conclusions "on incomplete life cycle data," adding fuel to the fast fashion business model.

The fact is, polyester and high street are cozy bedfellows. Synthetics are cheap and do not take a year to harvest, which makes them perfectly compatible with fast fashion cycles. They are also easier to recycle than cotton and save energy in the process without compromising on quality. But they come from a non-renewable source (crude oil), are non-biodegradable and are created with catalysts such as antimony.

The good news is that there is no need for polyester in denim. Jeans had become one of the most popular staples in the world before polyester and spandex entered the picture. According to WGSN, a trend forecasting and consultancy agency, and to denim brands queried, a shift towards more authentic – that is, 100 percent cotton denim – is under way as consumers increasingly look for products that can last.

Also, as water efficiency improves at the farm level, the water argument alone may not suffice to offset polyester's disadvantages. Although it is true that the fiber consumes considerably less water in production, it ends up polluting water at its end-of-life stage.

Microplastics

What are these, exactly? They are fragments of plastics, usually smaller than 5mm in diameter, shed as debris from cosmetic products and synthetic textile fibers, among others. Polyester, rayon and acrylic are among the most common microplastics found in seawater and in autopsied animals.[57] Often mistaken for food by small and large aquatic organisms, including plankton and whales, microplastics cause digestive problems leading to starvation and negatively impact species' reproductive systems. Moreover, chemicals used in plastic production or found in surrounding water stick to microplastics, where they remain toxic as they move up the food chain. The particles have also been found to transport so-called persistent organic pollutants (POPs) into organisms, toxic to both humans and the environment. The EPA says that

> because they can be transported by wind and water, most POPs generated in one country can and do affect people and wildlife far from where they are used and released. They persist for long periods of time in the environment and can accumulate and pass from one species to the next through the food chain.[58]

Filter feeders such as oysters, clams and mussels are particularly at risk.

In other words, we end up eating the very toxins with our seafood platter that we release into the environment. Patagonia commissioned a study from the Bren School of Environmental Science and Management at the University of California that concluded that a city of 100,000 people produces 170–441 kilograms of microfibers from washing synthetic clothing per day. Of those, between 9 and 110 kilograms, depending on the wastewater treatment, end up in local water bodies daily, equal to about 15,000 plastic bags.[59] Further, Patagonia wanted to know what the impact of four of its bestselling fleece jackets was and had them compared to a budget jacket. The analyses showed that both the age of the jackets and the type of washing machine determined how much microplastic was shed. Aged jackets displayed 1.8 times more shedding, while top-load machines had 5.3 times the microfiber shedding of front-load machines. On average, synthetic jackets released 1,174 milligrams of microfiber from the washing machine, 40 percent of which slipped through local wastewater treatments.

Also, the generic fleece jackets lost about 170 percent more particles than Patagonia's higher-end product.

A similar study conducted by Mistra Future Fashion[60] showed how the construction of a garment impacts the amount of microfiber released. It found that shedding from polyester was reduced when garments were left unbrushed, when ultrasound cutting – comparable to laser cutting – was applied in the cut and sew process and when microparticles had already been removed at the production stage. Fabrics made from virgin polymers shed 126 percent more than fabrics made of recycled polymers.

Meanwhile, at Goteborg University, scientists noted that 90 percent of microplastics found on the Swedish west coast,[61] where a lot of debris ends up due to ocean currents, came from textile fibers, putting the apparel industry on the spot, which often argues that microplastic pollution stems mostly from packaging.

The study tested three materials – acrylic, polyamide and polyester – of which fleece (made of 100 percent polyester) shed the most. Consequently, the "sheddability" depended not only on the fabric type, but the yarn and texture as well. Regardless of garment construction, a higher fiber loss was registered when detergent was used and when the clothes were repolished to simulate used clothes. The researchers therefore suggested "the development of solutions such as construction of materials with less shedding and filters in washing machines and wastewater treatment plants, and to promote less use of synthetic textile fibers until better solutions are found."[62]

Given polyester's popularity, it is unlikely that the fiber and its microplastic problem will be phased out in a similar fashion as microplastic beads in cosmetics, following President Obama's "Microbead-Free Waters Act of 2015." In the meantime, the Bren study recommends putting synthetic clothing into a washing bag, such as the fully recyclable Guppyfriend, to prevent microfibers from going down the drain. Alternatively, Patagonia suggests installing a permanent washing machine filter such as Wexco's Filtrol 160 and disposing of the filtered microparticles with regular trash. They may not be recyclable, but it is still preferable to keep them out of the water streams and our food chains.

Energy

As the volume of polyester in the market grows, so does its carbon footprint. MIT calculated that under current conditions, which are slated to remain the same for the next 15 years until renewable energies take over, "the global impact of polyester fabric will grow from roughly 880 billion kg CO_2 today to a projected 1.5 trillion kg CO_2 by 2030."[63] It estimated that polyester production for textiles was responsible for over 706 billion kilograms of greenhouse gas in 2015.[64] This equals 1.6 billion barrels of oil (a two-year supply of oil for the US) or carbon stored in one year by 579 million acres of forest (the size of Algeria). By comparison, cotton emits 107.5 billion kilograms of CO_2, which amounts to four years of household energy supply for the city of Los Angeles, or carbon stored in one year by 88 million acres of forest (the size of Japan). MIT recommends using knit over woven polyester, which would slash energy consumption in production by almost half; sourcing fiber from suppliers with low-emission electricity grids; and using recycled PET (polyethylene terephthalate).

Antimony

Polyester is primarily made of polyethylene terephthalate, or PET, which is the same material used to make water bottles. PET requires a catalyst to speed up the chemical reaction, and the catalyst used worldwide in polyester fiber processing is called antimony. It's a heavy metal, which can be released during processes that involve heat such as dyeing or incineration (where most polyester clothing will end its life), or become a pollutant in air and wastewater. The International Agency for Research on Cancer (IARC), part of the World Health Organization (WHO), classifies antimony trioxide as a 2B agent, i.e. "possibly carcinogenic to humans," following evidence of carcinogenicity by inhalation among animals.[65]

Antimony-free polyester is available from TWD Fibres GmbH or Victor Innovatex, which also allows it to be safely recycled. Regular polyester retains its antimony when made into another fiber. So far, recycling technology does not permit antimony to be re-extracted.

DuPont, on the other hand, has come up with a new antimony-free formula of compostable polyester called Apexa®, with the primary goal to reduce waste. It is a standard PET combined with a monomer that creates weak spots in the polymeric chains, allowing them to degrade through hydrolysis. Naturally occurring microbes convert Apexa® polyester from large polymer molecules into smaller ones and finally into carbon dioxide and water.

As Samit Chevli, principal investigator of biomaterials at DuPont, explains: "It will be hundreds of years before regular polyester biodegrades. Apexa® decomposes in less than six months under industrial compost conditions." The fiber is also said to enhance performance, making garments more durable but with a softer hand feel than regular polyester.

Recycled polyester

The United Nations notes that we can expect to find "more plastic than fish in the world's oceans by 2050 unless people stop using single-use plastic items such as plastic bags and plastic bottles."[66] Plastics in general have a deplorable recycling record. Only 14 percent of plastic packaging is collected, with a loss of between $80 billion and $120 billion in material value,[67] according to estimates by the Ellen McArthur Foundation, even though they could be mechanically recycled with little to no loss in quality. PET, more specifically, has a higher recycling rate of 50 percent, but only 7 percent are recycled bottle-to-bottle. The overwhelming majority of PET bottles – 80 percent – are reprocessed into polyester fibers for carpet or clothing, which the foundation refers to as mechanical open-loop recycling, or downcycling, since it does not create a truly circular system. However, as long as there is no circular model in place, making fiber with waste is a better option than leaving plastic bottles in the oceans or the ground, as long as both manufacturers and brands/retailers advise customers on how to filter any microplastics during household washing.

Recycled polyester not only reduces plastic waste, but also saves energy and raw materials. Many such fibers are suitable for denim. Repreve by Unifi, for instance, reuses post-consumer plastic bottles via a mechanical recycling process. According to the company, it takes six bottles to make a shirt and 50 bottles to make a fleece jacket. Teijin's Eco Circle Fiber is done through chemical recycling, which operates in a closed loop. Here, polyester textiles are collected, broken down and processed into new polyester fiber without any loss in quality.

Mechanically recycled polyester is said to be of slightly lower quality than virgin, depending on the raw material used as input. The fibers are chopped up, which makes them lose strength. They will at some point become useless, which is why this process only temporarily diverts waste from landfills. Cradle-to-cradle fiber specialist Annie Gullingsrud also warns that "the demand for used PET bottles is now surpassing supply in some areas, and reports indicate that some suppliers are buying new bottles to make polyester textile fiber that can be called recycled." [68] Some materials in this process also need to be bleached and re-dyed.

Chemically recycled polyester retains its quality and makes infinite recycling possible. The process is based on the idea of breaking up the polymers into their molecular structures and putting them back together again. This technique does use more energy than mechanical recycling, and the chemistry used needs to be monitored to make sure it does not lead to more pollution. This is true for synthetic fibers as well as natural ones. So far, new chemical recycling methods are being explored to separate cotton from polyester, which would allow the creation of both regenerated cotton and polyester yarn from a cotton/poly blend. The initiative Worn Again is currently partnering with Kering, Puma and H&M to make the technology available on an industrial level.

Some fabrics can be recycled neither mechanically nor chemically due to certain finishes or chemical ingredients found in them. It is therefore imperative to design clothing with recyclability as a premise.

Spandex/Elastane

Contrary to common belief, stretch is not a fiber, but a performance quality. Stretch means elastic, and the elasticity is mainly achieved through a fiber called spandex or elastane. Like polyester, spandex is a synthetic, oil-derived material, which is not renewable and sheds microplastics. It is essentially synthetic rubber. It wears out quickly and therefore produces garment waste, in addition to its high-energy consumption. Elastic garments serve a range of purposes, which can be convenient. They are not imperative, however, to a good pair of jeans. In denim, stretch has become an aesthetic fad, especially with the emergence of skinny jeans. But as spandex is most often blended with other fibers, it stands in the way of being recycled in a closed loop – that is, fiber to fiber. Moreover, the production of spandex is linked to toxic substance emissions, since many of the solvents used in the manufacturing of spandex are considered hazardous.[69]

It is therefore imperative to opt for more eco-friendly, bio-based alternatives as they become available.

Sorona® stretch fiber

One is the Sorona® stretch fiber, developed by DuPont. Sorona® itself is made from 37 percent plant-based ingredients. Compared to competing products such as

Nylon 6, the PTT (poly trimethylene terephthalate) polymer uses 30 percent less energy, emits 63 percent fewer greenhouse gases during production and requires no antimony. It is certified by the independent OEKO-TEX labelling system and is compatible with other fibers, which is what the mills like about it. However, its recyclability is limited due to its synthetic component, and the fiber is neither bio-degradable like Apexa® nor compostable.

To create stretch, DuPont mixes Sorona® with polyester, resulting in a bi-component fiber that allows between 10 and 30 percent stretchability.

Sorona® is billed as breaking down less quickly than regular spandex, resulting in less bagging, fewer washes and more durability. "It has excellent recovery of 80% or more, even after 25 washes, or two to three years of life, while Spandex has 40 percent," explains Akshay Kumar, engineer of biomaterials at DuPont.

Unlike other stretch fibers, Sorona® is UV- and chlorine-resistant, which makes it retain its shape and color longer. While regular polyester needs to be dyed at 125 to 130 degrees Celsius, Sorona® requires 20 degrees less at the dye-ing stage.

LYCRA® T400® EcoMade

Among the companies using Sorona® is Invista, which made the fiber part of its LYCRA® T400® EcoMade formula. "Different from an elastane, this is a bi-component fiber," explains Jean Hegedus, the company's Global Segment Leader for Denim. "Fifty percent of the fiber is made from recycled PET such as water bot-tles. Another 18% of the fiber is made from a renewable plant based material (corn). The remaining 32 percent contains traditional petrochemicals." Invista is billed as the world's first manufacture of bio-derived elastane, which it introduced in 2013. Its original stretch fiber was 70 percent derived from dextrose made of corn, while the remaining 30 percent was traditional petrochemicals, though there is currently no commercial offering due to lack of demand. Initial interest in LYCRA® T400® EcoMade fiber has been strong, on the other hand, says Hegedus, "so we are opti-mistic about its future."

The ultimate goal would be to create "a compostable denim," says Simon Candiani, marketing manager at Candiani SpA, "which means that it is not only biodegradable, but that once it biodegrades, it does not release any harmful sub-stances into the soil."

Weaving

Much can also be done in the weaving department. Former denim mill ITV, which sadly went out of business in 2017, had already developed a stretch quality it called "stretch-no-stretch" made of 100 percent cotton. The construction rendered the fabric on the lower end of the comfort stretch zone at between 10 percent and 13 percent stretch. According to ITV, the technology will live on in future collabo-rations with other mills.

Lyocell/Modal

Lyocell is also a man-made fiber, but it's natural. It's made of wood pulp, much like viscose and modal. And much like cotton and polyester, its sustainability level depends on who makes it and how. Turning cellulose into textile fiber is a chemically intensive process, but it can be done in an eco-friendly fashion, by a) keeping chemicals in a closed loop and b) using sustainably sourced wood, as modeled by Lenzing. The Austrian manufacturer has developed a system that recovers and recycles 99 percent of a chemical solvent called NNMO, used in its lyocell manufacturing, along with its water. Meanwhile, more than 99 percent of its wood and pulp is Forest Stewardship Council (FSC) and Programme for the Endorsement of Forest Certification (PEFC) certified. The company is being audited by Canopy, a non-profit organization that focuses on the protection and conservation of ancient and endangered forests. Lenzing says the bioenergy derived from the wood is used to make its facility partly self-sufficient in terms of energy. "Due to the vertical integration of pulp and fiber production, energy is used highly efficiently," it claims in its Sustainability Report.[70]

According to Canopy,

> every year, 120 million trees are logged for fabrics including rayon, viscose, modal and other trademarked textiles. That number is projected to double by 2025. Too many of these trees are over 1,000 years old or provide forest homes to threatened species [and] to indigenous people. [...] Furthermore, ancient and intact forests absorb carbon, storing it in soils and standing trees. Their continued existence is vital to stabilizing the world's climate and helping us all mitigate the growing impacts of climate change.[71]

Lenzing's lyocell fiber is branded as Tencel® and is mostly derived from eucalyptus trees, which grow quickly and don't require irrigation. Tencel® gives denim a soft feel and a light sheen.

The company has also introduced a new line of modal fabrics, made from birch trees, called Modal® Color. It's a spun-dyed fiber, meaning the pigments are embedded directly in the fiber matrix. The advantages are higher color fastness and a smaller ecological footprint, since garments made with Modal® Color no longer need to go through a conventional dying process, saving 50 percent in the energy and water departments respectively, which also results in 60 percent fewer CO_2 emissions. Modal® Black is particularly interesting to denim producers, who have been struggling with making black jeans retain their shade. Modal is derived from beech trees, which are considered soil enhancers with little appetite for water and better resistance to pests. This results in six times higher yields than cotton, according to Lenzing.

Bast fibers

Bast fibers are perhaps as old as clad mankind itself. They are extracted from the stems of the plants through a process called retting. Among the most common examples of bast fibers are flax, hemp and jute, but they also include ramie, bamboo, nettle and banana.

Hemp is perhaps the most obvious choice for denim. One of the first pairs of Levi's was reportedly made of hemp canvas, not cotton. Some sources indicate that as much as 80 percent of clothing was made from hemp until the 1920s,[72] before it was forced to take a backseat to both synthetics and cotton at the beginning of the 20th century. While a great deal of funding poured into making cotton a high-yield crop, the hemp industry got sidelined by unfavorable laws prohibiting its cultivation due to its links with narcotics, since hemp and cannabis are part of the same family.

Hemp comes with a series of advantages vis-à-vis other natural fibers. It grows extremely fast, some four meters in three months, resulting in the highest yield per acre of any natural fiber.[73] Three times the amount of hemp fiber can be produced from the same amount of land as cotton.[74] The plant is compatible with cooler climates and is an excellent rotation crop because of its fast growth and deep rooting system, which has been reported to up soil quality, increasing the yield of subsequent crops by 10 to 20 percent.[75]

It's also one of the strongest natural fibers, which makes it very durable, in addition to its natural antibacterial properties, breathability and thermal protection.

Hemp is low-maintenance. It does not require any artificial irrigation, pesticides or fertilizers due to its high resistance to diseases. Between cotton, polyester and hemp, hemp was found to have the lowest ecological footprint, which can further be improved by technological innovation.[76] Its biggest inconvenience is availability and outdated machinery. While in the 16th century Henry VIII compelled farmers by law to use one-fourth of an acre aside for hemp cultivation, by the early 20th century there was hardly any left. China has been the most consistent supplier, with some 6,000 years of experience under its belt. Consequently, most hemp today is grown and processed by China, though the European Industrial Hemp Association (EIHA), formed in 2005, is looking to revive the dormant industry in countries like Great Britain, the Netherlands, Germany and Italy.

"Hemp is as soft as a baby's bottom but super straight at the same time, which means spinning it is a real art," says Robert Hertel, CEO of HempAge, which has spent the last four years developing the next generation of hemp jeans.

> There is one machine that's 120 years old that can achieve the right quality, but it's an artefact. Most machines in use have been adapted from the cotton industry. Just imagine what we could do with modern technology. Hemp would be so much easier to process and cheaper. Yet no one's building it.

His own company is investing in optimizing the retting process with ultrasound. There are three types of retting:

- dew retting is the most eco-friendly, as it returns valuable nutrients to the soil, though it is unpredictable as it depends on the weather. Here, the pectin and lignin that holds the bast fiber and the stem together are separated though natural fermentation made of nothing more but bacteria, sun, air and dew;

- water retting steeps the stems in water, where bacteria can do their work, but the process requires large pools of water; and
- chemical retting involves boiling and immersing the plants in a chemical solution including sodium hydroxide and is the quickest way of extracting the fiber, but also the one with the largest ecological footprint.

It is imperative to treat the waste water from both water and chemical retting before releasing it back into nature.

More research and development are needed to bring down the price of production, which can be five to ten times higher than cotton or synthetics. With more demand coming from the denim industry, this is a viable business opportunity, as shown by the Freitag brothers, best known for their bags made from recycling truck tarpaulins.

They have created a new genre of denim from hemp and flax that they call f-fabric. It is spool-dyed rather than indigo-dyed to make their jeans fully compostable. Daniel and Markus explain:

> We use an eco-friendly reactive dye instead of a classic indigo dye. So after a year, the look of our denim will be different from a cotton raw denim. We probably can't convince the pure denim heads – raw denim freaks – of f-fabric. We don't compete with rough denim made with a Japanese shuttle loom. Our denim simply is different.[77]

Other than finding the right machinery, which is a challenge in Europe, they say

> the main issue with hemp is softening the outer part of the fiber. It's done with lots of chemicals. How do you solve this? We simply don't soften it in an extreme way. It's done mechanically and the weaving is what really matters. Our fabric is not as soft as cotton, but I really like the feel of it and it does get "softer" and more comfortable the longer you wear it.[78]

It took five years to develop the fabric, since the company that originally provided the fiber went bankrupt.

G-star, meanwhile, has experimented with nettle, until its Dutch supplier also went out of business, much to the brand's disappointment. Frouke Bruinsma, G-Star's sustainability manager, says,

> It was so experimental that is was rather expensive, but it worked well for denim, and it could work on a larger scale. Because nettle is a rain-fed crop, it doesn't need much water, and you can even grow it in your backyard. We are currently looking into where we could source it from for larger production.

The struggles of alternative fiber manufacturers underline the brands' and retailers' obligation to work more closely with suppliers and commit to their output.

Recycled cotton

To reduce the dependency of the apparel industry on raw material, recycled cotton is growing in importance. It is hailed as a long-term solution to growing demand and the scarcity of land. Swedish re:newcell is able to break down old cotton clothing and other cellulosic fiber such as lyocell into dissolving pulp; this allows new garments to be 100 percent made from recycled cellulosic fiber without any loss of quality vis-à-vis virgin fibers, as proven by the now-famous yellow dress that debuted on the Berlin Ethical Fashion Week catwalk in July 2014. The dress had been made of a pair of blue jeans recycled with re:newcell's technology. The chemicals used to dissolve and treat the textile waste are collected and reused in a closed loop. According to the brand, chemicals and dyes present in the fabrics function as input and are separated out and disposed of in accordance with Swedish environmental regulations.

With 80 percent of clothing ending up in landfill and an estimated 50 to 70 million tons of clothing thrown away each year, Austrian cellulose specialist Lenzing bets on Refibra, a new generation of Tencel®. It is made from cotton scraps – left over from cutting that would have otherwise ended up in the trash – and wood. Refibra is also done in a closed-loop chemical process.

Evrnu, meanwhile, has teamed with Levi's and is working on its own formula for chemically recycled cotton scraps; it is said to be constantly improving the quality of its fiber, according to market sources.

Bio waste and living organisms

Waste in general has enormous potential. Organic waste in particular could help reduce the toxic nature of our clothing and close the loop, mimicking nature, where the waste of one organism becomes food for another. The field is more experimental in nature, to be sure, but also most promising.

It can literally start with something as simple as the poop of bacteria. DuPont's Sorona®, for instance, is derived from the excrement of an organism that is fed with sugar from corn. This organic waste helps form the bio-version of a compound needed to make a polymer for textiles.

Natureworks takes a similar approach. It relies on corn, sugar cane and beets to capture and sequester a greenhouse gas like carbon dioxide and transform it into long-chain sugar molecules. Microorganisms then ferment those sugars into lactic acid, which eventually becomes a polylactide polymer (PLA) called Ingeo and can be made into biodegradable, plastic-free yogurt cups or apparel. The company is currently exploring ways of skipping the help of plants and training the bacteria directly to transform methane or carbon dioxide into Ingeo.

FIGURE 3.2   Indigo jacket by Biocouture
Source: Suzanne Lee

Both PTT and PLA are likely to become serious competition to polyester.

Bacteria are one of the most available organisms on the planet, and they do great work in the lab. Suzanne Lee, formerly of Biocouture and now chief creative officer at Modern Meadow, has been growing fiber with their help. Lee once created a Levi's look-alike jacket from microbial cellulose by feeding a sugary solution to a microbe, which then excreted the cellulose and formed sheets of material via fermentation.

> It's like brewing beer or kombucha. It's a mix of yeast and bacteria. You get this matter on the surface of the jar that is a nanostructured material that traps the oxygen inside the fermenting brew. We started taking that mass, which gives you a very pure cellulose material. You dye it in indigo – we even grew it in indigo – and the fibers that the cellulose is bringing together form the sheets, and then you can turn the sheet into a garment of some kind.

It feels more like a leather, but technically you could weave the sheets into denim fabric, she says (see Figure 3.2).

> The challenge is that cotton is cheap, so what you end up doing is competing with a commodity fiber that is stockpiled around the world, and these

technologies are really, really expensive to bring to market. Till the price of cotton goes up, it's just not possible to do it at the same price. Either you find a way to give the fiber radically different properties to plant-based cotton or it's not a go.

Speaking of slow fashion, it took two weeks for the denim-like jacket to form.

Textiles have also been made of cow dung by BioArtLab and wine scum by the University of Western Australia.

But this doesn't have to be as experimental. Waste from coffee grounds, for instance, is already used in denim on a commercial level. The coffee grounds are first carbonized, which turns them into fine powder, and then added in the extrusion of the polyester so they become embedded in the fiber. Prosperity Textile is among those mills that offer coffee-made denim, which it ups with quick-dry properties, anti-odor and UV protection.

The waste from citrus fruits, meanwhile, has been successfully employed by high-end fashion. Orange Fiber, an Italian company and brainchild of two Sicilian girls, produced a textile made by extracting the cellulose from the fibers found in orange rinds discarded during the industrial pressing and processing of oranges. In Sicily alone, where vast amounts of citrus fruits are grown, production results in some 700 tons of organic waste a year. Orange Fiber not only helps reduce that waste but also, through nano-technological techniques, infuses the soft, silk-like yarn with citrus essential oil, which the company says is able to nourish the skin with vitamins.

Technically, any waste from fruits and vegetables could find its way into fashion, reduce its environmental footprint and bring additional performance properties into the game.

An interesting proposal was made by Israeli scientists at the Hebrew University, which is working on a scalable process to produce nanocellulose, found in trees. "Of course, we didn't want to cut trees," says the project's lead Oded Shoseyov.[79]

> So we were looking for another source of raw material, and we found one – the sludge of the paper industry. The reason: there is a lot of it. Europe alone produces 11 million tons of that material annually. It's the equivalent of a mountain three kilometers high, sitting on a soccer field. And we produce this mountain every year. So for everybody, it's an environmental problem, and for us, it's a gold mine.

The nanocellulose discarded during paper production is both literally and figuratively a waste, given that it's ten times stronger than steel, though made of sugar. Adding only a small percent of nanocellulose to cotton fibers, for instance, increases its strength dramatically, says Shoseyov, noting: "This can be used for making amazing things, like super-fabrics for industrial and medical applications."

Bio-based technologies are not just a fad, but big business. Incubators like the Fashion Tech Lab (TFL) are specifically scouting early pioneers eager to scale up production. TFL, which has invested into Orange Fiber, has set aside $50 million to spend on cutting-edge technologies. Founded by Russian entrepreneur and fashion week fixture Miroslava Duma, TFL is part venture capital fund, part experimental lab. It is currently exploring bio, nano, wearable and other smart technologies by providing funding and hoping to "[hook] up these technologies and [bring] them extremely close to the $2.4 trillion industry of fashion."[80] To Duma, these innovations will be the driving force behind what she calls "the fourth industrial revolution." Anyone who doesn't jump on the bandwagon will get left behind.

Performance denim

One of the biggest worries of denim manufacturers is that denim is losing out to the booming segment of synthetic-based activewear. "The ath-leisure movement is taking ground away from denim, but this territory historically belongs to us," notes Adriano Goldschmied. The industry veteran has been blowing the trumpet for knit denim, which has shown good results when blended with other fibers such as Tencel® for a lightweight, comfy feel, crossing over from sportswear. But Goldschmied urges designers to think outside the box and treat the fabric in new ways, moving it away from the yoga-pants culture and into higher spheres. He says it's not true that comfort means only close to the body. "Comfort is not just leggings, it's fashion. That's why I say, 'Don't sleep, innovate,'" he argues.

Technologically speaking, the possibilities for adding performance benefits to denim are bountiful, and green at that.

Activewear is often required to be water- and stain-repellent – in some cases antimicrobial. These add-ons, however, are usually achieved through hazardous substances, including fluorochemicals and organotins, which tend to persist in the environment and in the human system.

Opting for biodegradable solutions is therefore imperative.

One of the companies making headway with cutting-edge finishes is Swiss textile innovator Schoeller, which also targets denim manufacturers. The company's Eco-repel technology, for instance, mimics the natural, water-repelling protection of a duck's plumage via its long paraffin chains, which keep water and even mud at bay. The Bluesign-approved technology is PFC (perfluorinated compound)-free and based on agricultural products not used for foodstuffs. Schoeller's water- and wind-repellent corkshell coating, on the other hand, is billed to have much higher thermal insulation properties than functional fabrics, while staying both breathable and comfortable. The coating is made of FSC-certified cork granulate, which is a waste product in the manufacturing of wine corks and is therefore biodegradable.

Antimicrobial finishes can be obtained from Polygiene Technology, which has calculated that bad odor leads to reduced confidence among 90 percent of people queried; this in turn "causes 30 percent of us to discard clothes prematurely."[81] Much like nature uses silver salt (silver chloride) to prevent bacterial growth, the company recovers the substance from recycled silver in electronic waste.

Polygiene-treated textiles, which carry the Bluesign seal of approval, don't need to be washed as often, which not only saves water and energy but also cost and time. Skipping just one load of laundry per week accounts for three days of free time gained a year based on an eight-hour week, the company says.[82]

Bio-based wicking and soft-hand finishes are also available from Beyond Surface Technologies, which resorts to bio waste as its raw material, with GreenScreen certification.

Patches, rivets, buttons

For the sake of recyclability and saving resources, special attention should be paid to manufacturing accessories relevant to denim, such as patches, rivets and buttons. There are a plethora of companies that offer more sustainable options. What is true for fabric is also true for the small parts of denim. Recycled is better and offers great potential in this category. Unrecovered copper alone – the material of rivets and buttons – is worth around €100 million per year. Meanwhile, at least 800,000 tons of leather waste are produced by the global leather industry each year, according to the UN.[83]

Green alternatives range from recycled leather to laser-printed patches. The Cadica Group offers decorative patches for customization in recycled felt microfiber, while Butonia provides recycled polyester buttons that look like horn. Corozo buttons, which are made of corozo nuts, have gained ground among indie denim brands. They are biodegradable, durable and also look like horn. At Bottonificion Padano, for instance, they are also GOTS (Global Organic Textile Standard)-certified.

Trim manufacturer Prym, on the other hand, has developed what it calls the Low Impact Finish Ensemble (LIFE) treatment for its buttons and fasteners, avoiding large amounts of water, chemical colorings and coatings.

"To manage 800 tons of raw material, you need 600,000 tons of chemicals," according to Marco Corti, Prym's director general.[84] The company's buttons and fasteners are therefore not electroplated and are free of heavy metals and coated with water-based paints. As a result, Prym has seen savings of 65 percent water, 16 percent electricity, 98 percent chemicals and 85 percent hazardous waste.

Hang tags, meanwhile, can be fully circular, as shown by Stitch & Trim, which has produced paper tags for jeans and other garments that grow into plants when dissolved in water and put into soil.

TABLE 3.1 Checklist for sustainable production

Recommendation	Alternative	Benefits	Limitations
Abstain from non-sustainable cotton.	Pick one or several sustainable cotton standards, e.g. organic, BCI, CmiA, Fairtrade.	Considerable reductions in toxic chemicals, water consumption and soil degradation. Reduced health hazards for the farmers. Positive impact on reputation and stronger position vis-à-vis shareholders.	Higher costs. Will require marketing to explain the benefits to customers and/or investment within the company.
Collaborate with denim mills and suppliers on the research and development of sustainable fibers and the recyclability of existing fibers to create a circular economy.		Collaborations bring competitive advantages and opportunity for marketing.	Nurturing relationships with suppliers requires time and dedication. It can also come at an additional cost, at least initially.
Only work with suppliers that have a recycling system in place for their left-over stock and discarded scraps of fabric.		Saves natural resources and cuts down on textile waste.	Opportunities for capsule collections and community projects.
Avoid conventional polyester.	Use biodegradable and antimony-free polyester. If not available, opt for recycled polyester.	Considerable reductions in chemicals and energy consumption. Reduced health hazards and microplastics pollution.	The price of sustainable polyester is higher, though may be as little as a few cents per meter fabric.
Promote non-stretch denim.	Promote a non-stretch aesthetic. Use bio-based alternatives. Explore new weaves.	Considerable reductions in chemicals and energy consumption. Reduced health hazards and microplastics pollution. Allows recyclability.	Will require marketing to explain the benefits to customers.
Blend cotton with other natural fibers. Abstain from mixing natural with synthetic fibers, e.g. cotton and polyester.	Use recyclable mixes, e.g. sustainable cotton and Tencel®.	Amounts to larger water savings. Allows recyclability.	The price of sustainable fabric blends is higher, though may be as little as a few cents per meter of fabric.
Commit to sustainable cotton and place orders in advance.		Ensures availability. Helps farmers, especially those transitioning into organic cotton production. Opportunities for marketing.	Requires advanced planning and determination.

Notes

1 Aspin, Christopher & Chapman, Stanley. *James Hargreaves and the Spinning Jenny*. Helmshore, England: Helmshore Local History Society, 1964, pp. 13ff.
2 Ibid., p. 9.
3 Ibid., p. 10.
4 Allen, Robert. *The British Industrial Revolution in Global Perspective*. Cambridge; New York: Cambridge University Press, 2009, p. 190.
5 Aspin & Chapman, p. 10.
6 Ibid., pp. 10–11.
7 Ibid., p. 14.
8 Allen, Robert. *The British Industrial Revolution in Global Perspective*. Cambridge: Cambridge University Press, 2009, pp. 183–184
9 Allen, p. 184.
10 Ibid.
11 Ibid., p. 182.
12 Ibid.
13 Fiber Year, The. *The Fiber Year 2017: World Survey on Textiles & Nonwovens*. Issue 17, May 2017. https://thefiberyear.com/fileadmin/pdf/TFY2017_TOC.pdf
14 Van Rhoon, Peter (ed.). *Book of Denim*, Vol. 1. Amsterdam Publishing Inc., 2016, p. 45.
15 World Wide Fund for Nature. *Thirsty Crops: Our Food and Crops: Eating Up Nature and Wearing Out the Environment?* Zeist, NL: WWF, 1996, p. 10.
16 Chapagain, A. K. & Hoekstra, A. Y. *Water Footprints of Nations: Vol. 1: Main Report*. UNESCO-IHE, 2004.
17 WWF, *Thirsty Crops*, p. 4.
18 Sinclair, Mark et al. *A Sustainable for Intensive Agriculture*. Grantham Centre for Sustainable Futures. 2015. http://grantham.sheffield.ac.uk/wp-content/uploads/2015/12/A4-sustainable-model-intensive-agriculture-spread.pdf
19 2017. Cottoninc.com
20 Ibid.
21 Fairtrade Foundation. *Fairtrade and Cotton*. March 2015. https://www.fairtrade.net/fileadmin/user_upload/content/2009/resources/Cotton_Commodity_Briefing_2015.pdf
22 Blackburn, Richard (ed.). *Sustainable Textiles: Life Cycle and Environmental Impact*. Cambridge; Milton Keynes: Woodhead, 2009, p. 34.
23 Pesticides: Economic nonsense? *Ecotextiles News*, June/July, 2016.
24 INRA Press release. Reducing pesticide use in agriculture without lowering productivity. March 16, 2017. productivityhttp://presse.inra.fr/en/Press-releases/Reducing-pesticide-use-in-agriculture-without-lowering-productivity
25 Pesticides: Economic nonsense? *Ecotextiles News*, June/July, 2016.
26 United Nations, General Assembly. *Report of the Special Rapporteur on the Right to Food*. January 2017, p. 3.
27 Ibid., p. 3.
28 Ibid., pp. 3–4.
29 Ibid., p. 18.
30 Fairtrade Foundation. *Fairtrade and Cotton*.
31 ICAC. *Concerns, Apprehensions and Risks of Biotech Cotton*. ICAC Recorder. March 2005.
32 ICAC. *Update on Refuge Requirement for Biotech Cotton*. ICAC Recorder. March 2015.
33 ICAC. *Update on Refuge Requirement for Biotech Cotton*. ICAC Recorder. March 2015.
34 Goodyear, David. Cotton Farmers Paying the Price of Disposable Fashion. *Fairtrade Blog*, April 20, 2015. http://www.fairtrade.org.uk/Media-Centre/Blog/2015/April/Cotton-farmers-paying-the-price-of-disposable-fashion
35 Compson, Sarah. *Failed Promises: The Rise and Fall of GM Cotton in India*. Soil Association. October 2017. https://www.soilassociation.org/media/13510/failed-promises-e-version.pdf

36 Ibid.
37 Ibid.
38 United Nations, General Assembly. *Report of the Special Rapporteur.*
39 Fairtrade Foundation. *Fairtrade and Cotton.*
40 Ibid.
41 Blackburn, p. 36.
42 Fairtrade Foundation. *Fairtrade and Cotton.*
43 Ferrigno, Simon. *A Insider's Guide to Cotton & Sustainability.* MCL Global, 2012, p. 21.
44 Soil Association. *A Sustainable Future for Cotton.* Oct. 12, 2017. https://soilassociation.org/news/2017/a-sustainable-future-for-cotton/Cobbing,Madeleine&Vicaire,Yannick.*Fashion At the Crossroads.* Hamburg: Greenpeace. 2017.
45 Ibid.
46 Nelson,Valerie & Smith, Sally. *Fairtrade Cotton: Assessing Impact in Mali, Senegal, Cameroon and India.* London: University of Greenwich, 2011, p. 4. https://www.nri.org/projects/fairtradecotton/docs/D6595-12_NRI_Fairtrade_Cotton_report_WEB.pdf
47 Ibid., p. 4.
48 http://aboutorganiccotton.org/
49 Textile Exchange. *Life Cycle Assessment of Organic Cotton Fiber – A Global Average.* 2014.
50 Cobbing, Madeleine & Vicaire,Yannick , p. 27
51 Pesticides Action Network UK, Solidaridad & WWF. *Mind the Gap: Towards a more sustainable market.* April, 2016.
52 Ibid., p. 4.
53 Carmichael, Alasdair. Man-Made Fibers Continue to Grow. *Textile World,* February 3, 2015. http://www.textileworld.com/textile-world/fiber-world/2015/02/man-made-fibers-continue-to-grow/
54 Olivetti, Elsa, Kirchain, Randolph, Greene, Suzanne & Miller, T. Reed. *Sustainable Apparel Materials.* MIT Material Systems Laboratory, October 7, 2015.
55 Kerr, John & Landry, John. *Pulse of the Fashion Industry.* Global Fashion Agenda & The Boston Consulting Group, 2017. http://globalfashionagenda.com/wp-content/uploads/2017/05/Pulse-of-the-Fashion-Industry_2017.pdf
56 Cobbing, Madeleine & Vicaire,Yannick., p. 10.
57 Aström, Lin. *Shedding of Synthetic Microfibers from Textiles.* Göteborg University. 2015.
58 https://www.epa.gov/international-cooperation/persistent-organic-pollutants-global-issue-global-response
59 http://www.esm.ucsb.edu/research/2016Group_Projects/documents/PataPlastBrief.pdf
60 Roos, Sandra et al. *Microplastics: Shedding from polyester fabrics. A Mistra Future Fashion Report.* 2017.http://mistrafuturefashion.com/wp-content/uploads/2017/06/MFF-Report-Microplastics.pdf
61 Aström, Linn. *Shedding of Synthetic Microfibers From Textiles.* Göteborgs Universitet. January, 2016.
62 Ibid., p. 4.
63 Olivetti et al.
64 Ibid.
65 Committee on Toxicology Staff, Board on Environmental Studies and Toxicology Staff & National Research Council Staff. *Toxicological Risks of Selected Flame-Retardant Chemicals.* Washington: National Academies Press, 2000. https://www.ncbi.nlm.nih.gov/books/NBK225647/pdf/Bookshelf_NBK225647.pdf /
66 UN News. *UN's mission to keep plastics out of oceans and marine life.* April 27, 2017.https://news.un.org/en/story/2017/04/556132-feature-uns-mission-keep-plastics-out-oceans-and-marine-life
67 World Economic Forum, Ellen MacArthur Foundation and McKinsey & Company, *The New Plastics Economy – Rethinking the future of plastics.* 2016.http://www.ellenmacarthurfoundation.org/publications
68 Gulligsrud, Annie. *Fashion Fibers: Designing for Sustainability.* New York: Fairchild Books, 2017, p. 255.

69 Gulligsrud, p. 123.

70 Lenzing Group. Sustainability Report 2016, p. 50.

71 http://canopyplanet.org/

72 MIT. The People's History. *The Thistle*, Vol. 13, No. 2 (September/October 2000). http://www.mit.edu/~thistle/v13/2/history.html

73 Gulligsrud, p. 40.

74 Cherrett, Nia. *Ecological Footprint and Water Analysis of Cotton, Hemp and Polyester.* Stockholm: Stockholm Environment Institute. 2005.

75 Haufe, Juliane & Carus, Michael. *Hemp Fibres for Green Products – An Assessment of Life Cycle Studies on Hemp Fibre Applications.* Germany: nova-Institute GmbH, June 2011. http://eiha.org/media/2014/10/Hemp-Fibres-for-Green-Products-----An-assessment-of-life-cycle-studies-on-hemp-fibre-applications-2011.pdf

76 Cherrett.

77 Van Rhoon, p. 140.

78 Van Rhoon, p. 139.

79 Shoseyov, Oded. *How We're Harnessing Nature's Hidden Superpowers.* TED Talk, May 2016. https://www.ted.com/talks/oded_shoseyov_how_we_re_harnessing_nature_s_hidden_superpowers

80 Ellison, Jo. Miroslava Duma's New Industrial Revolution. *Financial Times*, May 15, 2017. https://www.ft.com/content/d20b61ea-3954-11e7-821a-6027b8a20f23

81 Polygiene. How It Works. *Polygiene.com*, n.d. http://polygiene.com/how-it-works/

82 Polygiene. *Be Climate Smart: Wear More. Wash Less.* 2017. http://polygiene.com/wp-content/uploads/2017/11/poly_wmwl_a4_20151013_hi.pdf

83 Conti, Samantha. Burberry Foundation, Elvis & Kresse Prepare to Tackle Leather Waste. *WWD*, October 17, 2017. http://wwd.com/fashion-news/fashion-scoops/burberry-foundation-elvis-kresse-prepare-to-tackle-leather-waste-11028515/

84 Nieder, Alison A. Kingpins Transformers Tackles Industry Waste in Latest Roundtable Series. *Apparel News*, May 5, 2016. https://www.apparelnews.net/news/2016/may/05/kingpins-transformers-tackles-industry-waste-lates/

4

CHEMISTRY

Getting dirty with a clean conscience

Fans of the CBS television series *The Big Bang Theory* (BBT) will know this: It was Albert Einstein who established the theoretical foundations for the laser in 1917, in his now famous paper "On the Quantum Theory of Radiation." Einstein could have hardly foreseen that it would become a pivotal tool in an industry as banal as fashion or, as the hilarious BBT characters put it: that it would "be bitchin'"[1] like that.

Nothing pointed in the direction of a potential partnership with fashion.

The most outrageous thing that happened in fashion in 1917 was Coco Chanel's introduction of the striped Breton jersey top (a look previously reserved for sailors) to the fine ladies of the French High Society, who took the habit of vacationing en masse in oh-so-chic Deauville. Even more outrageously, Chanel paired the piece with wide-legged pants and big, masculine belts, raising the eyebrows of the Belle Epoque, which preferred its women under yards of ruche and flounces.

Although by that time the French couture houses had already evolved so much as to have a fashion calendar showcasing their collections twice yearly according to seasons, the Great War was still raging. Europe's streets were marked by misery and despair. How quantum physics could help save fashion from its own destructive ways in the future was therefore hardly on Einstein's mind.

And yet, his theory would become indispensable for future denim manufacturers in their quest to rid the industry of its dependence on toxic chemicals and large amounts of water. Trust the physicist who also noted that it is impossible to solve current problems with the same thinking that was used to create them.

This couldn't be truer for the laser and the creative potential it offers to denim finishing today.

Chemistry, of course, is everywhere. It's in the coffee we drink, the cheese we eat and the air we breathe – and that's a good thing, unless you are lactose intolerant or trying to kick your addiction to coffee. But it's also in our clothes. In denim, specifically, we apply chemicals at every step of manufacturing. It starts with the cotton crop in the form of pesticides – a perennial cost to farmers – and continues through the weaving, dyeing and finishing processes. The key is to know when and under what circumstances chemicals become toxic. To keep it brief: It's complicated. Of approximately 80,000 defined chemical substances and mixes in use today – each of which has several by-products – approximately 3,000 have been studied for their effects on living organisms.[2] And some of these molecules have proven fickle little friends. Once they're washed off, they can reappear under certain conditions through chemical reactions, which makes them difficult to measure. Some amines such as aniline, for instance, display such behavior. Very closely related to indigo, aniline is an organic compound considered the "mother molecule" of indigo. Highly controversial, it has divided the industry into two camps. While minimum amounts of aniline are considered acceptable by some, others contend that the compound is too volatile to be used in proximity to humans. Aniline has been classified by the EPA as a Group B2 probable human carcinogen. It mainly affects the lungs through breathing in contaminated air, but can also be absorbed through the skin and affect the blood.[3] Because aniline is a flexible molecule, it is difficult to substitute, and is present in many industrially produced products such as paracetamol and rubber. But it is the quantity that makes a difference. It is assumed that "the use of aniline as a starting material for the synthesis of indigo would not affect the environment because the quantity of it would be below critical limits."[4]

Nonetheless, even for aniline there are alternatives on the market today, such as indigo-free dyes.

Regulation

One of the main weak spots of the global textile industry is that the use of chemistry is at the moment very poorly regulated. No universally binding international legal framework exists for denim manufacturing specifically. Instead, regulations have been driven by some forward-thinking companies and NGOs. Following the Detox Report by Greenpeace, for instance, which exposed global clothing brands and their toxic water pollution practices, the Zero Discharge of Hazardous Chemicals (ZDHC) initiative was born. It aims to phase out the use of hazardous chemicals by 2020 and provides a so-called manufacturers' restricted substance list (MRSL), which sets acceptable concentration limits for chemical substances used to process materials within the supply chain. This differs from the so-called restricted substance list (RSL), which sets those limits for finished products only, prioritizing the safety of the consumer rather than the entire supply chain. The adoption of those goals is the responsibility of each individual brand that is a member of the initiative, which currently includes G-Star, Levi's Strauss & Co. and Gap Inc., among others.

ZDHC also issues guidelines for wastewater, which have been endorsed by the Sustainable Apparel Coalition (SAC) and built into the Higg Index.

The SAC was founded by Walmart and Patagonia as an industry-wide alliance between apparel, footwear and textile companies to measure their ecological footprint. The Higg Index is currently working on a set of tools for brands, retailers and facilities along the supply chain that will allow them to score their sustainability performance (see also Chapter 7). It contains among others the MSI (Materials Sustainability Index), which lists 79 base materials as well as their impacts based on chemical content, global warming potential, water usage, etc.

There is a legally binding regulation known as REACH, set up by the European Union to manage the risk posed by chemicals imported by or manufactured in the EU. REACH applies to all chemical substances – those in industrial as well as household use – and spans across industries, including clothing. It covers about 120,000 chemicals. Companies (manufacturers and importers of chemicals, though not retailers) are obliged to gather information on the substances they manufacture or import and identify the risks when the quantities in question exceed one ton a year. The final deadline to register these substances is May 31, 2018.

REACH consists of several lists. If a substance is on the Authorization list, its use needs prior permission from the European Commission. If a substance is on the Restriction list, its manufacture, placement on the market or use is banned or limited in the EU. Finally, there is the list of substances of very high concern, which obliges producers and importers to notify ECHA (an agency responsible for the coordination of the implementation of the REACH regulations) and gives retailers and consumers the right to enquire about those substances; if this occurs, an answer needs to be provided within 45 days. Non-compliance will result in legal penalties on the national level.

According to Rémi Lefèvre, scientific officer at ECHA, the system can help denim brands convince their supply chain partners to switch to greener options for dyes, solvents, rivets or buttons. Lefèvre notes:

> From discussion with various clothing brand representatives, [we know] REACH is a way for them to strengthen the system they have put in place to track the substances they have in their products. They can go back to their suppliers, say "you have to tell me if any of these substances are present" and to be strong about it. In other words, they use our list to forbid their suppliers from using them, and then they can communicate it to their customers, so it has a marketing advantage, as well.

If the chemical challenge isn't tackled properly, recycling and long-term circularity projects could become a "toxic recirculation nightmare," as Greenpeace warns in its recent "Fashion at the Crossroads"[5] report. Clothing done unsustainably, that is using hazardous chemicals, stays unsustainable even when it has been recycled.

To understand where green formulas and technologies can make a difference, it's useful to take a look at how a denim fabric is made in the first place.

Carding and spinning

Once you have the fiber, which for denim is still mostly cotton, you need to spin it into yarn. At the beginning of the spinning process, fibers from different origins are mixed together in order to achieve the right quality. The quality of the fiber is defined by color and cleanliness, on the one hand, and staple length, on the other. The longer the fiber, the better the quality of the yarn, which in turn has an impact on the feel and look of the final garment. For denim, one inch is sufficient, though high-end denim often uses one-and-one-eighth-inch.

Other parameters used to describe cotton's quality are micronaire, which measures the fiber's fineness, and tensile strength, which reflects the force required to break a bundle of fibers.

After the fibers are opened, cleaned and mixed in what's called the "blow room," they are taken to a carding machine, which "combs" them, resulting in the first cotton sliver (basically a big, white cotton spaghetti). The drawing frame smooths the fiber in order to take full advantage of the fiber length. From there, the cotton sliver is taken to the roving frame, where torsion is applied to the sliver, giving it enough strength to be spun on the final ring frame.

There are two ways of spinning the sliver into yarn: ring spinning or open-end spinning. *Ring spinning* is employed in quality denim as it adds strength and character to the yarn through an uneven, more authentic surface. In contrast, *open-end spinning* produces a weaker and more even yarn that is also cheaper and faster to spin.

In the case of slasher dyeing (see below), the yarn is wound onto a giant beam by the warping machine, which somewhat resembles a giant spider web and can hold up to several hundred strands of yarn. Once the beam is full, it is transferred to the dyeing department, where it joins other beams to make the dye lot.

Dyeing and sizing

The two most common methods of dyeing the warp threads are rope and slasher dyeing. Both have their pros and cons. In *rope dyeing*, yarns are twisted into between 12 to 16 ropes before being wound onto a beam. The process stands out for its high productivity and low waste of thread, but comes with lower flexibility in creating shades.

In *slasher (or sheet) dyeing*, the warp yarns enter the machine parallel to each other. This requires more technical experience, since the yarn is more prone to breakage, in which case the machine would need to be stopped and the yarns in the machine at that point would go to waste. However, if done with care, this process leaves more room for experimentation with a wider range of colors, since every yarn is dyed individually.

Before the yarn is dipped in a series of indigo dye baths, a wetting agent is applied to ensure even penetration of the dyestuff, and the yarn is scoured with caustic soda to eliminate natural impurities such as grease and dust that may interfere with the subsequent dyeing operations.

Dyeing, in general, is a water- and chemical-intensive operation. Up to 12 dye baths are needed to achieve a standard blue color, and it is a fickle operation in that it requires a constant monitoring of temperature, pH levels and concentration of chemicals involved. As mentioned in Chapter 1, indigo is insoluble in water and requires a powerful reducing agent (sodium hydrosulfite) along with an amount of alkali (such as caustic soda) to achieve a soluble state. When the yarn is immersed in the pre-reduced indigo vats, several dips of between 10 and 30 seconds are needed, followed by periods of oxidation (or skying), which last between 30 and 180 seconds (including the drying process). It is here, upon contact with air, that the indigo turns from green to blue. However, because the indigo molecule is too large for cotton fibers, it does not penetrate the fiber's lymphatic channel, but stays superficially on the yarn; this gives it the ability to fade, a property that has made denim so popular. To wash off excess dye and neutralize the chemicals, more baths with water are needed. It is therefore crucial for mills to have their own purification and water recycling systems to keep as much water as possible in the loop and only discharge what is clean.

Sometimes the yarn is dyed with a sulfur dye. When sulfur is applied before the indigo, the process is called bottoming, whereas when it's done after it's referred to as topping. This is done to create different casts (shades) of the final color. When looked at closely, some jeans display a red cast, while others are greener. Casts can also span from yellow to brown or from grey to black.

Finally, the yarn receives a protective layer in the form of a sizing agent, such as starch, which prevents the yarn from breaking during the strenuous weaving process. The woven fabric will later require desizing to get rid of the starch, which would otherwise render it stiff.

Weaving

The type of weave is one of the determining factors in denim's final look and feel. The most classic construction is a 3x1 twill. This refers to the path the threads travel as they are woven into a cloth: A white thread goes through the blue threads, skipping three blue threads at a time. The white or undyed thread is called the weft and runs horizontally; the blue, indigo-dyed thread is called warp and runs vertically – though, of course, other color combinations are possible.

These twill lines can go from left to right, which is referred to as right-hand twill and is a construction originally used by Levi's. Lee, on the other hand, has opted for a right-to-left direction, creating the so-called left-hand twill that distinguishes it from its competitor. Wrangler coined the broken twill, which has no specific direction. Today, the right-hand twill is the most common, though other patterns have emerged, such as herringbone and cavalry twill.

Denim can be woven on four different types of looms: shuttle, projectile, rapier or air jet loom.

Shuttle looms make about four meters of fabric per hour, measuring about 80 cm in width. They are slow, but have personality. The weft travels inside a shuttle across the loom, and instead of being cut, loops right back after reaching the end, producing a clean, self-binding edge that does not fray. This selvedge (or self-edge), as the fabric is called, is extra-durable and was the original denim until the Sixties. Connoisseurs swear by it and don't mind the higher price, which is returned in time due to the fabric's higher durability.

Projectile looms are the most expensive type and require the most expertise, but they are the most sustainable as they consume the least amount of energy and reduce waste. They can weave 20 meters of fabric per hour, which are on average 140 cm in width, and are therefore fit for large-scale production. Because the weft yarns are disconnected when they shoot across the warp, they leave an open edge that requires an overlock-stitch to prevent it from fraying.

In *air jet looms*, a jet of air propels the weft yarn. They are easier to operate but consume more energy, much like rapier looms. *Rapier looms* are also easy to navigate and are half as expensive as projectile looms.

Denim's character is also expressed via its weight, which is measured in ounces per square yard and can range from 2.5 to 20 oz. per square yard. Most denim is woven between 7.5 oz. and 15 oz.

Finishing

When the denim fabric leaves the weaving department it is in a so-called loom-state or dry state. This means it has not been finished with any additional processes, which are necessary to give the fabric dimensional stability in addition to the soft hand feel favored by many customers today.

Basic stabilizing treatments include:

- singing: the surface hair of the fabric is singed or burnt with a gas flame to remove the fluff and give it a smoother look;
- neutralizing: refers to the pH value of the fabric;
- skewing: fixation of the twill line in order to prevent the fabric from skewing; this is necessary to avoid leg-twist when the fabric is washed;
- sanforizing: pre-shrinking of the fabric by compression so that it doesn't shrink during laundry; and
- thermofixation: used for stretch fabrics to control their performance. The more heat is applied, the harder the fabric gets and the less it stretches.

After the basic finishing, the denim is still raw, a term coined by G-Star, which has made it part of its brand name.

Optional ennobling treatments include:

- foaming or coating: the wet application of color on the fabric, which results in an indigo and pigment blend into new shades to enhance the fabric's optical effect;
- desizing: carried out to remove the starch, which previously rendered the fabric stiff to prevent breakage, with enzymes; and

- mercerization: refers to dipping denim in a chemical solution that causes the cotton to swell, giving it a fuller, smoother look and more luster.

Laundering

Until the 1970s, all denim was sold in a raw state. It is by far the most ecologically friendly, as it requires no further chemical treatments, water or energy consumption. Today, however, most jeans are washed before they hit the retail floor. The customer demands it, craving a worn-in aesthetic that they associate with denim's irreverent, heavy-duty image. While all denim dyed with indigo will naturally end up looking used (the indigo will slowly fade, creating whiskers along areas of heavy crease – something the Japanese call *iro-ochi*), most customers today, especially in the mass market, expect brands to break their jeans in for them artificially.

This is done in large, industrial laundries, which are responsible for denim's negative image; most of these facilities are situated in countries with poor safety regulations, low technical know-how and insufficient auditing practices.

Depending on a given season's set of trends, different visual effects can be achieved through various laundry techniques. These effects include not only whiskers, but also stains, cuts and tears as well as an almost endless list of shades, the final sheen of which also depends on the dyeing and finishing techniques discussed earlier. It is crucial that the fabric is chosen wisely to match the final look of the product, as it can substantially reduce the time and resources spent in the laundry.

The most common laundry technique is *stonewashing*. It first entered the scene in the 1970s, when Marithé Bachellerie and François Girbaud were looking for a way to set themselves apart from American denim and offer their European customers the look they were most accustomed to: the worn-in style of vintage jeans made popular by G.I. Joes. Although other brands, including Edwin in Japan, were experimenting with washes at the same time, the French duo is credited with introducing the stonewash on an industrial level. The way it works is that jeans are thrown into the washing machine with pumice stones, which scratch the dye and give the fabric an old-school look. This process has a large ecological footprint. The stones (which are actually volcanic ash) have to be mined in volcanic regions and shipped across the globe, which translates into high carbon emissions. They damage the machines; small bits and dust need to be removed by hand and during additional washes, substantially increasing water consumption. Stonewashed garments are also less durable, since the stones damage the fabric and abrade the rivets and buttons along with the indigo.

In the 1980s, the industry was looking to create sharper contrasts and more visual effects. The *acid wash*, also referred to as marble, moon or snow wash, made its debut. Pioneered by Italian Candida Laundry in 1986 and commercialized by Rifle,[6] it involved soaking pumice stones with bleach, i.e. either *sodium hypochlorite* or *potassium permanganate (PP)*, both of which are powerful chemicals that come with health and environmental hazards and bioaccumulate in the food chain. PP spray is often applied to achieve localized fades, mostly on the thighs of trousers.

In contact with skin, it can cause irritation, burning and pain; in contact with the eyes, permanent loss of vision is a risk; it may further irritate lungs and cause kidney damage, cardiovascular disease and, ultimately, death.[7] PP needs to be neutralized, most commonly with *sodium metabisulphite*, which bears similar health risks, including lung cancer. Flawless ventilation in the facilities where the substances are used and protective gear for the workers are therefore essential, though these are often not implemented due to poor local regulations. Sodium hypochlorite is what gives jeans their vintage sky-blue color. It also needs to be removed from the fabric via chemicals such as sodium metabisulphite and reacts with water to form a pungent, poisonous gas. Both sodium hypochlorite and potassium permanganate can build up in the effluent, where they cause environmental pollution and are "very toxic to aquatic life with long-lasting effects,"[8] according to EU regulators.

Sandblasting is still used to create worn-in effects on denim. Here, the fabric is blasted with abrasive sand containing silica. When inhaled, the particles cause a deadly lung disease called silicosis. It is a cheap and quick garment treatment and the rigorous safeguards needed to protect factory workers were found to be not properly enforced. Therefore, in 2010, Levi's and H&M led a campaign to ban the practice from denim manufacturing. A report by the Fair Trade Center and the Clean Clothes Campaign concluded that the brands'

> decision to ban sandblasting shows that even where a comprehensive sand-blasting policy is in place, including demands that workers should be educated about the associated risks, companies cannot guarantee that they are in full control of the sandblasting methods used by their suppliers.[9]

In fact, as the report stated, when Turkey banned the practice following a number of deaths, the industry moved to less regulated countries such as China, Bangladesh and Pakistan, where similar conditions as in Turkey prevail.

The good news is there are safer, greener and, in some instances, even cheaper alternatives available. What is lacking is an adequate level of information among brands and their designers as well as consumers, who are unable to make smart choices as a result.

Jeans are first and foremost functional, but they are also part of a bigger system that is fashion, which places a large emphasis on aesthetics.

Much as in product design and architecture, where form ideally follows function, in fashion – and in denim more specifically – the question of whether aesthetics follow ethics has come up many times. As Stefano Aldighieri, creative director at Arvind and denim maverick, points out: "There is no limit nowadays for what is possible in terms of creativity." To think that ethics are at odds with aesthetics "is still an excuse and based on bad past experience," he deplores. He adds:

> We did not do a service to the industry ourselves, because in the early days when people started trying to be more environmentally friendly, they did not worry about aesthetics. I remember Esprit put together a small collection

two years ago, but the line did not look great, the fabrics were kind of rough and they did not use any new technologies. It flopped miserably. People were saying: "I don't want anything to do with it. That's the stuff that hippies wear." We did a disservice to the cause at that time, trying to push it when we did not have the resources. Today, you can create a fabric that is perfectly eco-friendly, do washes that are just as attractive as the toxic washes, without using any chemicals.

The best way to achieve attractive aesthetics is for brands, mills and laundries to collaborate on the creative process, which also brings benefits to the final cost of the product. "If you want to be sustainable and save money, everything starts with buying the right fabric," notes Alberto Rigo, who is in charge of the laundry lab at Candiani; they work closely with Tonello, a fellow Italian and laundry machine specialist, on innovative washes. Their joint objective is to pair technologically advanced fabrics with the right machinery for optimal results.

Because then you won't notice any difference in the final effect. But if you take the wrong fabric trying to achieve a final look that is not meant for that fabric's original shade, construction or stretchability, there is nothing you can apply or do, you will never get the look you want. This is why we try to educate our clients, explaining to them: "Maybe you spend €1 more on the fabric, but you save four to €5 in the laundry."

And the right laundry starts with the right equipment.

Green machines

Denim manufacturing and finishing techniques are generally split into two groups: *dry processes*, which include such activities as sandblasting, brushing, whiskering, destroying or grinding to create cuts, tears and scratches; and *wet processes*, which comprise dyeing, bleaching and washing. Currently, there is nothing as good as a laser to get rid of harmful dry processing techniques, while ozone and no-stone technologies have recently contributed to great water and chemical savings in wet state. Put differently, lasers can be used to determine the pattern of the abrasion, while ozone determines the color of the wash.

Over the last few years these have been fine-tuned to fit the denim industry's needs by two notable machine technology providers, Jeanologia in Spain and Tonello in Italy – evolving in craft and resource efficiency as well as cost effectiveness.

Laser

A laser is a device that produces a beam of light powerful enough to cut through stuff, including textiles. It's highly precise. It can work on the surface of a fabric without damaging it, producing patterns or fades, which are then easy to reproduce via a matching software. The creative options lasers offer are diverse and have not yet reached their full potential; they are waiting for denim designers to discover them further. "A good laser cannot work without a good designer. That's why we employ a laser designer," insists Alice Tonello, who is responsible for research and development at her family's company, which has been selling specialized machines for fabric finishes since the 1970s. To show the equipment's full potential, Tonello in 2017 collaborated with a group of fashion design student for a project called "Denim Gallery" (see Figure 4.1), which resulted in photo-sharp imagery and artsy denim surfaces.

"Laser technology evolved tremendously in the last 15 years. This is thanks to the evolution of software," confirms Enrique Silla, CEO of Jeanologia. "Initially it looked a little fake," says Silla, adding: "Today, laser can completely substitute PP

FIGURE 4.1 A look from the denim gallery by Tonello

Source: Tonello

spray, sandblasting, manual scraping or handsanding, it can reduce labor, impacting cost, while being ethical. We need to understand that craft made by hand is beautiful, unless you put health at risk."

Silla notes that an initial capital investment is necessary, but argues that the economical return is fast.

> I would say for the production of 10,000 jeans per day, the investment is about €1 million. The return on investment depends on the type of equipment, the costs of energy and labor in a given country, but the global average is 18 months.

According to Jeanologia, the fabric loses only 5 to 6 percent of strength after being treated with laser versus 20 percent with a traditional PP finish. The water consumption, which is kept in a loop, goes down by 70 percent from 100 liters per pair of jeans. In terms of chemistry, savings of 80 percent can be achieved in addition to 50 percent savings in energy.

The company recently has launched the Jeanologia Nano, a compact laser for fast and easy customization. Because it can be used directly in stores, with the right assistance it can help raise awareness among customers on retail level. The Nano is suitable for finishing tags, labels, breaks and pocket details.

Jeanologia, which has a market share of 85 percent in laser finishing for denim (Figure 4.2), says its next big project is to design laundries with zero discharge and therefore no need for water treatment.

FIGURE 4.2   Laser finish by Jeanologia
Source: Jeanologia

We will be able to have a laundry in London or on the 60th floor of the Empire State Building, there will be no limitation. We won't need to go places where regulation is low, because it will be cheaper to reduce the water at home.

Ozone

Ozone may have a bad reputation – think the ozone layer – but it can be very useful in controlled industrial settings. Thanks to its high oxidation abilities, ozone can substitute for conventional chemicals such as bleach and save water – some 30 liters per pair of jeans – as it also cleans the fabric before it's being processed.

Silla explains:

> To produce ozone we take something that is free which is air from the atmosphere, we eliminate the nitrogen, so we have pure oxygen. We then change oxygen into ozone – ozone cannot be applied by spray, because it is a gas that will escape, so the only way to apply it is in a closed chamber, and there it never gets in contact with a human. When ozone goes into the atmosphere, it gets destroyed and becomes air [molecular oxygen] in 20 minutes. We accelerate this process, so it happens in seconds.

According to Jeanologia, the quantity of ozone used has no negative impact and is comparable to a storm in the countryside. The machine is able to measure the amount and say when it is safe to open the chamber.

At Tonello, two different types of ozone technology are used: ozone dissolved in water and ozone dissolved in air, both of which can be combined in one machine. Tonello adds:

> The ozone in the air alone is sometimes flat. By mixing the two you can have a more natural look, while completely avoiding the use of bleach. Meanwhile, the water consumption is reduced by up to 80 percent compared to normal washing.

Stone-less technologies

One of the best-known looks in denim is undoubtedly stonewashed jeans. The look is achieved through washing jeans with pumice stones, which creates a vintage, bleached-out effect. The longer the washing cycles, the more distressed the look. Both the French designer duo Marithé and Francois Girbaud and the Japanese denim specialist Edwin are said to have experimented with the technique at the same time, though Girbaud is credited with having industrialized the process. Girbaud, today an outspoken critic of the denim industry's harmful ways, has denounced stonewashing as a "mistake," deploring its environmental impact. Pumice stones tend to disintegrate inside the washing machine, which makes it necessary to wash the garments several times in order to get rid of residue.

This also damages the machines. In addition to a high water bill, there are labor costs involved, as some of the grit needs to be removed by hand from both machines and jeans pockets. Some of it will end up in wastewater.

While many brands today still use traditional stonewashing, it is possible to achieve the same effects with a much lower impact. Tonello, for instance, developed the mechanical No Stone® technology in collaboration with Levi's, declaring the end of "the Stone Age" in denim. The company eliminates the use of pumice stones by replacing them with an abrasive drum that is attached to the inside of the washing machine.

A chemical substitute for stonewashing has been provided by Garmon Chemicals through its Geopower NPS technology. Geopower NPS is a sophisticated chemical compound based on enzymes, but unlike regular cellulase enzymes typically used to replace stones, it comes with no aesthetic trade-offs. As Alberto De Conti, Garmon's chief marketing officer, explains:

> Both cellulases and pumice stones break cotton fibrils and free up the indigo molecules. The breaking is physical in the case of stones and chemical (hydrolysis reaction) in case of the cellulases. The problem with cellulases is that the freed indigo tends to go back and re-deposits on the surface of the cotton returning that undesirable effect called "backstaining."

The technique makes wastewater treatment easier, eliminates the costs for sludge disposal or stone transport and has a higher production output, better consistency and fabric performance, while rivets and buttons stay protected, according to Garmon, which markets the technology via a catchy slogan: "Stones belong to nature, not in the washing machine."

Enzymes are proteins present in all living cells that can speed up chemical processes. They are biodegradable, leaving no waste products, and are accepted under Bluesign, but not GOTS, as they usually involve bio-engineering.

Alternative bleach

Fabrics are generally bleached to prepare them for subsequent dyeing (if needed) or to give them an aged look. The majority of garments are bleached with a chlorine-based substance such as sodium hypochlorite or with potassium permanganate, both of which can form toxic compounds that bioaccumulate in the food chain.

Most chemical companies today have an alternative to chlorine bleaches and PP. Garmon, for instance, has avol oxy white. Its competitor CHT Group has organIQ, while Huntsman developed Gentle Power Bleach, which is an enzyme-based peroxide bleach that allows garments to be bleached at lower temperatures.

Hydrogen peroxide is also considered less of a pollutant, though it has to be neutralized before being discharged, like all bleaching products and enzymes.

Ozone uses no water and produces no waste, though for a full-on bleach peroxide or peroxo salts may be still necessary.

Some of the above come with their own unique aesthetics, but can be mixed with other technologies for enhanced effects. Cue acid wash, a look that became popular in the 1980s. It refers to a stonewashed look but with a sharper contrast. For this, the pumice stones were soaked in chlorine or potassium permanganate, resulting in an even higher ecological footprint. There are several ways of achieving this with eco-friendlier methods – laser is one, but another is avol evanix, a new formula aimed specifically at acid wash lovers and slated to be released by Garmon in 2018. The substance, which is a new oxidizing agent, is expected to replace hypochlorite bleach and, in combination with Geopower NPS, imbue most denim fabrics with an acid wash look.

Meanwhile, a chemical-free method is practiced by such veterans as Adriano Goldschmied, who works on the yarn instead of the finish. "I get the marble look in the construction, not in the laundry," says Goldschmied, explaining: "I'm overtwisting the yarn that I put on the warp, so you have the effect already in the rinse wash, and that is the way to do it." The overtwisting reduces the surface of the yarn that goes into the dyebath and reduces the dye's migration to the core of the fiber – hence the more superficial dyeing. He does say he is also a fan of laser.

The human factor

Most chemicals used in conventional denim manufacturing are a hazard to human health. Factory workers can and should be protected with intelligent equipment. To wit: Tonello developed its first eco-spray robot in 1989, substituting human labor with a fully automatic spraying cabin (Figure 4.3). Its first brush robot, equipped

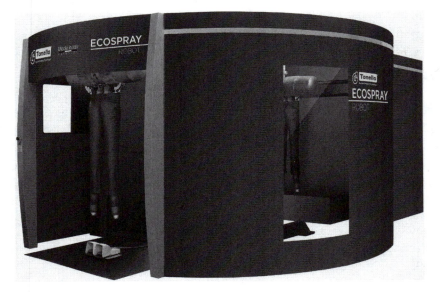

FIGURE 4.3   Eco-spray robot by Tonello
Source: Tonello

with large brushes for scraping fabric, followed a year later. Since then Tonello has perfected its technology and added more options, such as the water brush, which uses a high-pressure water spray to whiten denim instead of sandblasting.

Jeanologia's offering, meanwhile, includes the so-called Light Scraper, which incorporates a virtual sandpaper that replaces manual scraping and a Light PP spray that substitutes PP with laser.

It is imperative to only work with factories that invest in such equipment.

However, it is worth noting that while robots can protect humans by applying hazardous chemicals in a closed and automated environment, these substances can still be released via effluents and become toxic to aquatic life.

Green dyeing

Without blue, there are no blue jeans. It's a color that is imbued with history, legends, mystery and superstition, as seen in Chapter 1. And one of the reasons it has seen such rich storytelling unfold around it is because, chemically speaking, it's a tricky hue. Most of the blue in denim comes from indigo, which is insoluble in water. The dye was initially extracted from a plant, such as the *Indigofera tinctoria*, which grows in the tropics, or woad, which was most popular in Europe. It was ground into powder, mixed with a reductive alkaline waste like urine and left to ferment before being applied to the fabric. An Egyptian dyeing recipe from about the third century BC instructs:

> Take about 1 talent [approximately 25 kg] of woad, place it in the sun in a vessel with a capacity of at least 600 liters and pack it tight. Then add sufficient urine to cover the woad and let everything heat up in the sun. The next day tread the woad in the sun until it is thoroughly wetted.[10]

In the Hebrides, home to Harris Tweed, wool was dyed in urine vats well until the mid-20th century, "providing light shades of blue of unequalled fastness."[11]

A more elaborate technique was practiced by the Vikings, who also kept the vat alkaline, mostly with woodash, but fed it with wheat bran to keep the fermentation going. Inspecting the remains of the Vikings' former dyeing vats, scientists in Britain discovered that the active agent in the fermentation so the agent that actually chemically reduces the indigo is a bacterium called *Clostridium isatidis*, which feeds on sugars.

> Explains Prof. Philip John: We got some spores from the Viking woad vat that was dug up from the archaeological remains in York, dated to about 1,000 A.D., and we were able to reproduce their fermentation system to find that it was indeed the bacteria that were reducing the indigo instead of hydrosulfite.

The *Clostridium isatidis* matches the bacterium the scientists also found by reproducing a medieval woad recipe. Perhaps more interestingly, this woad vat formula also included madder. Madder is normally used to dye fabric red, though in this case the intention might have been otherwise. "What we discovered is that there is a very subtle chemical effect with the quinone compounds in madder that interact with the indigo and help break it up and make it more easily reducible," Professor John says. A similar practice can be observed in other parts of the world where indigo is used in dyeing. Natural indigo specialist Colors of Nature (see below) from India, for instance, uses traditional Indian seeds containing a similar quinone compound to that present in the madder as part of the formula.

Although the *Clostridium* bacteria could technically also reduce synthetic indigo, which makes up the majority of today's indigo market, nowadays dyeing with indigo is the result of a complex chemical formula. It took Nobel Prize Laureate Adolf von Baeyer to show that the dye could be produced synthetically and chemical giant BASF (Basische Anilin und Soda Fabrik) to make it economically viable.

Indigo is not a dye in the common sense. It is not soluble in water and therefore needs to undergo a reduction process first. Ancient cultures familiar with indigo used natural ingredients available to them through their environment, such as urine, lime, potash or sugar, and fermented indigo in a microbial vat. In today's formula, however, these natural substances and the fermentation process itself have been replaced by a range of chemicals, including the alkali caustic soda and, most importantly, the powerful reducing agent sodium hydrosulfite (also referred to as sodium dithionite), which comes with a large impact on the environment. Currently, the global indigo market is estimated at 66,000 tons a year, for which 65,000 tons of hydrosulfite are used, according to market sources.

Pre-reduced indigo

The impact of sodium hydrosulfite can be substantially reduced by employing a synthetic type of indigo that has been pre-reduced chemically before it arrives at the mill. The reduction is achieved via hydrogenation, the by-product of which is water, rather than sulfites and sulfates, as would be the case with regular synthetic indigo. According to Dystar, which offers the product branded as Indigo Vat 40% Solution, pre-reduced indigo is easier to handle and more reliable as it comes in the form of a liquid rather than the usual powder, which leaves a lot of dust. Usually, big bags full of powder indigo are mixed into giant water vats by workers, who then inhale the dust particles at risk to their health. Instead, the pre-reduced process is carried out in a closed system with minimum soiling and reduced sludge formation in the wastewater. The product also helps save resources (Figure 4.4): Up to 70 percent less hydrosulfite and caustic soda and 15 percent less indigo are required. On a global scale, this translates into savings of 55,000 tons of hydrosulfite, 27,000 tons of caustic soda and 4,000 tons of indigo per year.

Aesthetically, with liquid indigo the colors are more consistent.

The solution is certified by GOTS, Standard 100 by OEKO-TEX and Bluesign.

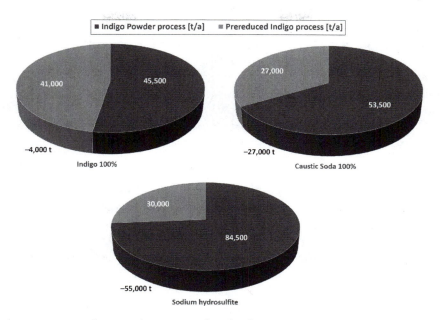

■ Indigo Powder process [t/a]   ■ Prereduced Indigo process [t/a]

41,000   45,500

−4,000 t

Indigo 100%

27,000

53,500

−27,000 t

Caustic Soda 100%

30,000

84,500

−55,000 t

Sodium hydrosulfite

FIGURE 4.4   Indigo powder vs. pre-reduced indigo
Source: Dystar

Natural indigo

Fabrics can, of course, still be dyed the old-school way, leaving synthetic chemicals entirely out of the equation. Natural indigo is available, albeit in much smaller amounts, which is why it is a better fit for fashion brands that have "small is beautiful" written into their manifesto. Almost every region in the world has its own variety of indigo plants, even Europe, where woad was particularly popular in the Middle Ages. With natural indigo, natural fermentation is key. Some mills tend to use natural indigo and advertise it as such, but mix the base with chemical reducing agents to speed up the process. Fermentation, on the other hand, is a recipe handed down from generation to generation. In places like India or Japan, every artisan has their own way of working with local, organic ingredients. Indigo masters in Okinawa, for instance, use sugar, Japanese sake and lime.

Denim connoisseurs swear by natural indigo, which gives the fabric a brighter, more brilliant color.

While it is true that additional land is needed to cultivate natural indigo, in India, where farmers grow indigo in their backyard or use it as a rotation crop, indigo plants grow very fast; this makes them economically viable, and they produce excellent high-purity indigo. Unlike woad in Europe, which is considered a hungry crop in need of nitrogen and can starve soil with time, *Indigofera* in India, of which there are roughly 700 species, can fix its own nitrogen from the atmosphere.

Natural indigo's main problem is the high water consumption, as it takes large baths to ferment the leaves. However, the water can be recycled. Colors of Nature, which was chosen as a fellow in the Levi's Collaboratory, a project that scouts more sustainable practices, is famed for having used the same dyeing water since 1993. The company's founder, Jesus Ciriza Larraona, is currently looking to up-scale the fermentation process to industrial levels. He says it's a method that can be used by both craftsmen and industries.[12]

The company currently operates with 40 vats, which equals 19,000 liters of indigo dye solution. Those vats can dye up to 30 kilograms of material per day, depending on the depth of colors desired. The company explains:

> We get our indigo cakes from a village only 60 kilometres from Auroville, which happens to be a world leader in natural indigo supply. There, indigo is extracted from *Indigofera tinctoria* leaves. On our site we grind the cakes, then add the powder to our vats. Since we wash using only biodegradable soap and have a water treatment system, all the water is re-used for our gardens. Once we start to cultivate indigo in [our] own field, we'll close the loop completely.[13]

The company's aim is to increase daily capacity to 1,000 kg. As the dyers note: "We also want to expand indigo cultivation on Auroville lands. This dye-yielding plant can revive barren land and provide income to rural women gatherers. Its' only by-product? Compost."

A similar revival project was funded by the European Union between 2000 and 2004, in which the re-introduction of woad was examined as a potential non-food crop. "The aim was to grow woad on an industrial level," explains Professor Philip John, who spearheaded the project Spindigo.

> At that time, farmers were looking for alternatives to food crops. We grew healthy crops in Finland and central Italy, and of course in Britain. The point is to get a good yield to make it worthwhile, you have to feed the crop, nitrogen in particular.

Finally, he says, the economics changed in Europe and it became more lucrative for farmers to grow food again.

Alternative reducing agents

Due to little availability and the slow microbial fermentation process of natural indigo, there are synthetic indigos in the market that forgo the use of hydrosulfite as a reducing agent, using sugar instead. Denim mill Prosperity, for instance, has developed an in-house version it calls "Sweet Indigo." It's less powerful as an agent but reduces water consumption, as no scouring is needed to prepare the fabric for the dying. "When you take hydrosulfite you need to prep the yarn by adding more chemicals for consistency in the dye. With sugar, you just dip it – that already saves two boxes of water," explains Bart Van de Woestyne, creative director at Prosperity.

Sweet Indigo produces an interesting vintage type of color, very much resembling natural indigo.

Swiss-based Sedo Engineering, on the other hand, substitutes the hazardous chemicals needed for the reduction process with electrical currents. "'Smart Leuco-Indigo' is produced in an electrochemical process consuming considerably fewer resources than existing methods, using only indigo pigment, caustic soda, water and electricity,"[14] say the inventors Herbert Guebeli and David Crettenand. Adds Guebeli:

> The denim industry is one of the major contributors to the pollution problems within the fashion business. And if we look at the size of this one section we realize how large the difference will be if the dyeing process of denim items is handled without the hazardous chemicals.[15]

These chemicals are discharged by the tons into the environment. In their own survey, Sedo Engineering calculated the total industry output of denim at 15 billion meters of fabric, 66,000 tons of indigo powder and 10 billion denim items (jeans, dresses, coats, jackets, etc.). Compared to the traditional method, Smart Indigo uses six times less energy[16] and allows for savings in wastewater management. It is said to have very good color consistency and is currently employed by Italdenim, among others.

The latest innovation comes from a partnership between Dystar and Pakistani denim mill Artistic Milliners. It's a combination of Dystar's 40 percent pre-reduced indigo with a newly invented liquid organic agent that substitutes sodium hydrosulfite entirely and runs under the commercial name Sera Con C-RDA.

Unlike hydrosulfite, the new agent is biodegradable and yields no salts as a by-product, which are difficult to remove from the effluent and make the recycling of indigo wastewater challenging. The agent also reduces the build-up of hazardous sulfates in the wastewater by 95 percent. Sulfates can release a harmful gas upon reaction with other chemicals present in oceans and rivers, harming aquatic life.

According to Dystar, the new formula, which it calls Cadira Denim, saves 30,000 tons of salt waste in a year, which equals 1,200 truckloads that would otherwise end up in landfill, and up to 3.25 billion liters of water, which equals the needs for drinking water of 3.5 million people per year. (The savings are calculated against the simple usage of pre-reduced indigo only.) The reduction of other chemicals used in the process, such as caustic soda, goes down by 70 percent.

Artistic Milliners brands the process as "Crystal Clear."

"This is very exciting," says Syeda Faiza Jamil, corporate responsibility and communications manager at Artistic Milliners. "The technology is in its infancy at the moment – we are exploring its range, but we reckon there will be little limitations in terms of shades if any."

There is currently an approximately 20 percent surcharge on the formula per meter of fabric.

Meanwhile, Cadira's aniline content is below 5.0 ppm, according to trials conducted for Dystar.

Indigo-free blue

For those looking for an industrialized blue dye that is entirely free of indigo and therefore aniline, there is an alternative dyeing process made available by Archroma called Advanced Denim (Figure 4.5). This concept is essentially an evolved version of sulfur dyeing technology that comes with great water and energy savings while employing zero indigo. The formula requires a single reducing agent, which is again a type of sugar, while the number of dyeing baths is reduced from ten or twelve boxes to four or even one, depending on the exact application. Unlike indigo, sulfur actually likes cotton, and so it bonds with the fabric more easily. This slashes water consumption by 92 percent, energy consumption by 30 percent and cotton waste by 87 percent, resulting in greater productivity. "The dyes no longer display any toxicological problems. They are 'bioremovable,' meaning they go through a biological treatment and are removed in the treatment sludges," explains Miguel Sanchez, global head of business development denim and casualwear at Archroma. The formula results in a novel type of blue, allowing for a wider range of shades, which makes it ideal for the fast-changing mass market. The products are GOTS- and Bluesign-certified and compliant with OEKO-TEX 100. The obtained dyed material is compatible with eco-washes such as ozone, which allows the colors to keep their initial cast while adding a naturally fading effect. Advanced Denim may also be worked with hydrogen peroxide, which is considered an eco-bleach as it leaves no harmful chemicals in the fabric but gives it a shiny, faded aesthetic.

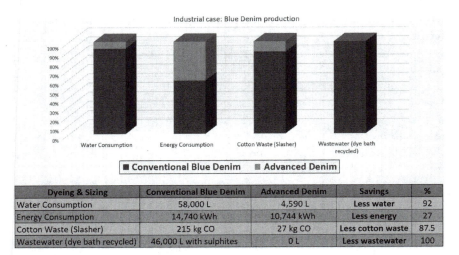

Dyeing & Sizing	Conventional Blue Denim	Advanced Denim	Savings	%
Water Consumption	58,000 L	4,590 L	Less water	92
Energy Consumption	14,740 kWh	10,744 kWh	Less energy	27
Cotton Waste (Slasher)	215 kg CO	27 kg CO	Less cotton waste	87.5
Wastewater (dye bath recycled)	46,000 L with sulphites	0 L	Less wastewater	100

FIGURE 4.5 Savings of Advanced Denim

Source: Archroma

Dyeing with waste and microbes

What's true for fibers is also true for dyes. Waste is a friend and can help keep valuable nutrients circulating inside the system.

The biosynthetic Earthcolors line by Archroma, for instance, is 100 percent based on raw materials from natural waste such as the shells of nuts and the leaves of plants such as saw palmetto, as well as herbal waste, including rosemary. Only the residues are used, leaving the other parts of the plant available for food consumption. The patented formula separates the shells, which are ground into a homogenous powder, creating no further waste, and are free of any petrochemicals. The colors range from beige to different shades of brown, mimicking the warm hues of nature. The raw materials are traceable with NFC (Near-Field Communication) technology.

Archroma is also producing a dye from cotton waste in collaboration with Cotton Incorporated. As Cotton Inc.'s Mary Ankeny, senior director of textile chemistry research, notes: "Byproducts of cotton harvesting and ginning have been utilized within the food and construction industries for decades, but we were intrigued by the idea of using cotton biomass to dye cotton fiber."[17]

This is billed as the first time that a cotton plant has been used to dye cotton fabrics, according to the company. Cotton Inc. and Archroma say there is "an ample supply of cotton biomass" from the industry that would otherwise go to waste.

> The global volume of cotton harvesting and ginning byproducts – which includes burs, stems, immature bolls, lint, sticks, and leaves – can be as much as three million tons per year. One 480 lb. bale of cotton, for example, can produce 150–200 lbs. of usable byproducts.[18]

The dye, too, is traceable with an NFC chip.

While dyeing with bacteria isn't new and has been practiced for thousands of years – natural indigo dyeing is nothing more than a fermentation process performed by microbes – tweaking bacteria to produce indigo is something different altogether. For instance, Genencor, a subsidiary of Dupont, uses microbes to help generate an environmentally friendly type of indigo. According to the EPA, Genencor's biotechnological process

> uses an intergeneric microorganism, glucose and other microbial nutrients instead of hazardous reagents including aniline, formaldehyde and hydrocyanic acid to create this commercially important dye. Eliminating the use of such hazardous chemical feedstocks via replacement with a more environmentally friendly process reduces exposures, releases, and risks otherwise associated with the traditional starting materials.[19]

This could eliminate the need for petrochemicals altogether, though for now the process is in dire need of scaling up. To wit: Though Genencor was able to produce some 400,000 square yards of bacteria-dyed jean material for Levi's,[20] the costs proved non-competitive with cheap synthetic dyes.

Several other science hubs are currently working on similar systems, including French start-up Pili and Berkeley University. German design firm Blond & Bieber, on the other hand, has been eyeing microalgae and their properties to produce a wide range of colors, a process they call Algaemy.

Last but not least, *Clostridium isatidis* itself could be an important ingredient of the future formula. As Professor John, who isolated the bacterium *Clostridium isatidis* from old Viking vats, suggests, "*C. isatidis* could be employed in a future bio-technological indigo-reduction process."[21]

Like with all new research, it will take time and patience. Perhaps the key to speeding up bacterial dyeing lies in the sound of music. Two Dutch textile designers found that sound frequencies can help accelerate the pigmentation process. In their research project, the bacteria happily used any fiber as a dance floor — except bamboo.[22]

Black denim

Denim's second favorite color is black; the black in black denim is normally achieved through sulfur dyes, which as mentioned earlier are sometimes combined with indigo to produce different casts. Sulfurs are an old class of dyes that were originally associated with the pungent smell of rotten eggs due to sodium sulfides present in the formula. This changed in the late Eighties when a type of sugar became the preferred choice for the reduction process, as offered by Archroma, for instance. However, as some mills still use cheaper sulfur containing reducing agents such as sodium hydrogen sulfide and other sulfides harmful to the environment, it is imperative to check with suppliers and encourage them to switch to greener options.

With new fibers entering the market, new dyeing techniques suiting the fibers directly are emerging as well. An example is Modal Black, in which the pigments are embedded directly in the fiber matrix, reducing both the consumption and pollution of water in the dyeing process. It is billed as having exceptionally high color fastness.

Many of the technologies mentioned have been adopted by mills, put to use and developed further, often in collaboration with brands and chemical companies. To move the needle of sustainable innovation forward, it is imperative for the industry to work together (Table 4.1). Among a group of companies that makes substantial investments into the development of greener technologies is Candiani SpA in Northern Italy. The mill is billed as one the most transparent in the industry.

CASE STUDY: CANDIANI SPA

Candiani is a family mill. Four generations of denim weavers have lived and worked on the premises, which look like a Slim Aarons photograph come to life. The building complex is unusually located in a natural reserve at the foot of the Italian Alps, which has influenced the mill's green mindset. Each Candiani has brought his own signature to the family business. Luigi, who founded the company in 1938, focused on workwear; his son Primo introduced denim in 1963; Gianluigi tapped into the zeitgeist with premium stretch denim in 1984; and his son, Alberto, is currently leading the mill's sustainable revolution.

The 35-year-old is the goalie of his local ice-hockey team, and as you would guess, his style matches his hobby. You can easily spot him at various denim trade shows, often sporting an L. A. Kings cap paired with loose-fit, black or dark blue selvedge jeans and a flannel shirt. One of his main features is that he doesn't shy away from teaming up with partners outside of his company, even if it means collaborating with a competitor. This is unusual in an industry so fixated on guarding its secrets.

His most recent coup is a strategic alliance with Canepa, a fellow Italian textile manufacturer that provides him with Kitotex®. This is a novel sizing agent, replacing the more conventional mix of starch and PVA (polyvinyl alcohol), which when washed off breaks down into microplastics in the wastewater. Candiani and another neighboring mill are currently the only ones with a license for Kitotex® in denim production.

Candiani says that "when it comes to R&D you have to collaborate with the suppliers to come up with something good, and you don't start by thinking about the cost first." It's a technique he learned from his grandfather, who together with his buddy, an engineer, developed the slasher machines the mill still uses today; these machines helped create the mill's unique range of dyes, including the eco-friendly N-denim, which thanks to its nitrogen formula delays the oxidation of indigo.

The N-denim process increases the penetration of the dye in the yarn, reducing the amount of chemical agents needed to achieve a deeper color. Instead of seven baths, one or two dyeing baths are sufficient. In 2016, the process helped save the mill 9,450 kg of auxiliary chemicals, including hydrosulfites.

For the opposite scenario – when a faded, vintage look is desired – the weaver invented Indigo Juice®, which penetrates the yarn only superficially, making it easier to launder and allowing the mill to save 2,300 cubic meters of water per year and to produce 44,000 cubic meters fewer of methane gas. Considering that Candiani turns out 100,000 meters of denim fabric per day, the savings appear even more substantial.

One magic formula, of course, is not going to save the blue world, and Candiani knows that. He is somewhat of a DIY guy, who likes to "play," as he says, with various formulations available throughout different industries and adapt them to denim. To illustrate the point, the company recently produced two sets of jeans—one made the "conventional way," the other using a volley of newer, greener technologies.

The result: Depending on the color, the conventional pair required about 90 liters of water and 0.62 kilograms of chemicals, to sum up the dyeing and washing stages of manufacturing. In contrast, the sustainable pair used only 22 liters and 0.2 kilograms, saving 75 percent and 65 percent, respectively.

In the laundry, the conventional jeans went through a laborious 11 steps, including stone washing, bleaching and potassium permanganate spraying, consuming a total of 0.12 kg of chemicals and 70 liters of water. The Kitotex® and Indigo Juice® combo, on the other hand, slashed chemical consumption by 60 percent to 0.05 kilograms and squeezed the amount of water by 83 percent to 12 liters, which is a little more than one toilet flush (Figure 4.6).

ENVIRONMENTAL IMPACT ⚡ OF WASH PROCESS

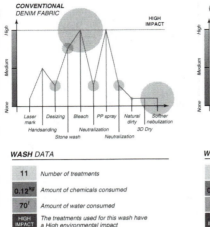
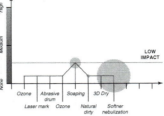
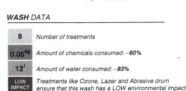
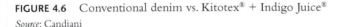

FIGURE 4.6 Conventional denim vs. Kitotex® + Indigo Juice®
Source: Candiani

Even skeptics would agree there were no visual trade-offs between the two pairs.

Candiani challenges other manufacturers to communicate their sustainability efforts in a similarly transparent way.

"Most guys will say: 'Oh, let's do organic cotton,' or 'We use 30 percent less water.' It means nothing. Thirty percent of what exactly?" he laments, adding:

> We live in the communication era, there are so many ways of showing customers what you do. Take people to the mill, to the laundry. Make a mini-movie. Everybody should have the balls to say, "We used to do it this way, now we have improved, don't point at me because I cared less. Now I care more."

Candiani is adamant about proving that sustainability is worth going the extra mile. "We have to understand sustainability as the new premium. No one really goes to the original meaning, which is: you pay extra to get a better product. By better, I mean both cleaner and nicer. It's an added value." Candiani, who is popular among the denim specialist brands for his rich range of weave and color combinations, says the difference between conventional and green fabric is set between 15 and 80 cents per meter.

> Trust me, not many customers are willing to pay that. I say "I'm giving you something that is tangibly better, has more performance, way less pollution in the fabric making process and in the laundry, because all these new products are easier to wash, so you will definitely save those f****** 80 cents at the laundry, I promise."

Over the last 12 years, the family mill has invested €100 million into research and development.

> Our yearly turnover is about 120 million, that means all profit goes into new investments. Sustainability does cost more because you have to invest, so it does mean that we are taking hits along the way, but we do it with a long-term strategy in mind. I think that in five to 10 years from now we will have a more competitive advantage. If we use less water and chemicals, it's worth it. Also, when you look at [our generation] it feels like no one gives a s*** about sustainability, but the 20-year-olds are really into it; they grew up with organic chicken and green smoothies. So if you are a big corporation and you are scared of being sustainable because it is interfering with your margins, then you belong to the past century.

Denim making is a global undertaking. The path of a pair of jeans is often scattered across several continents. The cotton can be grown in Australia, the fabric woven in Italy and dyed with German dyes, the CMT outsourced to Bangladesh, the laundry done in Pakistan, with the final garment then shipped to a brand's warehouse in the US. It will therefore take a global effort to streamline the processes and facilitate the implementation of cleaner systems. Otherwise, too many missed opportunities might be the consequence, as the example of Jeanologia's e-flow technology shows.

Normally, where there are chemicals, there are large amounts of water involved since water is needed to dissolve the chemicals and clean the waste. Jeanologia's e-flow uses air instead of water to transport chemicals onto the fabrics in the form of nanobubbles. Approximately one million bubbles can be found in one square centimeter. The technology is compatible with a variety of enzymes, denim softeners and water repellents, though Silla notes that some of the more conventional chemicals cannot be used in the process.

> Nobody is developing specific chemistry for that technology, so we are using existing chemistry, limiting its potential. But the advantages are unbelievable. We are talking about completely eliminating the use of water, and reducing chemistry by 75 percent, that's also a competitive advantage.

Currently with the combination of laser, ozone and e-flow manufacturers can finish a pair of jeans with only one glass of water rather than the industry average of 70 liters.

TABLE 4.1 Checklist for sustainable production

Recommendation	Alternative	Benefits	Limitations
Abstain from washes where possible.	Leave denim raw/ unwashed.	Denim will age naturally, creating a higher emotional and unique aesthetic value.	Will require marketing to explain the benefits to customers.
Collaborate with denim mills and laundries on sustainable research and development.		Collaborations bring competitive advantages and opportunity for marketing.	Nurturing relationships with suppliers requires time and dedication. It can also come at an additional cost, at least initially.
Only work with suppliers that treat their wastewater and keep water in a closed loop where possible.		Saves water consumption and prevents water pollution.	Wastewater management is mostly regulated by governments, though audits may still be necessary to ensure compliance.

Avoid conventional indigo.	Use pre-reduced liquid indigo, naturally fermented indigo, hydrosulfite-free indigo, aniline-free dyes or biosynthetic alternatives.	Considerable reductions in toxic chemicals, water and energy consumption. Reduced health hazards.	The price of sustainable indigo is higher, though may be a little as a few cents per meter of fabric. Natural fermentation and biosynthesis are also more time consuming for the moment.
Avoid chlorine-derived bleaches and potassium permanganate.	Ozone, laser, enzyme-based bleaching formulas or hydrogen peroxide.	Considerable reductions in toxic chemicals, water and energy consumption. Reduced health hazards.	The price of sustainable bleaching agents is higher, though it may be as little as a few cents per meter of fabric. Ozone and laser require initial investment in machinery, but have quick return on investment.
Avoid stonewashing.	Abrasive drums, enzyme-based bleaching formulas, manipulation of yarn.	Considerable reductions in energy consumption, labor, costs for sludge disposal and wastewater treatment.	Requires initial investment in the drums. Enzymes come at a slightly higher cost.
Reduce number of sample requests.	Match fabrics with desired final color.	Comes with considerable reductions in resources. Saves time and costs.	Requires planning and determination.
Seek assistance of certifying bodies and NGOs, e.g. Bluesign, GOTS, OEKO-TEX.		Will provide lists of allowed and prohibitive chemicals and practices and/or issue certification.	Not free of charge. Price will depend on the size of the company and services provided.
Play and promote difference.	Some green techniques may not be compatible with others. Be open to experimenting with new looks. Green techniques provide great room for creativity.	New hues and effects offer potential for marketing and telling stories.	Though some technologies like laser create great consistency, others, especially when certain chemicals are involved, may give off heterogeneous effects. This in turn can be an opportunity to market an item as unique.

Notes

1 The Lunar Excitation. *The Big Bang Theory.* Season 3, Episode 23. Air Date: May 24, 2010 on CBS.
2 Braungart, Michael & McDonough, William. *Cradle to Cradle.* Vintage Books, 2009, pp. 41–42.
3 Aniline. *EPA.gov*, January 2000 [April 1992]. https://www.epa.gov/sites/production/files/2016-08/documents/aniline.pdf
4 Muthu, Subramanian S. (ed.). *Sustainability in Denim.* Oxford: Woodhead Publishing, 2017, p. 395.
5 Cobbing, Madeleine & Vicaire, Yannick. *Fashion At the Crossroads.* Hamburg: Greenpeace. 2017, p. 6.
6 Turk, Piero (ed.). *From Here to There: Denim in Motion.* Tonello, 2016.
7 Muthu, p. 184
8 https://echa.europa.eu/substance-information/-/substanceinfo/100.028.874https://echa.europa.eu/substance-information/-/substanceinfo/100.028.790
9 Riddselius, Christopher. *Fashion Victims: A Report on Sandblasting Denim.* Fair Trade Center and Clean Clothes Campaign, 2010, p. 4.
10 Seefelder, p. 21.
11 Cardon, p. 350.
12 LS&Co. Unzipped Team. Meet Benita and Jesus, Levi Strauss & Co. Collaboratory Fellows. *Unzipped*, October 10, 2016. http://levistrauss.com/unzipped-blog/2016/10/meet-benita-and-jesus-levi-strauss-co-collaboratory-fellows/
13 http://thecoloursofnature.com/natural-dyes/at-the-colours-of-nature/
14 Stay Informed about Smart-Indigo™. *SmartIndigo.com*, 2018. https://www.smartindigo.com/news/
15 Guebli, Herbert. In: *Smart Indigo Booklet.* https://www.smartindigo.com/fileadmin/Dateiliste/downloads/Booklet_Smart-Indigo_2017_01.pdf
16 *Eco Textile News.* Electrochemical Pre-reduced Indigo – a Greener Alternative? June/July 2016, p. 25.
17 Cotton Incorporated & Archroma Redefine "100% Cotton." *Cotton Incorporated*, September 12, 2016. http://www.cottoninc.com/corporate/Pressroom/PressReleases/2016/100-Percent-Cotton-Redefined.cfm
18 *CottonInc. & Archroma.* Press release. Cotton Incorporated & Archroma Redefine "100% Cotton." September 12, 2016. http://www.cottoninc.com/corporate/Pressroom/PressReleases/2016/100-Percent-Cotton-Redefined.cfm
19 Reviewing New Chemicals Under the Toxic Substances Control Act (TCA): P2 Recognition Project. *EPA.gov*, n.d. https://www.epa.gov/reviewing-new-chemicals-under-toxic-substances-control-act-tsca/p2-recognition-project
20 Onion, Amanda. Scientists Make Bacteria-Dyed Jeans. *ABCNews.com*, October 15, 2015. http://abcnews.go.com/Technology/story?id=97864&page=1
21 Padden, A. Nikki, John, Philip, Collins, M. David, Hutson, Roger & Hall, Allan R. Indigo-Reducing *Clostridium isatidis* Isolated from a Variety of Sources, Including a 10th-Century Viking Dye Vat. *Journal of Archaeological Science*, Vol. 27 (2000), pp. 953–956.
22 Luchtman, Laura. Living Colour: Dyeing Textiles with Dancing Bacteria. *Kukia Blog*, March 8, 2017. http://blog.kukka.nl/2017/03/living-colour.html

5

FROM RECYCLING TO CLOSED-LOOP PRODUCTION

Make me over

A curious event took place on October 16, 2001, in a London gallery in Mayfair, home to the city's commercial art community.

Damien Hirst, the most notorious of the Young British Artists (YBA), was showcasing his latest oeuvre. Britart's enfant terrible, who was already selling out shows with his provocative art often based on found objects, put together an impromptu installation of "half-full coffee cups, ashtrays with cigarette butts, empty beer bottles, a paint-smeared palette, an easel, a ladder, paintbrushes, candy wrappers and newspaper pages strewn about the floor."[1] The work was valued at "six-figures" by the gallery's head of special projects.

VIP guests mingled to marvel at the art, drinking and smoking and probably pondering in very sophisticated terms on the deeper meaning of what looked like a pile of trash. You could say the preview was a success.

The following morning, when the gallery staff returned, ready to open the exhibit to the general public, they realized someone had cleaned the rubbish, not knowing it was − well, art.

The culprit was soon identified as Emmanuel Asare, the gallery's cleaning man, who innocently explained: "As soon as I clapped eyes on it, I sighed because there was so much mess. It didn't look much like art to me. So I cleared it all in bin bags, and I dumped it."[2]

When Hirst heard about the incident he thought it was "hysterically funny." The gallery lauded the clean as a "healthy" debate about what is art and what isn't and duly reassembled the artist's installation from photographs taken the night before.

Naturally, Asare kept his job.

Charles Thomson, a painter and outspoken opponent of conceptual art, report-edly concluded:

> The cleaner obviously ought to be promoted to an art critic of a national newspaper. He clearly has a fine critical eye and can spot rubbish, just as the child could see that the emperor wasn't wearing any new clothes.[3]

To be fair, Hirst was not the first – and probably not the last – victim of ambitious clean-up acts. It happened to Joseph Beuys before him, whose dirty bath installation was scrubbed shiny by two diligent cleaning ladies at a museum. Similar incidents are reported of the art of Gustav Metzger, Martin Kippenberger, Sara Goldschmied and Eleonora Chiari, while the pioneer of ready-made art himself, Marcel Duchamp, must have seen his "objets trouvés" thrown away by cleaners more than once. His most famous items, including an upturned urinal and a bicycle wheel on a stone stool, disappeared a long time ago. "Were the originals simply chucked in the bin?,"[4] teased the *Guardian*'s Jonathan Jones.

Trash has been useful to many artists, who proposed an anti-establishment approach to art by diverting garbage from landfill to workshop. Pablo Picasso conceived his cubist constructions from recycled wood parts and frumpy upholstery. Anton Gaudí used waste ceramic pieces he had collected from factories to compose his architectural works, including the Sagrada Familia in Barcelona. And Robert Rauschenberg transformed industrial detritus into bestselling sculpture. Rauschenberg caught the bug after volunteering for garbage collection while still a student. The trash he later found in New York City's bins and gutters made its way into his treasured artwork.

As the art critic Kim Levin wrote, for most of the 20th century

> recycling was an oblique way of trashing the past during a period of optimism about the future [...] It wasn't until the 21st century that it really began to dawn on most of us: trash, detritus, and the results of what Robert Smithson called entropy are the by-products of the Industrial Revolution and the consumerism it engendered. Trash is the inevitable outcome of a century of disposal.[5]

As the incident in the Mayfair gallery shows, the line between art and rubbish remains a fine one, but it is even finer between trash and fashion. Curiously, Duchamp appropriated the art term "ready-made" from the clothing industry, which at that time had just started to move away from the sustainable art of custom-made garments to more accessible and disposable off-the-rack (or "ready-made") clothing. It was the first mark of the throw-away society we are drowning in today, following the Industrial Revolution.

Early fashion was pretty straightforward. Prehistoric humans covered themselves with whatever they could hunt or find lying around: raw animal skins and fur, flax, fleece and even vegetation. Having tracked down the evolution of lice, science assumes that humans must have started wearing clothes between 50,000 and 200,000 years ago, which is when the body louse, which feeds on human skin but lives in clothing, split from the head louse.[6] As it was made in small quantities of biodegradable materials, almost all of pre-historic clothing decomposed a long time ago.

Our current garments are unlikely to go down the same route.

Since 2000 there has been an explosion of fast fashion, helped by the rise of value chains originating in Europe, most of which favor cheap and synthetic but non-renewable and polluting fiber such as polyester, which is now the most popular in the world. In the first decade of the 21st century, clothing production doubled, in 2014 surpassing for the first time 100 billion garments a year, according to McKinsey.[7] MIT is even less conservative, estimating that already in 2010 the global apparel industry produced more than 150 billion garments – "enough to provide more than twenty new articles of clothing to every person on the planet." The university's Materials Systems Laboratory calculated that by 2015, the global apparel industry was likely producing more than 400 billion square meters of fabric per year, enough to cover the state of California annually.[8]

Today, the average consumer buys 60 percent more clothing but keeps it only half as long as 15 years earlier. By some estimates, shoppers treat "the lowest-priced garments as nearly disposable, discarding them after just seven or eight wears."[9]

In the EU alone, the cost of clothing fell by 26 percent in the first decade of the 21st century, almost doubling sales from $1 trillion in 2002 to $1.8 trillion in 2015; this is projected to rise to $2.1 trillion by 2025.[10] It's hard to resist when new collections drop every two to six weeks, encouraging more shopping sprees on the high street. To wit: Zara offers 24 new collections per year, and H&M produces 12 to 16 and refreshes them weekly, according to McKinsey.[11] Meanwhile, the average number of clothing collections among all European apparel companies has more than doubled, from two a year in 2000 to about five a year in 2011, the researchers say.

With the volume of product, waste also goes up. ReverseResources, which is developing a software solution for mills and garment factories "to map, measure and track their input and output of fabrics" to help them boost the remanufacturing and recycling of leftovers through a marketplace where they can be sold and traded, noted that "even according to our optimistic scenario, the world would create 40 billion square meters of leftover textile per year, almost enough to cover the entire Republic of Estonia with waste."[12]

As far as post-consumer waste is concerned, in the US alone, 24 billion pounds of textiles are discarded every year, of which only 15 percent are collected. In the EU, 80 percent of clothing is thrown away with household waste – most of it (56 percent) ends up in landfill; the rest (24 percent) is incinerated. Of the remaining 20 percent, only a fraction (10 percent) is resold as clothing; the rest is downcycled into lower-quality products such as insulation.[13]

Why is this a problem?

In landfills, clothes cannot decompose; they fuel the greenhouse problem through methane and CO_2 emissions and produce toxic leachate that finds its ways into our water systems; when incinerated, burnt waste causes air pollution via chemicals such as dioxin, which creates even more greenhouse gases. What's more, the primary resources contained in them go to waste as well and are lost forever, despite their scarcity.

No doubt, the potential for recycling is substantial: Speaking in greenhouse emission figures, recycling 2 million tons of clothing per year equals removing 1 million cars from the streets.[14] But it does not come without technical challenges and it has its limits. One of the bigger problems in recycling is that many cotton jeans on the market today are blended with polyester and spandex (elastane) to achieve stretch properties. Although desired by the consumer, that fiber mix cannot be separated for further processing at this point. Moreover, the copper rivets, leather patches, yarns, zippers and buttons are difficult to extract because they have not been designed for further use. Further, the chemicals present in the fabrics from dyeing and finishing create obstacles for the chemical safety of recycled products.

In the long run, simple recycling only defers waste and comes at a cost, logistics being one of them. Instead of being sustainable, it becomes high maintenance. The industry's favorite buzzword is a closed-loop economy. This includes fiber-to-fiber technology as well as water management. If done right, the savings in materials alone could top $1 trillion a year, according to McKinsey.[15] Companies that adopt circular-economy principles are expected to outcompete their rivals as the scarcity of resources exposes businesses to higher costs and unforeseeable risks.

A truly circular economy is tricky, because at this stage neither technology nor design is refined enough to make it happen on a global scale. Recycling is an important first step, but it's a split concept. It is divided into downcycling and upcycling, which are often used synonymously by the apparel industry, resulting in misleading communication towards the consumer. Downcycling turns recycled garments into products of lower quality and value. This happens when, for instance, a pair of jeans becomes insulation for cars or buildings. It eventually becomes waste with no options of being recycled further. Upcycling, on the other hand, turns one product into another product of equivalent value – for instance, by taking scraps of fabric thrown away during production and repurposing them into a collection of desirable fashion.

The ultimate goal here would be to unravel the fabric of old jeans, re-spin the fiber and re-weave into a new pair of denim. This is currently what re:newcell is experimenting with. In general, when recycling cotton, the fiber gets shorter and loses strength and therefore quality. Consequently, a pair of jeans can only have up to 30 percent of recycled cotton in it; the remaining 70 percent must be complemented by virgin cotton fiber. Dutch MUD Jeans and Spanish textile maker Recover recently managed to turn old MUD jeans into new MUD jeans, increasing the recovered cotton content to 40 percent. This may seem like a small victory, but research by Circle Economy and G-Star shows that by including only 12 percent recycled content in a pair of jeans, water usage falls by 9.8 percent, energy consumption by 4.2 percent and the CO_2 footprint by 3.8 percent.[16]

Smart design

The fact is, almost none of the product in use today was meant to be part of a circular system. Imagine trying to squeeze the SIM card of your old Nokia phone into a newer model – it won't fit, although technically speaking it's not broken.

As Michael Braungart and William McDonough pointed out in their eye-opening book *Cradle to Cradle*, waste, pollution and crude products (those that have not been designed to benefit either human or ecological health) are not always "the result of corporations doing something morally wrong. They are the consequence of outdated and unintelligent design."[17]

In a circular system, clothes don't ever become waste; their (re-)use phase is extended, preferably indefinitely, following the example of, well, nature. Earth's rich ecosystems know no landfills or incinerators. Everything has a purpose; all waste equals food for somebody else, creating a circular loop. In contrast, humans have adopted a linear approach, or "cradle to grave." We take the nutrients out of the earth, contaminate them and waste or lose them instead of safely returning them to the soil. This is a consequence of poor design, argue Braungart and McDonough. Yet, the authors are convinced that all human material on the planet is potentially "food" – either biological and technical.

They say:

> Consider this: all the ants on the planet, taken together, have a biomass greater than that of humans. Ants have been incredibly industrious for millions of years. Yet their productiveness nourishes plants, animals, and soil. Human industry has been in full swing for little over a century, yet it has brought about a decline in almost every ecosystem on the planet. Nature doesn't have a design problem. People do.[18]

This must sound like a worthy challenge to any fashion creative who calls himself a designer. It is up to the current and next generation of creatives, mills and suppliers to collaborate and come up with new designs that will fit a circular system. It can be as simple as Y/Project's detachable jeans that turn into shorts, which made headlines in national newspapers (Figure 5.1).[19] And yet this fashion-forward label has barely scratched the tip of the iceberg. Creating products that are versatile and therefore likely to be worn more than six times before being discarded is only the beginning.

No industry with a similar ecological footprint to fashion has a comparable level of creativity. This comes with an enormous potential for producing greener products that are more durable, more versatile, of higher quality and fit for quick disassembly, making them more recyclable while remaining aesthetically appealing.

Such a model will require the industry to switch from linear supply *chains* to circular supply *networks*. This starts with smart infrastructure. Lean is definitely clean. It is crucial to find smarter manufacturing methods; this can be done with software solutions such as Lectra's "factory of the future," which helps with streamlining

FIGURE 5.1 Y/Project: detachable jeans

Source: Y/Project

processes, saving time, money and resources in the making. Lectra notes that: "Any process that wastes time, resources or fabric is not an option if manufacturers are to continue operating a sustainable profit model."[20]

A pair of jeans can have up to 24 different measurements from waist to ankle; these need translation into a large number of sizes and fabric mixes, which all perform differently, and in turn need to be adapted to various markets. This normally takes a lot of trial and error that produces an unnecessary amount of samples and waste; all the shipping back and forth ups the jeans' carbon footprint. Software like Lectra's, however, combines 3D technology for prototyping and patternmaking with lifecycle management, connecting the design team with its supply chain and thus minimizing errors.

Jeans have not changed significantly in appearance or construction since the second half of the 19th century, when Jacob Davis tailored the first pair as we know it. Imagine what the software could do by searching for new patterns that enable a quicker and easier disassembly – without changing the beloved look.

Smart is also synonymous with long-lasting. This should be a category in which denim excels. Denim is durable. Aesthetically speaking, a classic pair of jeans is unlikely to go out of style any time soon – after all, it has persisted for almost 150 years unchanged. Historically, it's also one of the strongest pieces of clothing. There is a reason why gold miners used their old Levi's for lagging pipes to prevent them from bursting. The strength of jeans could be upped with new fibers as they come along. While Dyneema and Kevlar, which are among the strongest materials in the world and are found in ballistic and anti-stab vests, rely on petroleum-derived synthetics, biomaterials could do the trick in the future once their production has become more scalable.

An example is synthetic spider silk, a protein-based material created through a microbial fermentation process that does not depend on petroleum. With high mechanical strength and elasticity, this is a completely new type of fiber. Modeled after spider silk, which is 340 times stronger than steel, these protein fibers are environmentally friendly, highly customizable and very flexible. Spiber says:

> We have designed and synthesized over 600 types of original proteins, carefully analyzing their material properties to accumulate a massive amount of data. In the near future, proteins will be widely used as a basic industrial material, just like metals, glass, and plastics are used today.[21]

Since 2008, Spiber has been able to increase productivity 4,500 times, while manufacturing costs are currently 1/53,000 of what they were when the project started, moving closer to a scalable product. The Moon Parka by Northface, developed in collaboration with Spiber, is billed as the world's first piece of clothing made from synthetic protein material.

With such tools in hand, high-end denim has the potential to never be a waste product again. For lower-quality denim, it will be still imperative to design for quick and easy disassembly. This means that all parts and ingredients – from the fiber to the dye to the patch in the back – will need to follow an environmentally friendly recipe. Otherwise, when recycled, toxic chemicals will stay in the loop, leaching into the environment. Therefore, smart sourcing (fiber and its provenance) and smart technology (e.g. laser finishes) remain key.

Smart disposal

Our ways of disposing waste are among the most backward activities we engage in today as a society. Originally, our ancestors who roamed the prairies for plants to eat and meat to hunt left their garbage where it fell, which was okay because they lived in the wild where most trash decomposed in no time. Nutrients were returned to the soil as the hunters and gatherers moved on to new pastures. But as populations started to grow, so did the waste problem. American archaeologist Gordon Willey argued that the rise of civilization, or the advanced state of human society, was partly due to the need for organized garbage disposal.[22] But the methods of dealing with mounting piles of trash have been the same for thousands of years: dumping, burning, recycling and source reduction to save more valuable resources. The Maya, for instance, abandoned

> the practice of burying the dead with new or intact pottery, tools, and jewelry, and burying them instead with objects that were broken. In addition, they substituted "fake" for original – for example, clay beads covered with gold foil instead of beads of solid gold.[23]

Compared to that, our sacrifice of making one trip less to the high street per month seems banal. And yet the scope of our problem is significantly larger than that of the Maya. There simply isn't that much left. We've been too comfortable relying on resources that we thought would be available forever and on doing things the way we have always been doing.

For years now, we've been told to follow a simple formula: reduce, reuse, recycle. But in a complex system like fashion, this is too vague a concept.

In a circular system, clothes don't ever become waste; their (re-)use phase is extended – preferably indefinitely. Fortunately, because fashion is a creative industry, this can be done in a number of ways. In general, we have two types of waste to deal with: pre-consumer from manufacturing or unsold stock and reclaimed or post-consumer waste. As they vary in quality, the strategies for reducing them are different.

Pre-consumer

With an estimated 40 billion square meters of left-over fabric up for grabs every year, the potential for reducing pre-consumer waste is significant.

During manufacturing, cast-away material can be re-used and re-integrated into production at an early stage. A denim mill like Candiani, for instance, which turns out 23 million meters of fabric a year, recycles 100 percent cotton through the spinning, warping, dyeing and weaving stages, slashing overall waste significantly. "We dye 14 beams with 50,000 to 70,000 meters of yarn in one hit. The yarns go through the dyeing machine along a path of 500 meters," explains Simon Giuliani, the mill's marketing manager.

> This means that at any given time there are 500 meters of yarn in the machine. When we finish dyeing, we stop the machine, cut off the yarns in the back, take a new batch of 14 beams, knot them to the old yarns and start dyeing again. So the first 500 meters and last 500 meter of a dyeing lot are not

consistent in color. Normally, they would have to be thrown out. We collect those 1,000 meters, shred them back to fiber stage, mix with fresh cotton and re-spin them into our recycled collection.

Giuliani adds that the bigger the dyeing lot, the lower the percentage of fabric that doesn't make it into the main collection – something the mill is keen to get across to the brands and retailers it works with.

To make it easy: 500 meters plus 500 meters equals 1,000 meters of waste. If the dyeing lot is 50,000 meters, the waste accounts for 2 percent. If the dyeing lot were 5,000 meters, the waste would account for 20 percent. This is why we ask our clients for minimum orders of fabric, otherwise the waste is ridiculous.

The Turkish mill Orta, meanwhile, has teamed up with Circle Economy to tackle the problem of so-called "seconds," an estimated 750 million meters of fabric considered to be flawed and therefore waste. The mill is working on a detection and digital CMT (cut-make-trim) device that can map defects on the fabric, cut around them and minimize the meters that need to be discarded. However, Orta and Circle Economy jointly noted that

most importantly the industry needs to work together and create a demand for "seconds" in the market, which would ultimately bolster the value of this otherwise lost resource. [At the moment,] this tremendous amount of wasted denim is being sold at a fraction of its actual value, undermining the entire industry.[24]

Sometimes too much of a given fabric is produced and ends up in the warehouse despite being of top-notch quality. Brands such as Ink Inklusive and Double Eleven specialize in taking leftovers and turning them into limited-edition collections. "There is so much warehoused cloth from canceled orders or end of rolls, and it's just lying there," noted Alex Melgaard-Lewty, who founded the Amsterdam-based label Ink Inklusive with her husband Neil. They call it their "livestock" or "forgotten cotton." She added:

We see a lot of high-street fashion and design, but not much in the middle — something fun to wear, creative and exciting at the same time. And that's what we are working on. What we love about denim is that it's versatile – it's a twill. We do not work it like a denim, but like a woven fabric.[25]

Collaborations can be key. A good example is Blackhorse Lane Ateliers, an East London denim maker, which hands its fabric waste to British kids' wear label Fieldplay, which specializes in upcycled handmade clothing for children. The scraps perfectly fit a child's measurements. "We send Linda [Mackie – the founder and creator of Fieldplay] trash bags of our denim off-cuts, she upcycles them into onesies for children. If this was a big factory we would just throw these in the bin," says Han Ates, showing off a thick stack of large denim off-cuts, which he also turns into sports bags.

> We are also looking at ways to lay the patterns on the three meters to see how we can optimize it. When you do selvedge you have a less useful area in the middle of the meter. So we thought about how to lay out the parts – pockets, belt, loop, etc. – slightly differently, to make that center piece bigger and therefore have a larger off-cut as opposed to lots of small snippets which you can't do much with.

His small atelier, which also uses second-hand sewing machines from Japan, produces roughly 50 kilos of fabric waste a week. Given that the denim world as a whole turns out 3.1 billion pairs of jeans each year, and that most of them are done the conventional way, the missed opportunities are probably costing the industry millions.

It's great when not only mills but also established retailers take matters into their own hands, selling jeans from deadstock in collaboration with renowned labels. An example is Korean denim specialist Mode Man and its "Coworkers" series. Cue selvedge from Cone Mills deadstock done up by Railcar Fine Goods or Pure Blue Japan, among others.

Following the success of its Urban Renewal line, which upcycles vintage garments, in 2016 Urban Outfitters launched "ReWork," a new line of sustainable clothing made of remnant fabric. Dubbed the "anti-fast fashion label" by WGSN,[26] the limited-edition range drops three times a year, with each item labeled individually, many of which are denim. As Lizzie Dawson, the store's head of design, told *Vogue*, it always starts with the fabric, not the cut, which leads to novel levels of creativity:

> It's experimental and designed from what feels right as opposed to chasing trends. Fashion is fast and the landscape is constantly changing and evolving. By offering something like ReWork, I'm hoping that we can offer the new and unseen to our customers.[27]

Sadly, some initiatives don't last, such as Topshop's Reclaim, which had teamed up with Reclaim To Wear to create a system in which its pre-consumer waste could be upcycled into regular collections. The pilot resulted in three collections from 2011 to 2014 before being stopped.[28]

Post-consumer

Post-consumer waste is anything we have owned but no longer want to wear. Such old garments more often than not end up in the bin, where they will no longer reach other consumers; their ingredients won't be retrieved but will turn into pollution instead. This is a particularly hard loss in the case of denim. Denim is king in the textile category. High-quality jeans are durable and can be easily mended, which is why they should never finish their life in a landfill or an incinerator.

From L.A. to Riga, New York to London, there is an array of specialized repair shops, capable of stitching hard-worn jeans back together again and upping the ante with prolific customization techniques worthy of a designer brand. Examples include Atelier & Repair, Bulichev, Denim Doctor, Denim Surgeon or Triarchy.

Denim Therapy is one that takes matters very seriously:

> We know that there is more to denim relationships than meets the eye. Jeans are tried-and-true friends that represent unique memories. Which means no two denim relationships (or issues) are alike. That's why we painstakingly inspect and evaluate every article that comes through our doors before proposing a bespoke prescription.[29]

Swedish denim specialist Nudie has made a second business out of repairing and reselling its old products. The brand repairs 40,000 pairs of jeans a year, with their Repair shops generating one-third of the company's turnover.

If you're up for it, you can try to revive your jeans yourself. Levi's teaches how in a series of DIY tutorials on its website. Tips on how to repair, taper, customize, pintuck and crop are among the informative 01:20 video snippets it proposes.

If Picasso, Gaudi and co. were okay with making their hands dirty, there is no reason why fashion designers shouldn't go down the same route. The notion of reusing what someone else has worn before has arguably suffered from a frumpy image and the advent of celebrity bling culture in recent years. But there is indeed a great source of creativity hidden in recycled fashion.

Elevating post-consumer denim to new level is Re/Done. The L.A.-based label specifically scouts vintage Levi's jeans at rag factories, taking them apart and putting them together again into a modern fitting pair of jeans – a concept so effective, it prompted *Vogue* to ask: "Are these the perfect jeans?"[30] Cofounder Sean Barron explains: "We don't think of this as a denim brand, it's a movement we've started towards making heritage brands become relevant."[31] His partner Jamie Mazur, brother of Hollywood stylist Jennifer Mazur, says he can "pretty much make any shape out of a 501," of which he estimates there are around 400 million in circulation, making the business with vintage Levi's a truly circular economy. Re/Done is slated to venture into collaborations with other covetable brands.

Vintage Levi's denim is no stranger to the runway, either. Cue buzzy Paris-based label Vetements, which famously offers jeans and jackets cut and patchworked together from multiple swatches of old Levi's that the team scavenges at vintage markets. The pants, which boast Vetements' signature high-rise pattern, fetch £1,000 and more often than not sell out in one day. This sustainable idea was born out of an economic necessity. Vetements designer Demna Gvasalia says he just couldn't meet the minimum volume required to place an order with a factory.

What works at the higher end works at the lower end just as well. British online retailer ASOS is going strong with its "Reclaimed Vintage" collection, offering repurposed clothing it sources from flea markets and thrift shops. This includes military and one-off denim items as well as rescued deadstock. The result is a collection of unique items with a vintage flair, and definitely not your homogenous high-street uniform.

Nobody says, however, that a pair of jeans absolutely needs to be remade into another pair of jeans. With denim taking off as a category, the options are plentiful. Cue knitwear designer Katie Jones, a Central Saint Martins graduate who transforms reclaimed denim into new fashion items, employing her signature crocheting, hole punching and hand embroidery techniques.

Less high fashion but more accessible and flexible are initiatives such as Annika-N, which connects customers with indie designers who can up an old garment's fashion credentials. The London-based upcycling collective specializes in providing creative solutions to all types of textile waste.

For post-consumer recycling to work, it would need to be done on a big scale. Large brands, including Levi's, H&M and Inditex, have take-back programs in stores, but their number is still very low. As Greenpeace has noted: "End-of-life logistics and technologies for recycling should not rely on corporate generosity but be made mandatory, ensuring that externalised costs are internalised and linked to the volumes of output, if they are to have any structural value."[32] Take-back initiatives also need to be developed and coordinated strategically, the NGO noted.

An example is EcoTLC in France, a waste management system for clothing, linen and footwear, which currently covers 93 percent of the industry. Companies selling their own product on the French market "are considered responsible by law for providing or managing the recycling of their products at the end of their usage."[33] They can either "set [their] own internal collecting and recycling program accredited by the French Public Authorities or pay a contribution to Eco to provide it for them."

Interestingly, these payments are calculated against the companies' efforts to tighten the loop. For instance, using a minimum of 30 percent pre-consumer recycled fibers results in a 25 percent discount. A minimum of 15 percent post-consumer content adds up to a 50 percent discount.

So far, members of the initiative include A.P.C., C&A France, Louis Vuitton and Zara France, among others.

EcoTLC is slated to introduce discounts of up to 75 percent for durability, starting with the shoe category in 2018, followed by jeans, jumpers, T-shirts and sheets later.

Meanwhile, H&M has gathered more than 40,000 tons of clothing (equivalent to more fabric than in 150 million T-shirts, it says) since it launched its take-back program in 2013 with partner I:CO. I:CO sorts the batch into two categories: reuse (sold as second-hand) and recycle (downcycled into other products such as cleaning cloths or insulation).

More importantly, the retailer has invested into re:newcell, a Swedish startup, which is able to upcycle used garments as well as cast-offs with high cellulosic content (i.e. cotton, lyocell and viscose) "into a new, biodegradable material" it calls "re:newcell pulp"[34]; this is fed back into the textile production value chain, allowing a garment to be made from 100 percent recycled fiber.

"This is the link that has been missing from the production cycle. re:newcell has closed the loop," the company's CEO, Mattias Jonsson, declared in October 2017, adding that this could transform fashion into "a never-ending loop in the future."[35] re:newcell also follows a closed-loop production system for chemicals and water and uses renewable energy. Its current production capacity, however, is still small, with 7,000 tons of pulp a year.

Inditex, parent company of Zara and Massimo Dutti, too, is rolling out a global take-back program that allows customers to drop off their worn clothing, which will then be sorted for repair, resale or recycling in cooperation with local non-profit partners including Caritas, the Red Cross, Oxfam and China Environmental Protection Foundation (CEPF). The retail giant plans to achieve its "target of zero waste to landfills by 2020,"[36] while also entering into a strategic partnership with Lenzing. An initial 500 tons of textile waste generated by Inditex is to be converted into premium textile raw materials by the Austrian specialist of cellulose fiber. Inditex plans to up the amount to 3,000 tons within a few years, enough to contribute to the manufacture of 48 million garments. The group said it is also partnering with MIT and Spanish universities to push research into technology for the creation of new textiles from recycled garments.

According to UK retailer Marks & Spencer, which has launched its PLAN A strategy for sustainable business in 2007, recycling its own waste pays off. The retailer not only achieved zero waste to landfill in 2012 in its UK and Republic of Ireland markets, but also gains around £6 million per year as a consequence, e.g. by saving on landfill costs.

On the downside, Greenpeace estimates that only 10 to 12 percent "of the best quality clothes are re-sold" locally in the EU, while much of the rest is likely exported to the Global South,

> a trade which has risen dramatically since the year 2000, with 4.3 million tonnes traded in 2014, mainly from the USA, Western Europe and parts of Asia to countries such as Pakistan, Malaysia, Russia, and India – where some of it is re-exported to Africa.[37]

The NGO notes that "large amounts of used clothes are unsaleable due to poor quality - often associated with the greater use of synthetics and polyester/cotton mixes," which leads to downcycling.

One of the most rigorous strategies for dealing with post-consumer waste can be attributed to Eileen Fisher and her "Renew" collection. The brand encourages customers to bring back old Eileen Fisher clothes to the store, where the brand will find them another home. Clothes that are in good condition are cleaned and resold on the brand's website. Those that have stains or minor flaws are overdyed and sold again. Clothes damaged beyond repair, which constitute about 25 percent of the take-back load, are resewn, i.e. the damaged parts are cut away and the remaining fabric is stitched together to create a new design. Finally, the left-over scraps are felted or saved for later, waiting to be used as raw material, while the brand is investing in new technologies to create future fibers from waste.

Waste is by no means a high street and mid-market concern. The second-hand market for designer apparel and accessories is booming. Vestiaire Collective, the leading marketplace in Europe for pre-owned luxury fashion, including top-notch brands such as Chanel, Dior and Hermès, is growing at a rate of 60 percent a year, with the firm's founder and chief executive officer Sébastien Fabre estimating the global second-hand market at $200 billion. "If we address only 10 percent, it's going to be big. There's really room for growth," he told WWD.[38]

Stella McCartney, meanwhile, is taking matters into her own hands. A sustainability pioneer among the more established fashion designers, she has forged a partnership with the fashion resale site The RealReal, a member of the Ellen McArthur Foundation, which promotes circular economy. McCartney, who already uses regenerated cashmere scraps previously been considered waste to produce her arresting runway looks and reduce her dependency on virgin cashmere fibers, says:

> We believe that consignment, and recommerce can play a significant part in reducing the amount of raw materials that are required each year from our planet. This is key in our commitment to becoming part of a more circular economy. By ensuing that our products are used for the entirety of their lifecycle it is possible to begin to slow down the amount of natural resources currently being cultivated and extracted from the planet for the sake of fashion.[39]

Other luxury brands, however, have been hesitant about consignment. "The fear is that we're cannibalizing their business. Stella's not worrying about that, because she knows it's not true," The RealReal founder and CEO Julie Wainwright told WWD, adding: "We're using up the planet's resources at a rate that's truly unsustainable. If other brands follow suit, it will be awesome."[40]

Smart investing

Innovation moves fast, and any novelty is quickly labeled as revolutionary. But in reality, only a few technologies will bring about the seismic shifts that are needed to turn the fashion industry around. Spotting where these disruptions take place and adopting them early will put companies a step ahead of their competition, save costs and improve quality.

In a recent study, McKinsey Global Institute identified 12 disruptive technologies that in the coming years could "transform life, business, and the global economy" as we know it:[41] mobile internet, automation of knowledge work, the Internet of Things (IoT), cloud technology, advanced robotics, autonomous and near-autonomous vehicles, next-generation genomics, energy storage, 3D printing, advanced materials, advanced oil and gas exploration and recovery and renewable energy. The researchers estimate that these technologies will generate between $14 trillion and $33 trillion a year by 2025. That's a lot of money and a lot of opportunity, not least for the clothing industry.

One of the biggest issues with recycling textiles is that it has to be done by hand, which makes it a costly endeavor. Advanced robotics could enhance sorting systems as they get smarter and more dexterous by identifying color and blends and helping to disassemble items into fabrics, buttons, leather patches and rivets more quickly and efficiently. I:CO sorts clothing according to 350 criteria; as Paul Dietzsch Doertenbach, head of sales and marketing, says,

> The biggest challenge for us is the identification, of the fabrics that we have in front of us, the problem is how to get the manual sorter to make the decision, we don't have the time to look at labels, and cannot trust all of these label, like our white cotton T-shirt test shows.

I:CO did the test.

> We had white cotton t-shirts that were labelled as 100% cotton, recycled them mechanically and made new yarn with our partners. It all looked good. And then we dyed the fabric in black. Suddenly we had greyish spots all over which represented some sort of oil-based fiber which doesn't absorb the black color as natural fibers do.

With mobile internet growing increasingly capable, advanced display technology is just a step away. Along with the automation of knowledge work, which can help sort through big data via artificial intelligence and IoT's advanced sensors (applied to garments via RFID (radio frequency identification) tags), manufacturing, transport and recycling could be optimized on a much larger scale. This could be accomplished, for example, by communicating the content of a garment and how to best dismantle it, or using smart meters to save resources such as water and electricity, which are already used in cotton farming and help in streamlining irrigation processes.

And this could go further. In the US, the cities of Cincinnati and Cleveland put RFID tags on household garbage and recycling bins, which not only helped crews to eliminate pickup routes and cut operating costs but were also instrumental in implementing so-called pay as you go programs, which make residents pay extra if they put out too much garbage that doesn't fit the bin. As a result, residential waste volume in Cincinnati dropped 17 percent, while recycling volume surged 49 percent.[42] Putting out the wrong kind of garbage – such as denim – could equally be identified.

Scientists at the SENSEable City lab tagged trash via wireless location markers, tracking where our stuff goes after we got rid of it and thus making the removal chain more transparent. With the project, MIT is hoping "to promote behavioural change and encourage people to make more sustainable decisions about what they consume."[43] On a more low-tech level, this is already happening with jeans. Hiut Denim has come up with the History Tag. Each jean comes with a unique number and can be tracked via an application. Jeans owners upload their jeans' journey in the form of pictures, for example, so that when the jeans are handed down to the next owner, their memories go with them, building up an emotional connection to the garment.

Sensors could also be used to track garments through the supply chain and connect with the retail floor, avoiding excess inventory. What isn't needed wouldn't be produced in the first place, thus avoiding waste and the wasteful use of natural resources in the first place.

In design, 3D printing has the potential to bring a number of benefits. It could make on-demand production possible, allowing more local production (and therefore shorter transportation) while eliminating waste. As the range of materials expands, reliance on polyester in 3D printing is shrinking, possibly creating opportunities for alternative stretch fibers. TamiCare's CosyFlex fabric, for instance, claims to be stretchy and biodegradable. London start-up Unmade, meanwhile, is translating its knowledge of 3D printers into knitting machines, producing knitwear on-demand in a range of designs. McKinsey estimates that 3D printing could save manufacturers 35 percent to 60 percent in costs per printed product while enabling a high level of customization.[44] The price for a home 3D printer is already 90 percent lower than four years ago. In fact, it is to become so widespread that Greenpeace warns there is a danger it might uphold the current trend of overconsumption.

Another disruptive technology that should be of interest to the fashion industry is the production of advanced materials, which can up a garment's sustainability factor by allowing an array of superior characteristics. For example, silver nanoparticles, which have been studied for their antimicrobial properties, are already woven into denim to reduce odor. Now, scientists at Shaanxi University of Science and Technology have taken inspiration from nature's self-repairing organisms and have experimented with self-healing (for now PET) materials, which they say are suitable for mass-production.[45] Imagine a pair of jeans that can mend itself. Nanomaterials may also enhance the performance of chemicals and catalysts and help with environmental issues such as water shortages. Graphene is a material the industry is eager to see become more cost-effective. Graphene could be employed in filters that turn salt water into freshwater and remove impurities. Nanoparticles, however, still require more testing to ensure their non-toxic nature.[46]

Q&A WITH PAUL DIETZSCH DOERTENBACH, GLOBAL ACCOUNT MANAGER AT I:CO

Q: Why are some countries masters of recycling, while others lag behind?

A: In most countries there are no solutions to deal with textile waste. In Germany roughly 75 percent of textile waste is recycled after being collected mostly by charity organizations. Then there are markets where there is close to zero collection, mostly emerging marketing, but also in the US for example, where only 15 percent of textiles are collected. The UK is a very good example. They have through WRAP [Waste and Resources Action Programme] and SCAP [Sustainable Clothing Action Plan] come up with very good campaigns introducing the topic and the values of textile recycling to consumers. In general, once you are aware of the value you don't throw it away very easily. And then it has to be convenient to drop off your unwanted clothes, because nobody will walk the extra mile. In the UK, in every Tesco you have a drop-off – that makes it easy.

Q: How much textile waste do you sort for reuse, how much for recycling at I:CO?

A: We collect 20,000 t a year, our mother company SOEX Group roughly processes 100,000 tons a year. [Fifty-five] percent of collected clothes are reusable versus 45 recyclable. Recycling means we tear the garments apart mechanically to win back the fiber, which is used for insulation material. Most is sold into the automotive industry – roughly every car carries 40kg of recycled fibers in it, depending on the size of the car. What we are working towards is to ideally recycle that fiber bound in our clothing in a way that can be used to make a new yarn or fabric, so we are aiming at closed-loop recycling, which is an ambitious goal however.

Q: Where are the biggest obstacles?

A: Staple strength is one. The fibers are getting short, the quality decreases. The next big challenge is to come up with a chemical recycling solution. That would also enable us to separate mixed fibers from each other in order to get secondary raw material. Denim for instance is often mixed with polyester or elastane to make it stretch. We are able to mechanically recycle these and use it for insulation, but denim-to-denim recycling requires 100 percent cotton or a natural fiber like wool.

In chemical recycling there is an enzymatic approach, it can be a chemical bath where you use solvents to break apart the fiber, it remains to be seen which chemical recycling process will win here. When I hear chemical solvent that doesn't sound too good. Fact is, we need to change something, we need recycling innovation to kick in. One is not allowed to be pessimistic in a brainstorming sessions [sic], it's too early to judge.

But most importantly, we still need to collect far more clothes to ensure circularity; we are not collecting enough to close loop at the moment.

Q: Where do the garments you deal with come from?

A: We place collection units at the points of sale of your partners and we are encouraging our partners to give incentives to customers to come in and drop them off.

We are all very ambitious, but very lazy as well. Right now we have 63 retail partners, including H&M, Levi's, Timberland, Northface. Our mother company's core business is to organize the sorting and recycling of the goods, so they work with other collectors like charities.

Q: What kind of governmental regulation would you like to see in place?

A: In Germany, if you are retailing electronic goods you are required by law to implement strategies to take those back. All our retail partners that are collecting clothes are doing it on a voluntary basis. But it would be great if it became mandatory for apparel brands to do so. I think in the EU we will see something there by 2025. Customers need to learn that there are valuable resources bound into our clothes. In Denmark or Germany, for instance, you don't dump plastic bottles any more. There is a pant system. When you buy a bottle you pay 25 cents more, when you take the bottle to the store you get your 25 cents back. That does not exist for clothing – yet.

Smart consumption

The fact is, we produce more than we can sell and buy more than we need, wasting finite resources. Driven by impulsive shopping behavior that only brings temporary satisfaction, the result is that we throw away the stuff we bought after only a short period of usage.

The notion of a throw-away society is a faulty one because everything stays with us in one form or another. We are competing with our waste for space; our food chain is competing with our waste for space, as evidenced by the current state of our oceans. According to projections, by 2050 there will be more plastic in the oceans than fish. And as fish feed on the plastic we consume and throw away recklessly, we will almost certainly end up eating our own waste, too..

Trash is also expensive. According to Edward Hume, "American communities spend more on waste management than on fire protection, parks and recreation, libraries or schoolbooks. If it were a product," he argues, "trash would surpass everything else we manufacture."[47]

As discussed throughout this chapter, denim is the perfect candidate for reuse, offering both fashion-forward and sustainable solutions. But it still lacks the technology to be truly circular on a significant scale. Until there is a way of turning a pair of jeans into a nutrient for a biological or industrial circle, there is only one option: to consume less.

This doesn't mean that you have to stop wearing jeans. On the contrary, you can alter one pair to become another by seeing a denim doctor or turning your jeans into another equally valuable garment. Fabric is fabric; it will fall apart eventually and you will need to buy a replacement, but as the old gold miners would attest, denim can really last a long, long time, provided you invest in a quality fabric in the first place.

If you are fed up with your old jeans, just donate or resell them.

Some brands will actively encourage you to reduce your consumption by only buying what you really need. In one of the most buzz-worthy advertising campaigns in apparel history, Patagonia urged its customers: "Don't Buy This Jacket." The ad ran in the *New York Times* on Black Friday, when millions of citizens engage in a collective buying frenzy. Patagonia's reasoning:

> Businesses need to make fewer things but of higher quality. Costumers need to think twice before they buy. Why? [Because] everything we make takes something from the planet we can't give back. Each piece of Patagonia clothing, whether or not it's organic or uses recycled materials, emits several times its weight in greenhouse gases, generates at least another half garment's worth of scrap, and draws down copious amounts of freshwater now growing scarce everywhere on the planet.[48]

Patagonia resells its worn wear as "Common Threads" on eBay as well as its own website, asking customers to look there first before buying new gear. Its mantra: Reduce, Repair, Reuse, Recycle, Reimagine. What this means is: First, you buy only what you really need from a brand that you assume produces products that really last. Second, if a zipper breaks, the brand can fix it, instead of you throwing it away. Third, what you no longer need or desire, you sell on eBay through the Common Thread Initiative. Fourth, what can no longer be worn, you return to Patagonia to be recycled into new fiber or fabric. Fifth, by engaging in steps one through four, you help create a new system and divert waste from landfill. Patagonia describes the initiative as "reimagining commerce" or "a world where we take only what nature can replace."[49]

According to eBay, no major retail brand "has persuaded customers to choose used products over new ones" before.[50]

Other models suggest never really owning anything at all, which might be a good option for those obsessed with trends, however short-lived they may be. Dutch MUD jeans offers its jeans for lease. You pay a monthly fee of €7.50 for 12 months, after which you can return the jeans and MUD will recycle them into new denim. "Rumor has it – on average 30 percent of garments in our closets have not been worn for almost a year," the brand argues on its website, adding: "Lease a Jeans is a guilt-free solution for conscious people that have a desire for newness."[51]

Swedish brand Filippa K follows a similar strategy, allowing customers to lease anything they want, including denim, for four days at 20 percent of the full price, cost of cleaning included, though for now this is only possible at one of its physical stores in Sweden, Belgium, Denmark, Finland, Germany, the Netherlands or Norway.

For more upscale pieces and special occasions, there is Rent a Runway. To wit: For a four-day rental of a pair of Derek Lam culottes made of denim, the company asks $110 compared to the item's $650 retail price.

It's not that we are not capable of buying less and buying better. When the great recession hit, people changed their behavior in a heartbeat. Suddenly quality was favored over quantity. It was a necessity. Value was considered an investment. This time it is not our personal wallets that are affected, but the earth's resources, which are everyone's common good.

Notes

1 Hoge, Warren. Art Imitates Life, Perhaps Too Closely. *New York Times*, October 20, 2001.
2 Ibid.
3 Blackstock, Colin. Cleaner Clears Up Hirst's Ashtray Art. *Guardian*, October 19, 2001.
4 Jones, Jonathan. Modern Art is Rubbish? Why Mistaking Artworks for Trash Proves Their Worth. *Guardian*, October 27, 2015.
5 Levin, Kim. Talking Trash. *Artnews.com*, January 6, 2011.
6 Nuwer, Rachel. Lice Evolution Tracks the Invention of Clothes. *Smithsonian.com*, November 14, 2012.
7 Remy, Nathalie, Speelman, Eveline & Swartz, Steven. Style That's Sustainable: A New Fast-Fashion Formula. *McKinsey&Company*, October 2016.
8 Olivetti et al.
9 Remy et al.
10 Cobbing, Madeleine & Vicaire, Yannick. *Time-Out for Fashion*. Greenpeace. 2017.
11 Remy et al.
12 How Much Does Garment Industry Actually Waste? *Reverse Resources*, August 31, 2016. http://reverseresources.net/news/how-much-does-garment-industry-actually-waste
13 Cobbing & Vicaire.
14 Bailey, Paul. Clothing and Textile Recycling Has Major Impact on Reducing Greenhouse Gasses According to EPA and S.M.A.R.T. *PRWeb*, September 26, 2013. http://www.prweb.com/releases/2013/9/prweb11166628.htm
15 Bonini, Sheila & Swartz, Steven. Profits with Purpose: How Organizing for Sustainability Can Benefit the Bottom Line. *McKinsey&Company*, July 2014.
16 The Future of Denim. *Circle Economy*, May 9, 2017. https://www.circle-economy.com/future-denim-industry/#.WjKCJrQ-fOQ
17 Braungart & McDonough, p. 43.
18 Ibid., p. 16.
19 Hosie, Rachel. Opening Ceremony Launch Detachable Jeans That Turn into Shorts. *Independent*, May 19, 2017. http://www.independent.co.uk/life-style/fashion/opening-ceremony-launch-detachable-jeans-shorts-brand-shop-summer-a7744581.html
20 Friedman, Arthur. Lean Manufacturing Detailed in Lectra Study. *WWD*, June 17, 2016. http://wwd.com/business-news/business-features/lean-manufacturing-detailed-lectra-study-10458975/
21 www.spiber.jp
22 Rathje, William & Murphy, Cullen. *Rubbish!: The Archaeology of Garbage*. Harper Collins, 1992, p. 33.
23 Ibid., p. 34,
24 Orta Anadolu: Finding Value in Flawed Fabrics. *Circle Economy*, n.d. https://www.circle-economy.com/case/orta-anadolu-finding-value-in-flawed-fabrics/#.WjKFb7Q-fOQ
25 Szmydke, Paulina. Ink Inklusive Opens in Amsterdam. *WWD*, July 27, 2015.
26 WGSN Insider. Urban Outfitters ReWork Collection: The Anti-Fast Fashion Label. *WGSN*, June 30, 2016. https://www.wgsn.com/blogs/urban-outfitters-rework-anti-fast-fashion/

27 Conlon, Scarlett. Urban Outfitters Launches ReWork. *Vogue*, June 21, 2016. http://www.vogue.co.uk/gallery/urban-outfitters-rework-collection-interview-reveal
28 TOPSHOP Reclaim to Wear 3d Collection. *Reclaim to Wear*, n.d. http://www.reclaim-towear.com/2014/topshop-reclaim-to-wear-3d-collection/
29 About Us. *Denim Therapy*, n.d. http://denimtherapy.com/about-us/
30 Milligan, Lauren. Are These the Perfect Jeans? *Vogue*, April 7, 2015. http://www.vogue.co.uk/gallery/redone-jeans-founders-jamie-mazur-sean-barron-interview
31 Ibid.
32 Cobbing, Madeleine & Vicaire, Yannick, p. 7.
33 http://www.ecotlc.fr/page-297-information-in-english.html
34 https://renewcell.com/
35 Ibid.
36 https://www.inditex.com/our-commitment-to-the-environment/closing-the-loop/collect-reuse-recycle
37 Cobbing & Vicaire.
38 Edelson, Sharon. Vestiaire Collective's Profile-Boosting Campaign. *WWD*, September 28, 2017.
39 https://www.stellamccartney.com
40 Edelson, Sharon. The Real Real, Stella McCartney Team to Embrace Circular Economy. *WWD*, October 2, 2017.
41 Manyika, James, Chui, Michael, Bughin, Jacques, Dobbs, Richard, Bisson, Peter & Marrs, Alex. *Disruptive Technologies: Advances That Will Transform Life, Business, and the Global Economy*. Antwerp: McKinsey Global Institute, May 2013.
42 Shahrestani, Seyed. *Internet of Things and Smart Environments: Assistive Technologies for Disability, Dementia, and Aging*. Cham Springer International Publishing Imprint: Springer, 2017, p. 67.
43 Tracking Trash. *MIT News*. July 15, 2009.
44 Manyika et al.
45 Xue, Chao-Hua, Bai, Xue & Jia, Shun-Tian. Robust, Self-Healing Superhydrophobic Fabrics Prepared by One-Step Coating of PDMS and Octadecylamine. *Scientific Reports*, 6, article 27262 (June, 6, 2016). https://www.nature.com/articles/srep27262
46 Manyika et al.
47 Humes, Edward. *Garbology: Our Dirty Love Affair with Trash*. New York: Avery, 2013, p. 10.
48 Patagonia. Don't Buy This Jacket, Black Friday and the New York Times. *Patagonia.com*, November 25, 2011. https://www.patagonia.com/blog/2011/11/dont-buy-this-jacket-black-friday-and-the-new-york-times/
49 Patagonia.com
50 Wills, Jackie. Patagonia Urges Customers "Don't Buy New, Search eBay." *Guardian*, May 15, 2014. https://www.theguardian.com/sustainable-business/sustainability-case-studies-ebay-patagonia-recycle
51 http://www.mudjeans.eu/lease-a-jeans/

6

ECONOMY

To have or to be?

"To have or to be?" That is the question Erich Fromm explored in his work of the same title. The German psychoanalyst and philosopher pointed out that modern society favors "having" over "being" with dramatic consequences for planet and people.

At first glance, having seems pretty basic. Everybody owns something, such as a pair of jeans – or at least a loincloth. But while in some languages speakers manage without an equivalent for "to have" in their vocabulary, in consumption-oriented, Western cultures, *having* and *being* have somewhat become synonymous. Assuming that consumption is one form of having, the distinction between the two indeed becomes confusing, because the concept of consumption itself is ambiguous, as Fromm notes. "It relieves anxiety, because what one has cannot be taken away; but it also requires one to consume ever more, because previous consumption soon loses its satisfactory character." Consequently, he observes: "Modern consumers may identify themselves by the formula: I am = what I have and what I consume."[1]

This very much reflects what neuroscientists know today (see Chapter 2). As Peter Sterling writes:

> Satisfaction is brief and diminishes as a particular reward becomes predictable. This circuit design works well for the pre-industrial societies in which rewards are varied and unpredictable. But capitalism shrinks the diversity of possible rewards, leaving the remainder less satisfying, and making stronger doses, i.e., more consumption, necessary.[2]

This partly explains why the consumption of material goods, helped by an industry that promotes the activity for the sake of profit, was so easily allowed to spiral out of control following industrial and technological progress. Our pre-historic desire for more has created an economic model that is out of date, much like the design of the products that we use today. Fashion is a case in point. The current system, based on perpetual growth and a linear culture of "take-make-dispose," no longer corresponds to either human or environmental needs. It is simply not sustainable. Instead of a circular economy, we have collectively established a vicious circle in which we deplete natural resources, treat them chemically – putting human health at stake and causing pollution – and release them back into nature, not realizing that we depend on a healthy planet for prosperity. But being prosperous, in the current system, just means using up more resources, and the circle starts all over again.

This is nothing we have discovered only today.

Fromm recognized in 1976 that the "Great Promise of Unlimited Progress" has failed us. The whole point of the Industrial Revolution was to gain "unimpeded personal freedom" and "the greatest happiness for the greatest number," to dominate nature and enjoy material abundance – in other words: to be omnipotent like the gods who created us.[3]

But it turns out that the contrary is true: Our personal freedom is nothing but an illusion controlled by industries that tell us what to think, feel and taste through crafty advertising and ever-changing trends. We now know that raw materials are finite, as is our consumption; technical progress has threatened our ecosystems and therefore our own existence, while economic advancements have favored the few over the many, creating social unrest. And as far as happiness is concerned? Well, that has proven to be a fleeting pleasure.

We know today that material possessions do not create happiness, and of course we are still mortal, though that might change in the future.

Instead of clinging to a faulty system in which we still find ourselves trapped, Fromm sketched an alternative model of consumption for what he called "The New Man."

Among the main character qualities he proposed were: "confidence [...] in what one *is*" instead of what one *has*; "acceptance of the fact that nobody and nothing outside oneself give meaning;" "joy that comes from giving and sharing, not from hoarding and exploiting;" less greed; and "giving up the aim of conquering nature, subduing it, exploiting it, raping it, destroying it, but trying, rather, to understand and cooperate with nature."[4]

In what reads like a manifesto of some Notting Hill mom's lifestyle coach, Fromm managed to create the blueprints for a new economic model based on a high degree of decentralization and rejection of the free-market economy and unlimited growth in favor of selective growth, accompanied by a general spirit in which instead of material gain other, psychic satisfactions are effective motivators. Conditions would have to be created under which people experience well-being and joy, rather than the satisfaction of the maximum-pleasure drive.[5]

This manifesto for a post-modern Renaissance man echoes Tim Jackson's proposal for an economy that delivers prosperity without growth. Prosperity, Jackson writes, is "not synonymous with material wealth. [...] Rather, prosperity has to do with our ability to flourish: physically, psychologically and socially. Beyond sheer subsistence or survival, prosperity hangs on our ability to participate meaningfully in the life of society."[6]

Jackson acknowledges that the lack of growth is a tricky concept.

> Society is faced with a profound dilemma. To reject growth is to risk economic and social collapse. [...] Once consumption begins to falter the economy starts running into trouble. Investment falls, jobs are lost, businesses go bust, government deficits rise and the economy risks falling into a deflationary spiral. [But] to pursue it relentlessly is to endanger the ecosystems on which we depend for long-term survival.[7]

We already take out more than the earth can replenish. According to a report published by the Geological Society in London, of 40 metals, minerals and fossil fuels essential to the economy today, including iron, copper, silver, gold and oil, most have already reached peak production or will do so before 2050. Among the key policies the report encourages is recycling of metal and

> developing models for an economy that converges within the sustainability limits. It may be cyclical or steady rate, but it must and will stay within the limits of sustainability. If we do not do this, mass balance and thermodynamics will enforce it anyway.[8]

Or, as the Global Footprint Network calculated, the world's population on average would require 1.5 planet Earths to satisfy its needs, and if all nations were to live like an average American, 4.1 Earths would be necessary.

Similar to Fromm, Jackson proposes an economic model "fit for the purpose,"[9] respecting the boundaries of a finite planet while growing in alternative ways. Jackson does not think that producing more in a greener way is an option. He proposes an economic model that is not measured by GDP but actual happiness, one that helps us get out of our "iron cage of consumerism" by focusing on more intrinsic values of prosperity such as health, family and personal wellbeing. "It is sometimes possible to have more fun with less stuff. Consuming less, voluntarily, can improve subjective wellbeing – completely contrary to the conventional model," he writes,[10] noting how "people [are] persuaded to spend money we don't have, on things we don't need, to create impressions that won't last, on people we don't care about."[11]

Going to the park, for instance, instead of the shopping mall may sound banal, but it does reflect what neuroscientists have been telling us about conquering excessive consumption: "The path toward sustainability must include re-expanding the diversity of satisfactions."[12]

Jackson bets his cards on "the economies of care, craft and creativity,"[13] providing low-carbon footprints through more durable and repairable products that are embedded in the community.

That's good news for fashion, which already checks two of the three boxes.

But let's zoom back in on denim.

Unlike electronics, jeans can be repaired at a lower cost than the retail price of a new product, and through creative re-use strategies such as customization (see Chapter 5) can generate additional value.

While the planet's resources are indeed finite, the creative options for dealing with apparel are not.

Yet, the industry is taking it slowly.

One of the most pressing issues of sustainability is that no one really knows how to define it. For some, opting for BCI cotton does the trick; others go the extra mile and dye it with greener chemicals such as pre-reduced indigo. Still others put a green label on their product when it contains a percentage of recycled fiber. Either way, it seems sustainability means a lot of different things to a lot of different people.

The most accepted definition tells us to imagine it like a three-legged stool, one leg each for environmental, social and economic sustainability. In the past, we used to give to one while taking from another, simply shifting focus as it suited us or as it became necessary. Today, we understand that all three legs are very much interconnected. You remove one leg, the stool collapses.

For instance, if we achieved environmental sustainability in one country by outsourcing toxic production to another region where laws and regulations are lax, the stool would lose a leg, because the outsourced activity happened at the expense of local garment makers, violating basic social principles such as human health due to toxic manufacturing. This has been done on a large scale in fashion.

Christian Dreszig, head of marketing at Bluesign Technologies, grew up on the Lake of Constance and remembers how chemical pollution in Central Europe led to a major clean-up plan in the 1980s. This had far-reaching consequences for other geographies:

> Maybe 100, 150 years ago, there were as many as 2,000 textile companies in the region. In the 1980s, the lake was dead – there were no more fish. The governments of Switzerland, Germany and Austria tried to evaluate the reasons. They found that the agriculture, metal and textile industries were responsible for the disaster. So at the beginning of the 1990s new rules were set up. In Switzerland, the government started charging not only for the volume of wastewater, but the freight of wastewater, so the dirt that is inside. The price went up from 0.8 cents to 4.8 cents, roughly five times. Meaning: if you were a heavy consumer of water, you couldn't afford it anymore.

To offset their impact, the industry came up with new and improved end-of-pipe solutions such as partial stream digestion, which handles the wastewater from various parts of manufacturing (e.g. dyeing) separately, reducing the overall volume of pollutants in the process; another solution is anaerobic destruction, which uses microorganisms to biodegrade material in industrial effluent. As a consequence, "the Lake of Constance became clean again – the fish came back," says Dreszig.

> But here's the thing, while it's true that we improved our environmental situation in Europe, in exchange we exported our dirt with globalization. Companies closed. Around the Lake of Constance, we now have maybe five to 10 textile companies left. That's because we produce everything in China or Bangladesh, and the sad thing is that where the production went,

I see people handling chemicals as if it was water. There are no end-of-pipe solutions, they are working like we did 100 years ago. This is mainly because we showed them how to produce but not how to protect the environment and its people. In fact, we had higher levels of protection in the 1980s in Europe than they do in the Far East now. Of course, there are good companies in the region, but the bigger part of the industry is making stuff the conventional way.

By shifting the problem, the European textile industry caused the stool to break. Sustainability knows no geographic boundaries. Someone always ends up paying – like the farmer that switches from conventional to organic practices. The move will improve his health and his soil quality, but it will also put him at a financial loss, at least during the mandatory transitional period in which he cannot ask for more money for his organic cotton because it has not yet been certified. He will also not be allowed to spray his crop with chemicals, which are prohibited under organic regulations, to protect his harvest from pests. In the worst-case scenario, he will not be able to sustain himself and his family and will have to revert to conventional farming methods.

That is, unless brands and retailers agree to support him by (a) committing to buying his cotton and (b) paying what his product is worth.

But what is a sustainable price, and can we afford it without bringing the whole economy to a standstill?

While the environmental and social aspects of sustainability have been getting much-deserved attention, in fashion at least there has been a lack of focus on the benefits of economic sustainability. That's a shame, because this is the part that the chief executive officer or chief financial officer of any brand or retailer, however large or small, will want to know about first.

"Can we afford sustainability?" he will ask. It's a legitimate question. To answer it, we have to look at who is paying for sustainability, or the lack of it, and how (Figure 6.1).

The environment is paying for it in increasingly obvious ways. Other than the strain that fashion puts on air, land and natural resources, the extreme use of water is still apparel's largest sin. Water is needed to grow fiber and its presence is required to dissolve chemicals, which in turn contaminates more water and disturbs aquatic life. It is needed to wash large amounts of garments, most of which turn to waste after a few wears. These growing piles of textile waste in turn feed the greenhouse problem, and so on.

To wit: Fewer than 1 percent of global freshwater supplies are accessible, and 70 percent of it goes straight to agriculture. According to NASA, one-third of the Earth's largest groundwater basins are currently in distress because of human over-consumption. NASA researchers found that "13 of the planet's 37 largest aquifers studied between 2003 and 2013 were being depleted while receiving little to no recharge." Moreover, little reliable data is available on how much is actually still left in those aquifers, making the future of water a very uncertain one.[14]

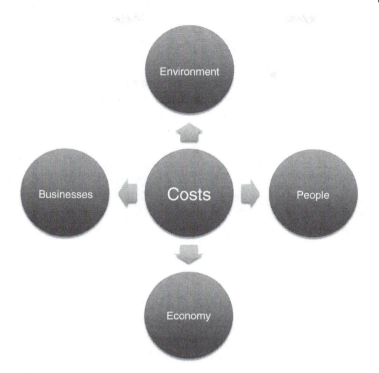

FIGURE 6.1   Can we afford sustainability?

The World Economic Forum calculated that by 2030 global water demand will exceed sustainable supply by 40 percent[15]. No wonder mega-banks like JP Morgan, Goldman Sachs or Barclays are investing in water. Water is the new oil.

The economy depends on it. In the US alone, one-fifth of all business would grind to a halt without a reliable and clean source of water. In terms of manufacturing, 46 percent of water consumed in the US is used to produce the products we buy and dispose of just as fast.[16]

Brands and retailers have substantial room to maneuver. They can control their use of water through their choice of fabrics, colors and finishing processes, and yet most production is still done the conventional way and is expected to increase. According to the Pulse Report[17] presented by the Boston Consulting Group and Global Fashion Agenda in Copenhagen, the fashion industry takes out 79 billion cubic meters of water – enough to fill 32 million Olympic-sized swimming pools – every year. That water use is estimated to increase by another 50 percent by 2030. In monetary terms, €32 billion are at stake, unless fashion can find a way to curb its consumption without using more than it does today.

Consequently, asking whether a business can afford sustainability without hurting its profits is beside the point. If a brand wants to stay in business, it cannot afford not to be sustainable. Because eventually the water bubble will burst and fashion, as a non-essential good, may be the first to go out of business.

People are paying. As discussed earlier, green manufacturing in one country means health risks for factory workers in another. Loss of arable land because of chemically intensive agriculture leads to environmental migration, something we will see more of in the future. The International Organization for Migration (IOM) suggests in a report that by mid-century, 1 billion people will be displaced due to environmental challenges.[18] Bangladesh, where 50 percent of the population lives fewer than 17 feet above sea level,[19] is among those countries most at risk. Bangladesh is also the second largest garment producer in the world, after China.

One man's profit is another man's loss. Minimum wages in apparel are one-half of what can be considered a living wage, and non-compliance with minimum wages can be as high as 87 percent, says the Boston Consulting Group. This concerns Asian countries, but also Eastern Europe and Turkey. If this systematic failure continues, more than one-third of workers in the sector are projected to be paid less than the minimum wage by 2030. The number of injuries is projected to rise from 1.4 million a year to 1.6 million, costing another €32 billion. Rana Plaza, a devastating accident that cost the lives of more than 1,100 people, most of whom were garment factory workers, could just be the beginning. As Andrew Olah, industry veteran and founder of Kingpins, put it: "Two dynamics create these incidents: the ridiculous corporate addiction for cheap clothing and the lack of enforceable laws in developing industries or nations."[20] Olah argues that

> corporations absolutely have the ability to know what is going on, or to enforce regulations if they wish. The answer to many of the problems is for retailers and brands to settle down and continually use the same suppliers and not constantly shop like maniacs for a penny cheaper on cut, make, trim (CMT) and give orders out only based on prices. In the long term, the answer has to be that we as consumers insist on transparent manufacturing, so that we know everything there is to know about our products.[21]

In addition, customers should be paying for sustainability, but are not. Though polls indicate that shoppers are willing to pay more for greener and healthier products, their actual behavior on the retail floor suggests otherwise. When offered two products they like equally, one of which is cheaper than the other, the cheaper one always wins. This has been explained as due to consumers' tight pockets and lack of altruistic behavior, but there is another reason. Brands and retailers do not brand their green denim accordingly, leaving consumers no points of distinction other than price. Which pair of jeans would win the fight if one was branded as green in big, flashy letters and the other pair came with a long list of chemicals, water and unfair social practices remains to be seen. But only then could the customer make an educated choice and learn to seriously weigh the pros and the cons of his or her own actions.

Clear branding is necessary because the price tag alone does not reflect a product's green factor. "There was a time when premium just meant expensive — and tough to sell," notes Olah. "But over the years, it has become difficult to understand what premium really is." It's not enough to be expensive and beautiful, he argues. "Premium has to have something exceptional to offer from the social, ethical and environmental points of view. How dare they sell something at £250 [...] if it was not washed in a sustainable way?" he asks.

With prices ranging between £7 and £1,000 at retail, a green pair of jeans does not need to strain anyone's pocket. L.A.-based brand Everlane advertises its jeans as "Ethically made. Perfectly Fit. $68." Made by Saitex, where 98 percent of industrial water is reused and comes out "so clean you can drink it" – the Everlane founder actually tasted it and put up a video to prove it – the jeans are also air-dried, saving 80 percent of CO_2 emissions (Figure 6.2). In monetary terms, the "true cost" of its $68 jeans is $28.02, says the brand – the lion's share goes to materials at $12.78, labor costs at $7.50, transport at $1.90 and duties at $3.70, while hardware adds another $2.15 to the bill. The difference, says the brand, lies in the mark-up. While conventional retailers mark their products up five to six times, which would result in $140 at retail, Everlane is content with a double to triple mark-up.[22]

A green product is likely to cost more until the price of sustainability itself goes down, which it will with time. Not paying a green premium could eventually cost the consumer through other channels. Michael Braungart and William McDonough, who coined the term cradle-to-cradle, warn of what they call "products plus," e.g. an average piece of polyester clothing that contains antimony, a toxic

FIGURE 6.2 Aerial dry at Saitex

Source: Saitex

heavy metal. "As a buyer you got the item or service you wanted, plus additives that you didn't ask for and didn't know were included and that may be harmful to you and your loved ones."[23] The researchers suggest that such clothing should have labels that say: "Product contains toxic dyes and catalysts. Don't work up a sweat or they will leach onto your skin."

Businesses are paying. On the one hand, businesses with a green agenda pay into the pot of sustainability through investments in R&D, better raw materials, costs of compliance and novel infrastructure – and some of these costs pay off more quickly than others, such as infrastructure. But on the other hand, they also pay in ways they perhaps didn't consider. Waste, for instance, can be very costly. The worth of unrecovered copper – the material of rivets and buttons – is estimated at around €100 million per year.[24] In total, the Pulse Report calculated potential savings for the global economy at €160 billion per year if a more efficient use of resources can be put into practice.[25] This is equivalent to 11 percent of the current retail value of the global apparel and footwear sector, or 90 percent of its current profit pool.

Energy prices will certainly be heartfelt by the apparel industry due to its dependence on polyester. With energy accounting for about 6 to 10 percent of production and material costs, the estimated spike of as much 3.5 percent in energy prices is unlikely to go unnoticed. The report foresees that by 2030,

> fashion brands will see a decline in EBIT margins of more than 3 percentage points if they continue "business as usual" – that adds up to approximately €45 billion per year of profit reduction for the industry as a whole. If energy, water prices, and labor costs grow strongly, the industry's profitability will be under even more pressure. Factoring in the negative externalities of increased water use (such as health impacts from water deficiency) in the price of water puts another 2 percentage points of fashion brands' margins at risk. The high-case assumption for labor costs adds another 2 percentage points and the same assumption for energy costs inflates that figure by an additional 9 percentage points.[26]

Fortunately, there are remedies. Timely investments in water, energy, waste efficiency and labor productivity will be able to balance out some of those negatives, the authors argue.

It is imperative that these investments are evenly shared between those businesses that supply the ingredients for the production of a pair of jeans and those who end up selling the final product. To wit: A chemical company like Garmon invests 25 percent of its budget into marketing and 60 percent into certification and analysis, which is required by the industry, with just 5 percent left for reformulations. At the same time, the company has seen its compliance costs go up 1,700 percent between 2012 and 2016. "That's not sustainable," says chief marketing manager Alberto de Conti. "This regulatory schizophrenia is a big problem for chemical companies. But is it only their problem? While the costs are going up, innovation and control are going down. That's a problem for us all."

In 2016, global R&D spending reached $679.8 billion, though only three out of ten industries – led by software and internet – increased their R&D spending during that period. In the chemicals and energy sector, spending was down 11.5 percent, according to PWC.[27] De Conti notes:

> The chemical companies are very often financially accountable for the compensation of others' mistakes. But the market is not willing to pay a premium for a chemistry of better quality, even though more conscious chemistry reduces customers' overall costs in the form of water, energy, time and dosage.

This creates a spiral in which a product becomes cheaper than its value, creating a ripple effect that is felt throughout the entire supply chain. Ergo, without all players sharing the costs of sustainability, greener chemicals may never see the light of day and organic cotton farmers won't make a living.

Because the system is circular, *the economy as a whole is paying.* The environmental impact of doing business costs the economy $4.7 trillion a year,[28] according to the TEEB for Business Coalition, which is part of the UN. Every year, the economy depends on $72 trillion worth of "free goods," which are not included in financial statements and are therefore poorly managed.[29]

What these costs suggest is that there is great potential for savings. Smart design, or making products that can be easily dissembled for easier recycling, can and will save money, as will choosing the right fabric for the right color in denim.

Smart sourcing, technology and infrastructure can make or break a garment's ecological footprint, which will eventually translate into monetary value.

McKinsey has forecasted that companies that adopt circular-economy principles will outcompete others because the shortage of resources will expose companies that do not to higher costs and unforeseeable risks. Their savings in materials could top $1 trillion a year.[30] It was Ford Motors that once noted how it takes some 55,000 pounds of raw materials to make a 3,000-pound-car. That's a lot of waste and a lot of money.

But what doesn't get measured, doesn't get managed. New accounting methods have appeared such as E P&L (Environmental Profit & Loss), developed by Kering, the parent company of brands such as Gucci, Saint Laurent, Stella McCartney and Alexander McQueen, in cooperation with PricewaterhouseCoopers (PwC). The tool translates environmental business impacts into monetary value, which Kering insists makes it easier for it to stay competitive in the long run.

In 2015, Kering's environmental impact stood at €811 million, up 1.03 percent versus 2014; in the same period, revenue grew 4.6 percent to €11.58 billion. The group understands it still has a long way to go, and bringing its impacts down remains a challenge if revenue growth continues to be a priority. But Kering's impact is still 40 percent lower than an average company in the same industry, according to PwC.[31]

The largest impact for the group came from the supply chain at 92 percent – mainly raw material production and processing.

In Kering's case the biggest culprit was leather, where most of its revenue comes from. Leather comes from animals. Animals need land to graze and they produce methane gas; ergo, 93 percent of the group's total impact were driven by land use and greenhouse gases (GHG) emissions associated with farming. The rest was due to energy use and water use by tanneries. The impact of plant fibers such as cotton, linen and viscose, on the other hand, showed Kering its challenging relationship with water consumption and water pollution.

Kering reacted by announcing its intention to switch the whole group to organic cotton. In 2014, 73 percent of denim used in Stella McCartney's collections, for instance, was already organic. Why organic? Because the E P&L accounting revealed that the organic cotton the group was sourcing slashed the amount of water by one-third and needed less than half of the fossil fuel energy than the cotton it sourced conventionally. More precisely, conventional cotton from its Indian farmers had an E P&L impact of €6.30/kg, which is more than six times higher than that of its organic cotton farmers at €1.00/kg. The group explained the significantly higher water footprint with geography: Much of the conventional production occurs in arid regions where the value of water is higher, and its use affects the amount of water available for local communities.

The shortcomings: Kering increased its overall footprint because it sold more stuff, which will not jibe well with more conservative voices saying that what we need is a sharp slowing of consumption. On the other hand, most of Kering's products fall into the luxury segment, which is on the opposite end of throw-away culture. Luxury items tend to stay inside the loop for decades, generating billions in second-hand sales. That said, luxury designer brands depend heavily on seasonal trends, which feed into the fast fashion frenzy by creating desire for similar low-cost goods, which are subsequently delivered every few weeks.

The question is this: If we can actually put a price tag on the cost of unsustainable business behavior, why are more businesses not adopting a greener model? McKinsey went ahead and posed the question to business leaders in one of its surveys. It found that half of all executives give in to the pressure of delivering short-term earnings, which is at odds with sustainability initiatives, because those require initial investment. The survey estimates that "only one in five S&P 500 companies sets quantified, long-term sustainability goals; half do not have any."[32]

At the same time, research suggests that once the initial step is made, the efforts pay off. The Deutsche Bank has found that

- companies with high ratings for CSR (corporate social responsibility) and ESG (environmental, social and governance) factors have a lower cost of debt and equity;

- while 89 percent of studies examined by the analysts showed that companies with high ESG ratings outperform the market in the medium (3–5 years) and long (5–10 years) term.[33]

On the flip side, McKinsey notes:

> Sustainability initiatives can be challenging to measure because savings or returns may be divided across different parts of the business, and some benefits, such as an improved reputation, are indirect. It is important, then, not only to quantify what can be quantified but also to communicate other kinds of value. For example, an initiative might improve the perception that important stakeholders, such as consumer groups, nongovernmental organizations, or regulators, have of the company. This can help to build consumer loyalty, nurture relationships, and inform policy discussions.[34]

This corresponds to an example Braungart and McDonough quote from past experience.[35] The duo was asked to come up with a new formula for a shower gel that would be healthy for the skin and the ecosystem of the river – the Rhine in this case, where it would end up. They managed to squeeze the formula down to a total of nine ingredients, but the company refused to adopt it because the new chemicals were more expensive. "But when the company considered the entire process, it came to light that the new soap was approximately 15 percent cheaper to make, thanks to simpler preparation and storage requirements," they said. Also, they exchanged the bottle for pure polypropylene after Braungart discovered that antimony from the original PET was leaching into the soap.

Much like that outdated design, most businesses are still looking at sustainability through the lens of mid-20th-century vocabulary – that is, in terms of marginal costs and benefits of abatement and crude products, which are defined as benefiting neither human nor ecological health.[36] GDP, for instance, only looks at economic activity, instead of taking into account long-term effects such as ecological impacts or cultural activity, note Braungart and McDonough. The term, after all, emerged at a time when natural resources were considered unlimited, which we now know is not the case. "Maximising profits for anonymous shareholders while manipulating consumers into buying more products,"[37] as the *Fashion at the Crossroads* report put it, is an obsolete way of making business – a "caricature" that calls for a systemic change.

What if executive bonuses were linked to sustainability performance, for instance? Currently only 1 in 12 companies follow that scheme; and only 1 in 7 companies reward suppliers for good sustainability performance, according to the UN Global Compact.[38]

In the end, whether the environment or the people are paying, it all comes back to businesses and the economy. In fact, the only positive balance comes through the investment in sustainable manufacturing, as shown in this chapter's two case studies.

CASE STUDY: SAITEX

Building homes with recycled steam

Sanjeev Bahl is a man with a cunning sense of humor. The founder and chief executive officer of Saitex, billed as the cleanest denim sewing factory and laundry in the world, likes to tell the story of the "Four Wise Monkeys" to explain what is going wrong within the apparel industry today.[39]

Bahl says he went out to meet the first monkey, a successful entrepreneur who runs a large textile operation. "He was in a great mood until I pointed out that the wastewater from his plant is being discharged directly into the local river and that it was devastating the local environment." The sludge from the plant was hazardous and after being dumped in a landfill leached into the ground-water, which is why people were getting sick. Meanwhile, the dormitories of the factory workers were crumbling. There were safety issues. But the monkey shrugged and said: "Everybody does it, and the cause for this is the ridiculously low prices my clients keep thrusting on me every single day. I have to survive."

Bahl went to visit the second monkey, a powerful fashion mogul. "He was also in a great mood," says Bahl, "until I pointed out that the NGO 'Redpeace' has branded his brand as a Detox loser. He brushed aside my comments and said that his organization had plans to move from Detox loser to greenwasher and eventually to a Detox leader. He had bought time until 2020." However, when Bahl pointed out that hundreds of people had already died in a factory fire in a place that sounds suspiciously like Rana Plaza in Bangladesh, where most of the monkey's production took place, the second monkey was annoyed, but refused to take the blame. He pointed the finger at the lawmakers, stating that the factories he hired were legally registered and that he, the monkey, was giving local people work, for which he should get credit.

The lawmaker was the third monkey Bahl went to see. He acknowledged the problems and added that he was also worried about the hazardous emissions from landfills, which are overflowing with textile waste, all leftovers of point-less mass production. He suggested that the global industry work together to create an environmental law that is binding to all. He said he discussed the topic in Parliament, but that these things take a lot of time. Disappointed with the politician's inefficiency, who asked him to vote for him, Bahl left to meet the fourth monkey.

Within the space of a couple of years, the fourth monkey managed to build an orphanage with revenue generated from converting rejected jeans into shoes. Once the children turn 18, they are provided with an equal opportunity and equal pay job at the factory he runs in the most eco-friendly way. With his plant, he is on the verge of recycling 100 percent of water, employing reversed osmosis, desalination and nano-filtration, which turns his wastewater into a purer product than recommended by WHO standards. The water is free of substances such as fluorite, arsenic or chromium, and whatever excess is left is shipped to places stricken with drought.

The sludge the fourth monkey's plant discharges has been tested non-hazardous and is subsequently converted into bricks to build houses for the homeless.

It's not long before the audience gets it: The fourth monkey is Bahl himself. Unhappy with the industry's standards, the Indian-born entrepreneur tore down his factory and built a brand-new plant in Vietnam, which is currently the only Bluesign-certified denim laundry in the world. In terms of water alone, he invested $2 million into efficient use and wastewater treatment, breaking even in less than four years and saving money ever since. According to Bahl, Saitex uses 12,000 m^3 of water per year versus 1,800,000 m^3 in a conventional factory of the same size. It produces 240,000 kg of sludge versus 1.5 million kg; its sludge is non-toxic and comes with only $24,000 in disposal costs versus $525,000, which is what a conventional plant would have to pay for secure landfill, packing and storage.

With the extra cash from its green practices, Saitex has invested in cleaner technologies to scale up production, including lasers, robots, ozone and nano-bubbles. The factory got rid of the 1:20 liquor ratio "belly" washing machines, which consume 140 liters of water per pair of jeans, and replaced them with 1:4 liquor ratio jet washing machines, which need only 6 liters per pair.

The plant also switched to greener chemicals, which can be processed at room temperature instead of with heated water. Solar power provides energy, while reversed air engineering recycles hot air and steam from machinery to dry denim, a practice that is not only eco-friendly but comes at no extra cost. (Even its marketing video footage uses recycled images).

With these measures, Saitex has managed to cut its CO_2 emission by nearly 80 percent and reduce its energy use by 5.3 million kilowatts per year, which is equivalent to powering 400 homes and taking 600 cars off the streets. This saves the company $376,000 annually in energy costs. Moreover, carbon neutrality has been achieved through the mass planting of trees instead of carbon offsets. One percent of its top line revenue is donated towards hunger alleviation.

"We live in precarious times where there seems to be no limits on greed. Factories and societies have become extremely selfish," says Bahl, noting the dire consequences this comes with. There is a lot at stake for Vietnam, especially, which has already overtaken Bangladesh as the second largest supplier of apparel to the US. The entrepreneur is convinced that by mid-century environmental refugees will be a reality, and they won't be buying jeans or cars or new smartphones.

Bahl has ambitious goals for the future: His aim is to grow his own cotton and indigo and produce biodegradable components that will eventually fertilize mother earth. It's obvious that to him, sustainability is no monkey business.

In its promotional video, Saitex appeals to other companies of its size to come together. It argues that it would take 1,000 like-minded businesses to provide clean water to 2 billion people. According to the WHO, which estimates 2.1 billion people lack safe drinking water at home, this might just do the trick.

CASE STUDY: PATAGONIA

Urging customers to buy less

Patagonia is a healthy company. It regularly logs double-digit growth and makes some $750 million in profit. It has a solid customer base, great brand recognizability and it's made a – somewhat reluctant – billionaire of its founder.

You could argue that's the definition of a successful business.

Curiously, Patagonia has done so by urging its customers to buy less, not more, and by giving away millions to environmental projects. Yvon Chouinard, who founded the company in 1973, says he never wanted to end up this way, viewing growth as a nuisance rather than a blessing. "I only have this business because I'm pessimistic about the future,"[40] he says, fully aware of the fact that every product he or anybody makes comes at a cost to the planet. But he figures if people buy more of the good stuff, then that could actually tilt the balance towards the positive.

Patagonia's message of anti-consumerism climaxed in a now legendary campaign that ran as a one-page ad in an edition of the *New York Times* in 2011. Accompanied by a picture of one of its signature outdoor staples (a fleece jacket), it pleaded: "Don't Buy This Jacket."

Interestingly, this only led the company to sell more of it.

The campaign was inspired by the recession of 2009, which made people redefine their relationship with stuff, including clothing. As Rick Ridgeway, Patagonia's vice president of environmental affairs, explains:

> There were a number of people recognizing that you actually save money if you buy things that last longer and if you were buying fewer of them as a consequence. And we wanted to provide a service for those people.[41]

Convincing the sales team within Patagonia was no cakewalk, he quips. "You can imagine, you go to them and say 'ooh, we wanna run this ad to ask people not to buy our stuff,' and they go: 'You wanna do what?'" But then when he put the idea into context, he says it made sense. "It's not 'Don't buy the jacket,' it's 'Don't buy the jacket if you don't need it.'"

Patagonia has since followed an elaborate strategy of reuse and resell, only then recycling garments that cannot be repaired, helping the company to use fewer resources and create less textile waste. "I'm a little suspect about making any product that is climate-positive, but it is possible to approach climate neutral," Ridgeway notes.

Regardless of whether the firm makes a profit in a given year or not, it has been donating 1 percent of its annual sales to grassroots environmental groups since 1985. That's $7.1 million in its latest fiscal year. Chouinard says: "I don't look at it as philanthropy. It's a cost of doing business, it's a cost of non-renewable resources, cost of living on this planet."[42] It's not an exclusive club. Any company is free to become a member at onepercentfortheplanet.org.

On Black Friday in 2016, the busiest of all retail holidays, the company went a step further, donating the totality of what it made that day globally in both brick-and-mortar and online sales to NGOs, working to clean up water and air and providing healthy soils on a local level. Ridgeway refutes the argument that customers don't care and shows the brand's Black Friday performance as proof. So many of its customers turned out in support that Patagonia ended up with record sales of $10 million, far exceeding the projected $2 million for the day.

Patagonia preaches that if it can show to the community that an apparel company can be successful while slowing consumption, more businesses will follow suit. It suggests that its growth comes thanks to tapping into new pockets of like-minded consumers, not through existing consumers buying more, because they don't need to.

The brand is not about flashy fashion but functional industrial design, which Chouinard quotes as his "secret of success."[43] But how revolutionary would it be if an established fast-fashion retailer went down the same road, providing clothing that is both aesthetically appealing and long-lasting? The price tag would likely go up, reflecting the garment's real value and securing the retailer's financial position, but as a consequence customers would buy less and throw away less. "The problem with public companies is they are forced to grow 15 percent, forced to show profits every quarter. There is no public company that would voluntarily restrict their growth for the sake of saving the planet,"[44] deplores Chouinard. He made sure his would never become part of the pack. Patagonia's new status as a so-called "benefit corporation," or B Corp, provides a legal framework for its executives to pursue environmental and social benefits without feeling the pressure from investors, whereas public corporations are legally required to put the financial interests of their shareholders first. But Chouinard says, the planet is his main shareholder. Without it, there is no business.

Today, Patagonia's products are Fairtrade-certified, paying fair wages and premiums to the people who make them. Albeit small in volume, the brand's denim collection is likely the greenest on the market. Many of its styles are 100 percent organic cotton, boasting an outdoor comfort fit decoupled from any seasonal fashion trends. They refrain from extra washes, which eliminates chemicals from the equation and are dyed with Advanced Denim technology developed by Archroma, an essentially non-indigo, clean sulfur dye that saves up to 92 percent water, 30 percent energy and 87 percent cotton waste in the process.

Setting up a chemically conscious production did not come without risk. When Patagonia pioneered the organic cotton in 1994, Chouinard said his co-workers were terrified.

We couldn't just call a fabric supplier and say "hey, switch that order over to organic," because there wasn't any available, so in the beginning it did cost us double, but it doesn't now. Now, it's much more competitive in price and it puts us way ahead of the competition. Marketing-wise it was a smart move, although we did risk 25 percent of our sales by switching over and being the first one.[45]

In the end, it started a movement.

Additionally, in 2013, Patagonia set up a venture capital fund to invest in start-ups that provide environmental solutions. Since its inception, Tin Shed Venture has invested $40 million in 12 companies with double-digit financial returns. "The end-game is to fund the next-generation of responsible business leaders,"[46] says Phil Graves, head of Patagonia's corporate development.

Notes

1 Fromm, Erich. *To Have or to Be?* New York: Continuum, 1976, p. 23.
2 Sterling, Peter. *Why We Consume: Neural Design and Sustainability.* Great Transition Initiative. February, 2016. http://www.greattransition.org/publication/why-we-consume
3 Ibid., p. 1.
4 Ibid., pp. 139–140.
5 Ibid., pp. 141–142.
6 Jackson, p. 121.
7 Ibid., p. 161, p. 210.
8 Ragnarsdóttir, Kristín & Sverdrup, Harald. Limits to Growth Revisited. *The Geological Society.* https://www.geolsoc.org.uk/Geoscientist/Archive/October-2015/Limits-to-growth-revisited
9 Jackson, p. 140.
10 Ibid., p. 129.
11 Jackson, Tim. *An Economic Reality Check.* TED Talk, July 2010. https://www.ted.com/talks/tim_jackson_s_economic_reality_check
12 Sterling.
13 Jackson, p. 159.
14 Buis, Alan & Wilson, Janet. Study: Third of Big Groundwater Basins in Distress. *NASA*, June 16, 2015. https://www.nasa.gov/jpl/grace/study-third-of-big-groundwater-basins-in-distress
15 The World Economic Forum. *The Water Resources Group : Background, impact, and the way forward.* The World Economic Forum Annual Meeting 2012. Davos-Klosters: January 26, 2012, p. 16.
16 Water's Value. *The Value of Water.* http://thevalueofwater.org/the-facts/waters-value
17 Kerr & Landry.
18 McLeman, Robert. Climate Change, Migration and Critical International Security Considerations. *IOM Migration Research Series*, No. 42 (2011). http://publications.iom.int/system/files/pdf/mrs42.pdf
19 Weiss, Kenneth. Bangladesh: Before the Flood. *Pulitzer Center*, July 3, 2014. http://pulitzercenter.org/reporting/bangladesh-flood
20 Van Rhoon, p. 45.
21 Ibid., p. 47.
22 About. *Everlane.com.* https://www.everlane.com/about
23 Braungart & McDonough, p. 38.
24 *Cradle to Cradle – Nie mehr Müll. Leben ohne Abfall.* Die Story, WDR. 2010.
25 Kerr & Landry.
26 Ibid.

27 *2016 Global Innovation 1000: Software-as-a-catalyst.* strategy&, October 2016. https://
    www.strategyand.pwc.com/media/file/2016-Global-Innovation-1000-Fact-Pack.pdf

28 Fellow, Avery. Environmental Cost of Business Estimated at $4.7T Annually. *Bloomberg*,
    April 17, 2013. https://www.bloomberg.com/news/2013-04-17/environmental-cost-
    of-business-estimated-at-4-7t-annually.html

29 Kering. *Environmental Profit & Loss: Methodology.* 2013 Group Results.

30 Bonini & Swartz.

31 Kering. *Environmental Profit & Loss (EP&L).* 2015 Group Results.

32 Ibid.

33 Deutsche Bank Group. *Sustainable Investing: Establishing Long-Term Value and Performance.*
    June 2012.

34 Bonini & Swartz.

35 Braungart & McDonough, p. 146.

36 Braungart & McDonough, pp. 36–37.

37 Cobbing & Vicaire.

38 Bonini & Swartz.

39 A version of the story was heard at the Transformers conference at Kingpins Amsterdam,
    April 2015.

40 Interview with Yvon Chouinard in: *Gamechangers: Patagonia CEO Case Study.* Magazine-
    b.com. JOH & Company, 2015. http://magazine-b.com/en/patagonia/

41 Interview with Rick Ridgeway, in: *The Next Black: A Film About the Future of Clothing.*
    AEG, 2014. https://www.youtube.com/watch?v=XCsGLWrfE4Y&feature=youtu.be

42 Interview with Yvon Chouinard, in: *Patagonia: The Sustainability Champions.* https://
    www.youtube.com/watch?v=bB8ZWOKoygY

43 Ibid.

44 Interview with Yves Chouinard, Commonwealth Club. *Climate One*, October 27, 2016.

45 Interview with Yves Chouinard in: CNNMoney, CNN, April 14, 2010.

46 Interview with Phil Graves in: Change the World. CNBC, November 29, 2016.

7

ATTENTION CONSUMERS

Don't panic, it's organic

The first thing people ask is "How can I know which jeans are green?" The answer is: Not even the brands know for sure. The supply chains are too complex, the shop assistants not knowledgeable enough and the definition of sustainability varies greatly. In a survey conducted for this chapter, a 4-point questionnaire was sent out to a total of 103 global brands, ranging from denim specialists to high street labels and luxury designer companies that employ denim regularly in their collections. The brands were asked to describe how they were pushing the green agenda in the denim category, based on the following topics:

1. What type of sustainable *fibers* do you use? (organic, BCI, recycled cotton; recycled polyester/nylon, Tencel®, hemp, nettle, etc.?) What percentage of your denim collection would you say is made with sustainable fiber?
2. What do you *dye* your denim with? (natural vs. synthetic indigo; pre-reduced liquid or powder indigo; if you use alternative dyes, please specify which ones) What percentage is dyed sustainably?
3. How do you *launder* your denim? (stone/no-stone, laser, ozone, PP, bleach, etc.) What percentage is laundered in a sustainable way?
4. How do you deal with your *pre- and post-consumer* denim *waste*?

Out of 103 brands, 19 completed the questionnaire, which accounts for 18 percent of the brands queried. All brands that replied had made efforts to be more sustainable, though the scope of sustainability varied greatly.

In the fiber section, seven companies stated the totality of their collections (100 percent) was made of sustainable fibers, listing all fibers they had used, including organic cotton, BCI cotton, recycled cotton, recycled polyester, hemp and Tencel®, with recycled materials growing in importance.

The answers were vaguer in the dyeing department, though six brands specified they used pre-reduced liquid indigo at least some of the time and two brands mentioned indigo-free blue dyes based on water and chemistry-saving sulfur technology.

The companies put more focus on the chemical and water input in the laundry phase of manufacturing. Given the number of treatments available for denim, it is no surprise that most brands queried opted for more than one laundry option. The most popular were laser and ozone, mentioned a total of ten times each. Five brands said they used PP spray, followed by stonewash and bleach with four mentions each. Only two employed alternatives to stonewashing, and one brand admitted to still employing sandblasting, though it specified that it was only applied in a controlled environment – that is, a separate, well-ventilated room. In total, five out of 19 brands used only laundry techniques that were considered 100 percent sustainable.

All brands recognized waste as a challenge that requires special attention. Twelve of them said they were partnering with their suppliers or an outside organization to close the loop by working used garments into new products or developing new materials. Eight said they had in-store take-back programs in place, though one had to abandon the project due to a low volume of customer participation.

Though the survey is by no means an exact reflection of the industry's sustainability factor and more in-depth investigations into the realities of denim manufacturing are needed, it does give a snapshot of the current status quo. The findings are line with the market share data provided by sustainable initiatives, which estimate the market penetration of sustainable cotton at 13 percent and that of laser at 25 percent.

The diversity of green practices in denim manufacturing also shows the challenges brands and retailers face in communicating these to the end-consumer.

Standards

In the ideal case scenario, there would be "a tag" – physical or virtual – attached to each garment, jeans or otherwise, informing potential customers of the exact composition and provenance of an article, similar to what we find on food packages. With clothing, however, the level of information would need to lead a step further, grading the garment according to its environmental and social impact: fiber, dye, finishing and labor conditions are not equal. So far, the sheer complexity of sustainability has prevented such a system from taking roots. Where does sustainability begin? What are its minimum requirements? And when is it just green-washing? These are legitimate questions asked by retailers and regulators alike.

This complexity is the main reason behind the conundrum of eco labels and indices that have emerged over the past few years and decades. Comparing these standards poses the same problems as comparing an organic cotton grower in India to a BCI farmer in China, for instance. The methodology is never the same. To wit: The very popular Standard 100 by OEKO-TEX tests for more than 300 chemical substances, but only on the final textile product, while GOTS (Global Organic Textile Standard), another standard respected throughout the industry, gives its seal of approval when at least 70 percent of a textile product contains organic fibers, but does not rate the rest of the fiber mix in the composition.

Labels do have advantages – they can raise awareness among consumers and educate; they push for improvements and force brands to be more transparent – but they also compete against each other.

The next generation of standards will have to take a more holistic approach and consider the system as a whole.

"All these standards, labels, and systems came about because the law was not enough. There was a demand. Now, we have a lot of different kinds of standards, which makes it difficult for the industry and also for the consumer, and it costs a lot of money," says Christian Dreszig, marketing manager at Bluesign. Bluesign aims to eliminate hazardous substances that pose problems to people and the environment right from the beginning of a fabric's journey, omitting only the farm level. Established in 2000, the organization doesn't see itself as a standard but a "system partner." The idea is to set a movement in motion and create an environment of safeguards and sustainable practices that allows members to manage the risk themselves. Dreszig explains:

> We educate people and give them tools so they can produce more sustainably. First chemical companies, converters and mills have to prove that they are on a base level. We make a company assessment, then define a road map, they need to be in compliance and then we can certify. For a denim mill or denim manufacturer the base criteria include end-of-pipe solutions such as wastewater treatments, advice on proper storage and handling of chemicals.

The service also includes the famous Bluefinder, a positive list of some 8,500 chemicals that can be safely used, 400 of which are set aside for denim laundry alone; according to Dreszig, these allow manufacturers "to dye all colors, all fibers, get all effects, also for fashionable and high-performance items." In this industry, he says, there are quite a lot of chemical substances, maybe more than in other industries. Of those we have on our Bluesign substance list about 900 to 1000 are considered hazardous, probably 600 are banned form use or have requirements for limits of use. For denim, we would probably find 400 to 500 substances here.

Bluesign has seen success with outdoor brands that tend to rely more heavily on technical material, but the organization is eager to move into fashion and denim as well. So far, only two mills (Prosperity and Calik) and one launder (Saitex) are certified, but it expects denim brands to carry the logo as well, starting with G-Star, which is slated to become the first Bluesign denim brand.

Bluesign itself is a member of the Sustainable Apparel Coalition (SAC), born in 2009 out of an unlikely alliance between Walmart and Patagonia; the goal is to "develop a universal approach to measuring sustainability performance"[1] across the apparel, footwear and textile sector. The SAC is currently working on the Higg

Index, "a standardized supply chain measurement tool for all industry participants,"[2] including the end-consumer. The tool consists of three different types of assessment, once each for brands and retailers, products and facilities. The product tool, which will give consumers an idea of what they are buying, is slated to launch as early as 2019, according to SAC's chief executive officer, Jason Kibbey.

Just don't expect it to be a regular tag. "We are encountering pretty significant barriers to implementing worldwide tagging," says Kibbey. "The paper alone in 100 billion Higg scores would be quite something," he notes, adding that the first place for the information to show up will be on a brand's on product pages, helped by some "pretty cool" advances in visual identification of product. "You can essentially point your cell phone at a product, even on a person and using AI and machine learning to figure out what type of shirt that is, while it pulls up a product page of the shirt," he said, quoting Malong Technologies as an example. The Chinese start-up says its computer can recognize clothes much like a fashion designer.[3] "That's more likely where we will be going rather than in the direction of deep, deep labeling, which is probably lower in value than making it accessible online."

Kibbey admits that "scoring is notoriously challenging," since a lot of the parameters are values-based rather than quantitative. "How do you combine, for example, social labor and environmental – do you weigh them equally and then within that how do you compare something like fair wages vs. freedom of association?" one of the reasons polyester and other synthetic manmade fibers score exceptionally well on the Higg Materials Sustainability Index (MSI) is that the issue of microplastics is tough to measure and compare. "Microplastics is an important issue but relatively new, there is no way right now to quantify it, and nobody even knows how to measure it. This is an R&D topic for the whole industry."

For the moment, the MSI is conceived in a way that allows designers to make quick and easy choices during product development. The consumer score will be more focused on footprinting outputs and assessing how many pounds of carbon or gallons of water went into one garment rather than another.

Kibbey notes that standards are a necessity, but rationalization would be a plus.

> We are not in the business of suggesting which standards should stay or go. We work with many of them like ZDHC, Bluesign, GOTS or Cradle-to-Cradle. It's a delicate balance where you want to have innovation and flexibility for the industry, but generally there is much more need for standardization, because it is too confusing.

Often the bigger challenge, he notes, is individual brand programs that make very specific requests from manufacturers, which struggle to keep up with the costs of compliance and number of certifications.

Eventually, all will be taken care of by smart computers, algorithms and artificial intelligence. But for now, the only relevant question for consumers is: "Which jeans are green?" Regardless of what information brands make available and what standards they sign up for, there is a set of simple guidelines, based on common sense, that anyone can follow when purchasing a pair of jeans. These rules can also be easily translated into categories other than denim.

Rule No. 1: Don't waste. Take it from Carrie Bradshaw, one of the most discernable fashion icons in TV history, who found herself without a home following a life-long shoe addiction. When she couldn't make a down payment to buy her beloved apartment after it went from controlled rent to condo, Bradshaw famously deadpanned: "I've spent $40,000 on shoes and I have no place to live? I will literally be the old woman who lived in her shoes!"[4] In other words, don't waste your money on what in the end is just stuff. Ask yourself if you really need a new pair of jeans or if you could spice up what is already in your closet. There is no item of clothing more versatile than denim. There are customization techniques aplenty, and these can contribute to a healthy creative economy. Many brands have in-store customization stations and trained staff to help pick a new look. What's more, buying less will also help save resources and cut down on waste. If you can't live without stretch, go for a high-end stretch that will bag out less quickly, serve you longer and make you wash it less – in the case of denim, this should never be at higher temperatures than 30 degrees Celsius. Note, however, that stretch is tricky. While jeans are truly democratic, skinnys are not. They are of questionable aesthetic value to most people. If you thought non-stretch denim couldn't be sexy, think again. Bradshaw pulled off straight-legged, wide-cuffed denim by pairing them with heels, and so can you.

Rule No. 2: Ask for transparency. Trusting that a brand is doing the right thing is not enough. You gotta ask for proof. Some brands post elaborate sustainability reports on their websites; others keep mum about their efforts in fear of making less sustainable products in their collections look bad. Either way, it's up to the consumer to apply pressure. Pressure forces brands to become more active in the field – a technique that has proven efficient in the past. "You have to call brands out like Greenpeace did [with the Dirty Laundry report]. You call them out, they go green," says industry veteran and denim Kingpin Andrew Olah. Olah contends that brands know exactly how to change:

> The heads of these corporations have all the information that you have and they listen to it and they say to their colleagues: "We are not doing it." This is a value-less society. This has nothing to do with marketing, but with doing the right thing. There is no marketing for good manners, for not dropping your food when you eat, or for being polite. These are just fundamental human values. That's why you have to call them out. Because they don't want to be on CNN or BBC.

Rule No. 3: Be specific. You have a right to know what you are paying for. You don't want to end up with a "product-plus," to use Braungart and McDonough's term for an item that will either harm you or has already harmed someone in the process of manufacturing. Just because a pair of jeans is made of organically grown cotton doesn't mean it's green if, for instance, it was dyed or treated with harmful chemicals later. Brands are only slowly beginning to invest in staff that know a product's makeup. Asking for details may speed up the process. Start inquiring about the fiber. Is it sustainably sourced cotton, recycled polyester or a bio-based material? Then it's a go. Dyes and finishing techniques have a big impact on a pair of jeans' ecological footprint, with both water and chemicals playing a major role. Ask what the brand does to reduce the number of resources used in the process. With most indigo in the market synthetic, the least a brand can do is opt for pre-reduced liquid indigo. Cleaner industrial washing through new technologies such as laser and ozone is getting more widespread, but it's still well below 50 percent, so it's imperative to ask. A brand's investments in this department are also a strong indicator that they will respect workers' health in addition to reducing their impact on the environment. In case of doubt, go for an "unwashed"/raw pair of jeans and break it in yourself. It will last longer and feel more like a second skin.

Rule No. 4: Express your love. Alberto Guzzetti, sales manager at Tejidos Royo textile mill, put it best: "Which is the intensity of love that you are looking for? Because we can make it ethical, but how ethical do *you* want to be?" Sustainability is a question of principle. Even without many details provided by the brands, you can still make a series of distinctly honest decisions. Just how deep are you willing to go to express your values, is the question. If you care about the livelihoods of workers involved in making your jeans, then Fairtrade is your best bet. Are you worried about toxic chemicals? Go for organic, which avoids hazardous substances at crop level. If you are looking to reduce your carbon footprint, stay clear of man-made synthetic fibers such as polyester and elastane and buy brands that manufacture close to home. And if the health of aquatic life is your biggest concern, put polyester – virgin or recycled – on your black list. That's easier to do in denim than in sportswear, for instance, where most materials are synthetic. Water is a trickier question to tackle because it's the one resource that binds all of the above together. Here, it's best to go for a brand that has water-saving strategies built into its statutes. Strictly speaking, the cleanest pair of jeans that still looks like denim would be one that is made of 100 percent rain-fed, certified organic fiber that is also Fairtrade, dyed with the next generation of sulfur dyes and left raw (unwashed) for the user to break in. It will last longer than a pair that has been manually distressed and abused by chemical compounds and will have treated everyone as fairly as possible in the process, but it will require your patience if you are indeed chasing that vintage look.

Rule No. 5: Vote your conscience. A modern mill today has many options to produce denim in a way that would be considered green, but it won't manufacture anything that it cannot sell. Customers and the many brands and retailers who make denim around the world make their choices dependent on price. They will ask for a dozen samples and will pick the one that provides the best compromise between look and prospective margin, which can be in the high double-digit range depending on the market segment a brand operates in. Luxury brands tend to employ higher mark-ups and play up their image; value retailers tend to squeeze prices below socially sustainable levels. Either way, the price tag does not reflect the level of sustainability or quality. A pair of jeans can cost anywhere between £7 and £1,000. And within that range a £40 pair of jeans can be clean, while a £250-pair isn't. As Olah, who boasts five decades of experience in the textile business, notes:

There was a time when premium just meant expensive — and tough to sell. But over the years, it has become difficult to understand. It's not enough to be beautiful. Premium has to have something exceptional to offer from the social, ethical and environmental points of view. How dare they sell something at 250 pounds [$377.50] at Selfridges if it was not washed in a sustainable way?

Knowing what you are paying for is tough to find out, which brings us back to transparency. Your goal is to pressure brands and retailers to disclose the details of their pricing, as practiced by Honest By, for instance. On the other hand, Olah warns, "when you get a garment that costs 7 dollars, you know for a fact something evil is going on."

As an end-customer, you need to ask yourself just how much being clean is worth to you. A pair of jeans made of organic cotton will never cost as few as 7 dollars. "There are huge profit margins built into the model of fast fashion," says LaRhea Pepper, an organic cotton farmer from Texas and managing director of Textile Exchange.

> We did a whole cost analysis many years ago and laid it all out on the table saying why this was a fair price for us. They said they couldn't do it, unless they got a 6-percent margin on it. And yet you are asking me to live on a 2-percent margin? The price issue is the biggest barrier to the growth of sustainable cotton right now, and I don't care which cotton it is, whether organic, or BCI, Cotton Made in Africa or Fairtrade. In the future, clothing should cost more.

It's not like it's not doable.

> If you look at how much I paid for diesel or bread in the 50s – the amount of disposable income today and where that goes now in developed countries, we are spending so much less on those basics because prices are squeezed so far down. It's miniscule compared to what we used to spend. So the customers who are going to pay 7 dollars for a jeans are voting their conscience. Low price is where Bangladesh happens.

Bloomberg calculated it takes only 90 cents on a £14 pair of jeans to pay for factory safety and employee wages. Anything below that would compromise the standards.[5] Yet Pepper says:

> I heard conversations where it was said "if you want my business, I will only pay you 2 dollars 80 cents for that t-shirt, live with it or I will find somebody else who will." So there is incredible pressure, some of these manufacturers are only breaking even just to keep their factory people working, they are not reinvesting into infrastructure, better water treatments, new stairways and bathrooms for their workers, therefore there is crumbling buildings. You think those factory owners are bad guys. They are certainly trying to have a profit, but when there is so much pressure to deliver that 7-pound jean,

the only place that is negotiable is in the supply network of what I'm gonna pay to deliver your jeans, that's why manufacturing went from London to Bangladesh – and there is a price to be paid, and the people are paying it and the environment is paying it. It's not easy talking to these brands, but the change has to happen and the change starts with you. We need consumers that are aware.

Rule no. 6: Don't follow trends or seasons. Trends are tricky. For the most part, they are short-lived. In high-end fashion, which presents its offering on the catwalk and serves as an example for what high-street brands manufacture in bigger, less luxurious bulk for the masses, they often change from season to season. Skilled professionals such as department store buyers observe them closely, making predictions about what to purchase for the end-consumer. It's romantic florals one winter, crushed velvet another; carrot pants one summer, bell-bottoms the next. If one was to follow all trends meticulously, one would quickly ruin oneself. Think Carrie Bradshaw. Jeans are slightly less prone to the frantic changes of fashion, though in the last few years the category has made a stunning comeback. It's hard to resist the temptation. Until a few years ago, the choice was between straight-legged or tapered. Today, there is a difference between slim and skinny, high and ultra-high waist, 14" and 14½" leg openings. And that's just the basic cut options. Then there are color, fabric weight, wash, level of distress, which can get pretty artsy – cue paint splatters, tussles, patches, prints and embroideries on top of various stitching and weaving techniques, which produce contrasting hand-feels and surface structures. It's the versatility that makes denim great. But other than real fashionistas, most people just want a pair that fits. With such an array of ever-changing trends inspiring consumers to buy more, no wonder customers feel overwhelmed when shopping for denim and sometimes describe the experience as traumatic. There is too much of it. You can slow down the cycle by investing in a good pair of jeans. Trends tend to be cyclical. Ironically, one of the most persistent trends lately has been patchworked jeans based on a combo of contrasting scraps of fabric, something our grandmothers excelled in. Vetements, one the buzziest designer brands around, liked the concept so much it scrambled two pairs of vintage Levi's jeans together and is now charging €1,050 for a pair. Artisanal indigo printing techniques like shibori, batik or ikat, meanwhile, have been around for centuries and still haven't fallen out of style. Take it from *Vogue*, which teased: "The best-fitting pair of jeans you'll ever own may already be in your closet."[6]

The final rule should be: Whatever you do, don't just throw your jeans in the trash.

Fortunately, sustainability bears great potential for fashion from a stylistic point of view.

There are a bunch of brands that are taking denim to the next level, proving that ethics are indeed compatible with aesthetics. They have understood that products that are not designed for human and ecological health are not only unintelligent but inelegant. They are, by definition, "good" designers:

- Faustine Steinmetz
- G-Star
- JACK & JONES
- Reformation/Redone/Double Eleven
- Story mfg

Story mfg – Slow is beautiful

If you ask Bobbin Threadbare, one half of Story mfg – a hip, East London label with a knack for slouchy silhouettes and feel-good textures – about his design approach, he will say: "We are doing things the old way." Threadbare, who founded the company in 2013 with former WGSN trend forecaster Katy Katazome, is convinced slow fashion is the greenest fashion in today's hyperventilating apparel industry. The array of indigo and madder fabrics on display at the duo's Hackney studio indeed has a distinctly unique vibe. It looks, feels and even smells different. That's because the clothing is based on a detox formula boasting plants, lime, bacteria and the skilled manual labor of its rural artisans as the main ingredients.

The recipe goes as follows: Take a retired rubber or mustard seed farmer in Thailand. It's likely going to be an old lady for whom weaving those handsome and durable fabrics we consider luxury has been a pastime activity for generations. She will grow both the cotton and the indigo plant in her own backyard, pick the bolls, spin the yarn, ferment the indigo and dye and weave the fabric in her own four walls. Natural fermentation and hand weaving, of course, are time-consuming activities and the antipode to fast-fashion. Instead of trapping their workers in a hamster wheel of never-ending hours and poor working conditions, the brand simply looks for more people when needed. "We don't scale up, we scale out. We don't force people to work faster or introduce chemicals to make dyes work quicker – we get more ladies to do the same, spreading out our reach," says Threadbare, whose business has seen healthy growth, with 80 percent of its wholesale bound for Japan.

The designer knows there will be a limit to production, but he doesn't mind. He has created a micro-economy in a region with skilled labor and the right amount of resources. He is convinced: "People make stuff in the wrong places." In India, where the bulk of his production comes from,

> indigo grows like weed. Farmers use it as a crop rotation for a healthy soil. When they extract the indigo from the plant via fermentation, the plant matter that's left becomes manure, and because India is so hot, it dyes faster. We want to work more in collaboration with nature rather than against it. Nature doesn't recycle. A plant is planted, takes energy from the sun, dies and becomes nutrient-rich matter for the soil with all energy coming from the sun. It's not even a circle – it puts more into the soil than it took, the circle is positive. Recycling is not good enough, because there is always something left over, and what is left over is bad.

In their East End studio, the designer duo regularly organizes dyeing workshops, where people can witness how the magic of natural dyeing happens, bring in their old clothes and refresh them. "Being sustainable is not that hard and actually cool," says Threadbare.

> What sustainability needs is punk, be reactionary against the generation above us who f**k things up. Say "We are not like you, we are not going to buy this." You have to tap into that rebellion, that anti-establishment attitude. Don't talk about how negative the industry is because nobody wants to hear that.

He says sustainability for him pays off. Not doing washes saves costs, cutting well into the fabric saves scraps and not flying the fabric and garments around the globe saves on taxes:

> and I mean f******g loads. We saved thousands of pounds on duties in the course of a few months. Taxes are prohibitive. By making stuff vertical and not leaving a country, you end up not having to pay that stuff. We used to make fabric in Thailand, India and Turkey, fly it to Britain and make it here in a British factory. Now we make the garment within the vicinity where the fabric was made, everything is made within a small space, the shops pick up from there, there is no excess flying, they order it, we make it, they pick it up in India.

A pair of Story mfg jeans goes for 270 pounds, which is on par with less sustainable denim specialists and below most designer denim (Figure 7.1).

FIGURE 7.1   A look by Story mfg

Source: Story mfg

Reformation, Re/Done, Double Eleven – Talking trash

One person's trash is another person's treasure, they say. And that couldn't be more true for Re/done, which has built a new business model based on scooping up old Levi's jeans, taking them apart and stitching them back together for a new, more modern fit (Figure 7.2). "Thus far, we've repurposed over 75,000 vintage jeans that would have otherwise ended up in a landfill," says the brand. Nothing goes to waste in the process. "When we make shorts, we save the cut-off denim legs and incorporate them into our future designs," they say. The brand's portfolio is a treasure trove of unique cuts and styles, and, above all, colors – which are simply pigmented by their natural wear. It's as if someone broke them in for you and took them to the tailor's to have them refitted for a cooler, more contemporary look.

Free repairs are offered for life. Founders Sean Barron and Jamie Mazur say they want to encourage "consumers to get the most mileage possible out of the jeans instead of throwing them away."

Their concept means no virgin fiber – only a pair of old jeans or a scrap of recycled fabric can become a new style. "Our RE/DONE | Levi's are simply washed twice, once before we take them apart and once after they are reconstructed, as one would at home," which the company says takes about 50 gallons of water compared to the average 2500 gallons that are required to make a conventional pair.

FIGURE 7.2 A look by Re/Done

Source: Re/Done

There is a social component here, as well. The duo notes:

> We focus on local production to improve the sustainability of our products. Everything we make is manufactured within a 5-mile radius of our downtown L.A. headquarters. The employees who work in our factories are artisans. They are paid a living wage and enjoy good working conditions.

If you are worried that they may soon run out of stock, don't. "Levi's has been making the 501 for 40 years at around 10 million pairs a year, so there are 400 million pairs in circulation – give or take a few,"[7] Barron explained.

Every year, millions of hangers are discarded and end up as junk in landfill. According to Reformation, the typical lifespan of a plastic or metal hanger is about three months, which is why the brand uses only recycled paper hangers and wraps its goods in reusable totes instead of disposable plastic bags. Having calculated that 98 percent of clothing bought in the U.S. has been imported from abroad and that a single cotton T-shirt transported from Xinjiang, China to Los Angeles results in over 9,000 "clothing miles," which equals 2 pounds of CO_2, the L.A. brand is now sourcing 80 percent of its products locally and manufacturing all of its clothing in Los Angeles. Put differently, pick up a pair of high-rise cigarette Ref jeans and you will save 31 pounds of carbon dioxide, 1,460 gallons of water and 1.8 pounds of waste.

The math is not a trick, but stems from Reformation's strategy of using deadstock. Fifty percent of its collection is made from bales of denim cloth no one seems to have any use for. Further, the brand buys offsets to bring its water footprint to zero, and for every jean bought, it cleans 1,000 gallons of water via the BEF Water Restoration Program and the National Forest Foundation. So, here's a thought: If you could save up to 1,468 gallons of water with your purchase of a pair of green blue jeans and clean a thousand gallons more in the process, would you? It's 98 bucks.

Meanwhile, at Double Eleven, a newly launched men's wear brand by Rag & Bone cofounder Nathan Bogle, treasure hunting is on the company's daily agenda and is its only source of fabric. The brand rummages through libraries of denim, canvas and chambray for premium surplus stock. As they note:

> In Los Angeles, and all around the world for that matter, there are warehouses full of unused premium and vintage fabrics. They originate from Japan, Italy and the US, but have been discarded here by big brands or mills that clear their inventories from time to time.[8]

Its denim comes from such places as Candiani in Italy, Kaihara Corp. in Japan and Orta in Turkey. Bogle says the concept came to him as a moment of epiphany when he was sitting in a factory that made his leathers:

I was watching the guy cut the hide and basically utilize only 70 percent of it. And I just went through the calculation of the cow, feeding it and the food and water and it hit me like a ton of bricks and I thought, I've got to solve this.[9]

By not making any new fabric from scratch, the brand only takes a fraction of resources out of the earth while keeping production local. Ninety-five percent of its ingredients are sourced within a 15-mile radius and all garments are 100 percent made in L.A., eliminating long and carbon-intensive shipping of goods between mills, sample rooms and factories. To put it into numbers: Double Eleven estimates that a pair of jeans swallows about 2,500 gallons of water in its lifetime, including the growing of cotton, dyeing and industrial and home laundry. This is equivalent to the amount of drinking water a man consumes in six years, provided he follows the recommended amount of between two and three liters a day, which hardly anyone does. Seventy-four percent of that water goes into the production of fiber, a stage Double Eleven is skipping altogether. That leaves Double Eleven with 75 gallons of water per jean, or a total of 96 percent savings.

JACK & JONES – Denim 2.0

Mikkel Hochrein Albrektsen is a member of the very MI6-sounding "jeans intelligence team" at Danish men's wear label JACK & JONES, an uncommon department to have, especially for a high street brand and a member of a large retail group such as Bestseller.

The Dane says his team was getting increasingly frustrated by competing brands labeling a pair of jeans as sustainable just because it was made with organic cotton or polyester from recycled PET bottles, instead of focusing on a more holistic approach. He says,

> It seems like every brand is trying to put the flag on something, and it's easy to claim a garment is sustainable. Because when the average guy in the street hears organic cotton, he thinks "Great!" But what about the dyeing, what about the way the jeans were made? And so our aim has been to combine all threads into one package and inform the consumer on the whole cycle.

Six years ago, the brand started measuring its environmental impact via Jeanologia's Environmental Impact Tool (EIM), which divides products into three categories: high, medium and low impact. Albrektsen says,

> In the beginning, what we did was we fed the computer the type and number of treatments we employed, so for instance: one hour of stone wash plus

15 minutes of PP spray. The software then calculated the score at the end and every time we had made a pair of jeans that was low-impact, we added a small label to the jeans to mark the achievement. That is what the technology at that time was allowing us to do. Since then a lot has changed.

The possibilities have widened and the aesthetics of green technologies have improved. And so, with the accumulated knowledge, in fall 2018 JACK & JONES is launching a new line called Low Impact Denim 2.0. The formula will be based on 3 Fs – fiber, fabric, finish. On the fiber level, only organic cotton, recycled cotton and recycled polyester are allowed. Recycled leather is used for the jeans' leather patches; the rivets are non-galvanized so that they are more easily recyclable.

To dye the fabric in the least impactful way, JACK & JONES has teamed up with Orta in Turkey, employing its Indigo Flow formula, which combines the mill's Reserve Flow and Clean Flow technologies for cleaner wastewater and less water consumption. For the following collection, the brand will also include some Crystal Clear fabrics by Artistic Milliners (see Chapter 4). Finally, for the finish, the brand still relies on the EIM tool to be low impact, but is now entirely without the use of PP spray. The brand turned to CHT's OrganIQ Bleach, billed as a fully biodegradable bleaching agent. "It works amazingly well, the look and whiteness are just like in any other Jack & Jones jeans," confirms Albrektsen, adding that it took two years of development to create something that was authentic minus the PP.

> Because let's be honest. Not many people buy dry and raw. They want their jeans to be pre-washed. And if your jeans don't correspond to what the customer is looking for, you won't sell them, which in the end is not sustainable, because you need to produce volume within your sustainable initiative to make it work.

All its other chemicals are Greenscreen approved.

JACK & JONES is part of the club of brands that does not pass on the additional cost of sustainability to the consumer.

> The margin is smaller – at manufacturing level it's a difference of a few euros – but we see it as an investment. We need to industrialize the process. Once you start producing in a certain way, you get better at it and become faster and hopefully the price will go down.

Next on the JACK & JONES table: make elastane more sustainable. For the moment, says Albrektsen, the best he can do is to use recycled polyester from plastic waste.

> But I think in the future, we will be able to do a lot more with waste in general, so that every part of a jean either gets recycled or if it cannot be reused,

then it will go back into nature as a nutrient, so that nothing ever becomes waste again. And the same will be true for dyes, which people often forget about when they talk about recycling.

Faustine Steinmetz – The Denim Artist

Faustine Steinmetz' premise is simple: "We want to make those everyday clothes that you can buy anywhere really special again," she says. The London-based designer of French origin puts the same amount of effort one would expect from an haute couture dress into an ordinary pair of jeans. Her technique is impressive, her dedication admirable. She spends days applying complicated embroideries, tapestry, needle and wet felting to her unique denim creations. The designer treats her denim as transparent; she takes it apart thread by thread and puts it back together again, which in some cases takes on a web-like structure. The result is the type of denim you would find hard not mend when damaged or to throw in the garbage when no longer needed (Figure 7.3). The overwhelming majority of Steinmetz's pieces are

FIGURE 7.3   A look by Faustine Steinmetz

Source: Faustine Steinmetz

still handwoven in her atelier and stitched in London. It can take anything between three to seven days to obtain enough material for a pair of trousers. No more than 100 pieces per season are doable in this manner, though Steinmetz says she does have her sights set on making her line more accessible. She laments:

> Starting next season, if we can't make it ourselves, all other fabric is going to be recycled from denim by our Spanish partner Royo, which is a mill that also recycles its own water, so that nothing goes to waste. Waste really stresses me out.

The Royo fabrics will have 30 percent recycled content and 70 percent organic cotton. Steinmetz says she is not at all fixated on cotton. She likes to weave yarn as contrasting as mohair or copper into her outré denim creations. There is also a collaboration with African artisans who traditionally have woven only cotton, but under Steinmetz' guidance have widened their palette. "I particularly like this project because it supports a whole community and the artisanal ways are passed on to the kids." She explains:

> Cotton is complicated. There are many pitfalls. For instance, do you buy rain-fed cotton to save water but forego the issue of chemicals, or do you buy organic from the Middle East, where you know some of the proceeds will go to sustaining ISIS? In the end, every fiber has its own problem, and I hope that by the end of my career I will have figured it out. But for now nothing is perfect and I feel with the combination of recycled denim and organic cotton we have reached a good compromise. Because sustainability is always a compromise. We should all strive for it, but it doesn't really exist.

G-Star – Masters of raw

Much has changed in the ten years since G-Star set up its sustainability department. "During the initial stages, the focus was on social issues," reminisces Frouke Bruinsma, the brand's director of corporate responsibility, "but since then the industry has embraced a more holistic approach, which now includes environmental and technological improvements." Also, as Bruinsma notes, the industry has grown bigger, so it has become easier to place smaller orders closer to home, which is changing denim's carbon footprint.

G-Star, which coined the term "raw" thanks to its penchant for raw, unwashed jeans, stands out among the larger brands for its strategy not of focusing its sustainable efforts on single capsule collections but of integrating them into their bestselling items, such as the Elwood.

In spring 2018, the company is scheduled to launch its most sustainable denim yet (Figure 7.4). It is slated to only contain 100 percent organic cotton. For the indigo dye, the company partnered with Dystar and Artistic Milliners, resulting in a novel formula that is hydrosulfite-free. The dye is a combination of pre-reduced

100% ORGANIC
COTTON FABRIC

RESPONSIBLE
MANUFACTURING

WORLD'S CLEANEST
INDIGO TECHNOLOGY

ECO FINISH
JEAN BUTTONS

SUSTAINABLE WASHING
TECHNIQUES

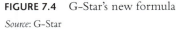

NO RIVETS
& NO ZIPPERS

G-STAR RAW

FIGURE 7.4   G-Star's new formula

Source: G-Star

liquid indigo and a novel organic reducing agent, which substantially reduces chemical inputs and toxic waste (see Chapter 4). Only sustainable finishes such as laser and ozone were employed in the laundry, foregoing entirely the use of PP and stones and in the end using only 10 liters of water per jean. To sew and wash the garments, G-Star worked with Saitex in Vietnam (see Chapter 6), which is known for recycling 98 percent of its water (the remaining 2 percent evaporates naturally). Saitex' jeans are partially air-dried, saving 85 percent of energy. Meanwhile, all components "not conducive to easy recycling," such as rivets and zippers, have been removed and replaced by eco-finished metal buttons from YKK. This means no electroplating baths, no use of toxic acids or other hazardous chemicals that would conventionally lead to a large amount of sludge in the wastewater. YKK says its end-waste is non-hazardous.

The Dutch denim maker has a reputation for trying out new stuff. It famously teamed up with musician and founder of Bionic Yarn Pharrell Williams in 2014 to transform ocean plastic into denim. Since then, Williams, who is also the UN ambassador of climate awareness, has become co-owner of G-Star as well its head of imagination (likely the most colorful title in the industry). Meanwhile, their joint RAW for the Oceans collection has started a movement, inciting a large swath of other brands and retailers to put out collections made of recycled PET bottles. "It was interesting to see how much awareness it raised and to show that you can reach the consumers by telling a story. They just didn't know there was so much plastic in the oceans," says Bruinsma. But the brand since ended the project.

> It was a very successful tool for raising awareness for plastic pollution. However, we discovered that there is a very big chance that when consumers wash their polyester garments, the polyester goes out of the product, and ends up again in very small particles in the oceans. Therefore, we moved on to see if we could work together with other brands to find solutions for those microplastics.

The Dutch denim specialist is a so-called system partner of Bluesign, with the goal to make its chemical record top-shelf in the industry. The company also makes no fuss about transparency. Following the Detox Report by Greenpeace, which exposed global clothing brands and their toxic water pollution practices, G-Star (though not explicitly mentioned in the report) was among the first to join the ZDHC initiative, which aims to phase out the use of hazardous chemicals by 2020 – a goal G-Star hopes to achieve in time under the ZDHC directive and with the help of Bluesign. True, its memberships in a series of NGOs cost a ton, but the company sees it as an investment. "We need to support these organizations so that they can set up the structures and so that we don't have to do it ourselves," says the exec.

As these examples show, there is a number of existing brands with serious green credentials. Instead of sifting through the hundreds of styles that inundate high streets every few weeks, perhaps the more customer-friendly solution would be to narrow down the search to those addresses where clean jeans are the rule, not the exception, and keep those anxieties associated with denim shopping at bay (see Chapter 2). Don't drive yourself nuts. As *Vogue* stated: "No one, actually, has a perfect jeans-body. We are *all* jeans-bodies: We just need to help our jeans along. Which is where tailoring comes in."[10]

Having your jeans made to measure will cost a few hundred dollars more and you will have to wait, but the garment will fit perfectly, and it will be a good investment. In its flagship London store, Levi's offers a bespoke service helmed by Savile Row-trained master tailor Lizzie Radcliffe, who cut her teeth under the aegis of tailoring legend Edward Sexton. French label Notify has made bespoke part of its brand identity. Notify founder Maurice Ohayon, who comes from a family of tailors, says it was the industrialization of fashion that forced him to branch out into ready-to-wear. "When I started as a tailor more than 30 years ago, we went months without eating," he explains.[11] He knew he needed an alternative to survive and stumbled across a guy who was selling denim and agreed to give him credit, so he started making jeans commercially, but, he says, "I have always regretted leaving tailoring this quickly. I was born into a family of tailors. My mother was a tailor, her mother was a tailor, my aunts worked in couture, someone was always sewing something around the house." And so today, "our strategy is no longer to grow through wholesale, but to set up retail posts that include a made-to-measure workshop."

At Notify, customers are not only measured as they would be at a proper tailor's, but are also involved in the design process, choosing anything from the washes to the plethora of patches, studs, stones and prints the label has to offer.

Independent tailors such as Paul Kruize are also entering the scene. Kruize, who has a penchant for selvedge, uses only one machine with a single-needle lockstitch. "There is no over-locking, no chain-stitches. It's all selvedge or hand-felled. All buttonholes are hand-sewn and I do a one-piece fly. It's really about the construction," he explains. It takes the Dutchman 20 hours to put together one pair of jeans compared to 20 minutes in a mass-production facility. "But it will last," he assures.

> I don't do fashion, I do tailoring. And I don't do big labels, what I do is sustainable to the core. When it's made for you, you know it's perfect, and it's sexy in the sense that people can see its different from what they normally see in the street. It has personality.

To increase his jeans' lifespan, he recommends to find a middle ground between not washing them, a technique preferred by denimheads, and washing them when needed. "Going without a wash for six months or putting jeans in a freezer is a myth. If you don't wash jeans, the dirt will break the fiber," he explains. Fortunately, there is a lifetime guarantee on patching and repair with Kruize.

What Kruize does fits retail's latest buzzword: "Competitive differentiation."[12] It is what drives Millennials, and they are currently the most coveted consumer group. According to the World Retail Congress, brand loyalty among Millennials is in rapid decline. "Millennials shift from big brands to local shops, boutiques and smaller brand name stores. At the same time, [they] tend to be loyal to brands that stand for the right values: namely, authenticity, transparency, and social responsibility."[13]

Q&A WITH DIO KURAZAWA, DENIM DIRECTOR AT WGSN

Q: Being an astute observer of the retail landscape, do you think consumers can change it for the better?

A: I really think Millennials *will* make a difference. They grew up with recycling and with H&M collaborating with luxury brands. These kids know J.W. Andersen because of Uniqlo, and they know Balmain because of H&M, which is ironically a good thing. We now find Millennials saving money to buy quality, which means they are buying less, so it's actually working. I doubt that this is what H&M thought would happen, but it did. So it's not all doom and gloom.

On the other hand, in 2017 we are still having discussions about how Patagonia is doing amazing things. And they are, but what about the rest? We are running out of time.

Q: Why is the industry not moving faster towards a sustainable business model?

A: Because no one at retail is *forced* to do anything. They know sustainability is coming, but they don't know what it is exactly. They are probably expecting it to be an easy transition from where they are now to where they need to be. They are used to doing denim in a certain way, and altering that process is hard. Meanwhile, some of those brands are going for the full-package from one-stop shop vendors that offer them ready-made jeans. They don't know what's in there. Brands like Patagonia are cutting-edge, because they want to, because they are passionate about it. It's a question of will.

Q: How could others be convinced?

A: The industry is not going to regulate itself. Regulation has to come from the top. It should mirror the food industry and give incentives. Take Google, for example. Google went to Ireland, because Ireland gave them tax incentives. The same incentives should be given to people producing denim in a responsible way. If you don't make certain requirements binding or give an incentive, nothing will change.

Q: In an ideal world, how would you build a denim brand and make a pair of jeans?

A: I would send everyone a DIY kit, like Burda did in the 70s. I would put the kit in a nice cylindrical canister and mail it out. As a customer, you would be able to take the jeans apart and put them back together again without a sewing machine. Snap buttons would make an easy assembly possible and you could decide how you want to wear your jeans and change them often. I would use a 3x1, but I wouldn't use indigo. I would keep it PFD (prepared for dyeing), so naturally white, and allow everyone to finish it in the bathtub at home using what is available in a household.

Q: I see you are a purist?

A: In my opinion, jeans shouldn't be washed, but I cannot cancel the designing department and the design department cannot cancel the buying department. It's a business and that is a problem. You have to embrace sustainability at the core. Otherwise, we do it on case-by-case basis and then it's like climbing the Mount Everest. Random nuances in color, for instance, should be acceptable, because it's denim. It's like an organic tomato. No tomato will look like another. But that's the beauty of it.

Q: It's not just the brands though. As consumers, aren't we buying too much, influenced by ever-changing trends?

A: I have a ridiculous amount of jeans, but that's for research. In my revolving arsenal of jeans that I actually wear, I have maybe three. The issue is: we are buying way too much sh*t. Slowing trends alone is not going to slow consumption. Sustainability should be a criterion when we report back from catwalks. And it's coming. But if catwalks were the only outlet for fashion, the world would be fine, because we are talking small volumes.

The problem starts when the catwalks get copied. Then it becomes just stuff that I know will never get sold – it goes to landfill. That's why at WGSN we only focus on influential brands. I remember back in the days when I wanted a leather jacket, I had to pay 300 bucks, period. Or I went to the [flea] market and got lucky. Now, I can get a jacket for 50 bucks. Who made the rule that we needed cheap clothes? Nobody was walking around naked, because they couldn't afford clothes. Why can't that just go away? You will still have shops, still sell product – not sell as much, which is not a terrible thing. But it means that companies need to re-adjust themselves so that they can make a profit selling less. Truth is, we don't need all these denim brands and we don't need to make that much new denim any more. There is already enough denim fabric in the world to break down the fiber and put it back together again.

Notes

1 https://apparelcoalition.org/our-origins/
2 https://apparelcoalition.org/the-coalition/
3 This Chinese A.I. Start-Up Focuses on Product Recognition. *CNBC.com*, November 3, 2017.https://www.cnbc.com/video/2017/11/09/this-chinese-a-i-start-up-focuses-on-product-recognition.html
4 Ring a Ding Ding. *Sex and the City*. Season 4, Episode 16. Air Date: January 27, 2002 on HBO.
5 Srivastava, Mehul & Shannon, Sarah. Ninety Cents Buys Factory Safety in Bangladesh on $22 Jeans. *Bloomberg*, June 6, 2013. https://www.bloomberg.com/graphics/infographics/90-cents-buys-factory-safety-in-bangladesh-on-22-jeans.html
6 Codinha, Alessandra. Why the Best-Fitting Pair of Jeans You'll Ever Own May Already Be in Your Closet. *Vogue*, April 20, 2015. https://www.vogue.com/article/guide-to-tailoring-denim
7 Milligan.
8 We Treasure Hunt. *Double Eleven*, n.d. https://doubleeleven.co/pages/we-treasure-hunt
9 Hughes, Aria. *Rag & Bone Co-Founder Starts Double Eleven Line*. WWD, December 12, 2016.
10 Codinha.
11 Szmydke, Paulina. Notify Expands Made-to-Measure Denim. *WWD*, May 25, 2016. http://wwd.com/fashion-news/denim/notify-denim-le-bon-marche-paris-maurice-ohayon-bespoke-made-to-measure-10437191-10437191/
12 LS Retail. The Future of Retail: 8 Key Predictions. *World Retail Congress Blog*, n.d. https://www.worldretailcongress.com/news/future-retail-8-key-predictions
13 Ibid.

8

THE FUTURE OF DENIM

Will it be blue?

Fast forward to 2068.

Fifty years from now, we will be looking at a very different world.

Climate change will be in full swing. Technology will match the sci-fi scenarios of decades past. We will be driving different cars, have different jobs and very likely be wearing different clothing. Geographically speaking, the earth will take on a new shape due to rising sea levels. More than 30 centimeters, or 12 inches, are expected by mid-century. Even if we were to stop pumping CO_2 into the atmosphere *right now*, the trajectory we are on would continue for some time. This means lots of flooding around coastal areas, especially in Bangladesh, the world's second largest exporter of garments; it is likely to be wiped out entirely, setting in motion a mass migration of people as well as a series of conflicts. Say good-bye to Malibu as well, which is expected to fall victim to high waves and erosion.

On the positive side, by mid-century renewable energy will have taken the lead. Solar and hydro are slated to achieve price parity with fossil fuels in the next ten to 15 years, until fusion is able to bring the power of the sun to earth.[1] Electrical vehicles will push fossil fuel cars out of the streets. They will probably be driverless and self-folding to save space. Our food will be grown more efficiently on the roof gardens of our skyscraper apartments, where waste and energy will be managed on site. Forget tedious grocery shopping. The fridge will restock itself, similar to Amazon's dash button, which can reorder your favorite product, though future technology will be more elaborate. Meanwhile, a new toothbrush will pop out of the 3D printer. Computer and TV screens will become a clunky thing of the past, making way for 3D imagery that helps the virtual world take hold. It is estimated that biotechnology will tinker not only with the genes of cotton, making it more versatile, but also with human genes. According to theoretical physicist and futurist Michio Kaku, the dreaded "designer babies" are on their way, scheduled to arrive by mid-century.[2] Kaku also foresees that cancer will be no more than a temporary hiccup.

It is possible that little nano-voyagers will travel through our bodies detecting diseases before symptoms arise, bringing cure where and when it's needed without the misery of life-changing side-effects or dangerous surgical maneuvers.[3] Life, in general, might be more carefree thanks to such technological amenities. There will be more time to indulge in space tourism, which could be flourishing by then thanks to a new generation of booster rockets.[4]

So, the question is: What will denim look like in a brave new world like that? Can we do without cotton and polyester? Can there be denim without indigo? Will there be more or less variety on retail level? Or will custom-made denim play a bigger part, including 3-D body scans and custom finishing? Perhaps in the future we will rent denim, while a list of ingredients just like we see in food today will tell us what's in it? Will we produce closer to home? And what more can bio- and nano-technologies do for apparel?

By mid-century, Kaku predicts the internet will be everywhere – "in wall screens, furniture, on billboards, and even in our glasses and contact lenses"[5] – so why not also in our jeans?

One of the main principles of sustainability is transparency. As discussed in the previous chapter, the brands themselves still have lots of untangling to do. But let's say they do manage to become leaner and cleaner, able to pinpoint exactly where their jeans took their pit-stops, what went into them and how much it cost. How to best convey that message to the consumer? Retailers say paper tags are confusing the customer; they are expensive to print and annoying to read because, let's face it: how much can you get across on a tiny piece of paper that is mostly read in a hurry, perhaps without adequate lighting on the shop floor? In the not-so-distant future we can expect tags to be available virtually, stating not only what ingredients were used to manufacture a pair of jeans, the journey it has travelled and who touched it before you laid your hands on it, but also if the pair will fit you even before you try them on. You might be looking at yourself in 3D in a virtual image appearing before you and possibly even experiencing what the fabric feels like on your skin. Avatar-like shopping apps already exist – cue Gap's collaboration with Avametric, or Carrefour's partnership with Fitle, though these do not allow touch and feel – yet. This is a real possibility in the future through thanks to haptic technology.

Digital information floating around us could truly transform the shopping experience. Just imagine people waving their hand in the air like crazy, scrolling through their virtual screens. The MIT Media Lab is already on it. Its researchers have developed the "SixthSense," a wearable device consisting of a pocket projector, mirror and camera that lets users import digitally stored information into the real world through natural hand gestures, using anything as a potential screen – the surface of a pair of jeans, for instance.

The device could propose ways to style a new pair, matching it with the shoes and tops and coats you already have in your closet. Call it your own personal stylist.

Staying "in touch" with your own wardrobe is no joke; it can help you make it greener, as Mark Brill knows. The British researcher has developed "The Internet of Clothes" (IoC) with his team at Birmingham City University. The IoC refers to a connected wardrobe that promotes sustainable fashion by reducing clothing consumption. Think of it as a smart tag. A radio-frequency identification (RFID) reader is attached to the wall of your closet, registering how often you take a piece of clothing out for a walk. The garments themselves can send reminders via an app, or they can tweet the user asking to be worn, because "clothes have feelings too," as the scientists say. If the clothes' pleas get ignored too often, they will automatically connect with a nearby charity, which will send an envelope to collect them. The Birmingham team notes that

> back in the 1930s, for example, a typical American owned nine outfits. Today, that number is 64. It's not just the US. Globally, we buy four times the number of clothes that we did in the 1990s. Yet it is estimated that we wear just 20 percent of our wardrobe regularly. [This] creates an impact on both the environment and exploitation of garment workers.[6]

In the future, the researchers want wardrobes to connect amongst each other, communicate their experience and create an economy of exchange among users.

Transparency, of course starts at the crop level. With everyone carrying a GPS in their jeans pocket in the shape of a smart phone, there is no reason why tracing a piece of a garment should be a problem. Tracking cotton from the gin through the supply chain is already in place. New York-based Applied DNA Sciences, Inc. has come up with a molecular barcode based on the plant's own DNA to prevent counterfeiting. Let's say you want to make sure you bought organic cotton, and you want to make sure it came from a country without forced labor but with fair wages. You can do it with SigNature T tag. The company already teamed with Woolam Gin in Texas and says the first molecularly verified organic cotton will be available in stores in spring 2018. James Hayward, president and CEO of Applied DNA, says

> in an environment where consumers are demanding more information about the origin and authenticity of their products [...] SigNature T assures that the organic cotton grown and ginned in Texas is not blended with other cottons from different origins or with non-organic cotton, thereby remaining pure throughout the supply chain, all the way to the consumer.[7]

Meanwhile, an MIT-incubated start-up called Sourcemap is working on a 2.0 traceability map, which is built like a social networking website. Sourcemap's CEO Leonardo Bonnani, who developed the concept as a student at MIT, notes that

> [a]fter decades of outsourcing, most enterprise databases don't even have address information for where the factories are in their supply chain. Today, there can be hundreds of thousands of suppliers in a chain [...] they can't account for all the different players in their network.[8]

The idea, he explains, is for companies to

> upload a list of their direct suppliers, invite them to our social network and ask them to map out their supply chains. This gets them visibility into the second tier of their supply chain, the third tier, and so on and so forth until they can map their entire chain to the sources of all their raw materials.

The mapping device could also function as a tool for sustainability, monitoring progress and measuring yields and inputs to compare the data efficiently, which currently constitutes a large obstacle in the complex cotton industry. Part of the service is also a risk exposure index, looking for weak spots in the supply chain in real time. The system can pull news feeds on an environmental disaster or political event that might have an impact on production and further alert executives to correct the course before it's too late.

Remember the tricorder from *Star Trek*? When Dr. McCoy moved his little scanning device up and down a patient's body to determine what its ailments were, he collected data and scanned the body for dangerous organisms. If Kaku is right, by 2068 doctors' appointments will be handled by a "robotic software program," in the comfort of our homes. Forget constantly alternating NHS consultants, hopelessly overworked and unfamiliar with your situation. The software will have your complete medical records and genetic information on file; it will simply ask us to pass a probe over our bodies – much like the tricorder – to detect illnesses, including tumors, before they turn into life-threatening situations. This function could even be performed by a pair of jeans. Already, denim fabrics are able to increase energy levels, improve blood microcirculation and prevent cellulite; they can cool you down or warm you up. For the moment, the denim industry is nervous about losing market share to ath-leisure, which gave way to such categories as knit denim and comfort stretch, the most popular type of jeans on the market. But in the future, performance will be much more sophisticated. Nano-sensors built into denim could turn out to be lifesavers. Let's say your jeans detect a change in your breathing or your brain activity, indicating that you have been involved in an accident or have had a heart attack; they could connect automatically with a first response center, requesting an ambulance.

"The blending of synthetics that bring technical capability – cooling, warming, wicking, protection of all sorts, will create a fortress around you," predicts Steve Zades, global vice president of transformational innovation VF Corp, who runs the group's Cognitive and Design Lab in California. He adds:

> When you are on the subway you won't have to worry about germs, denim will protect you in the urban environment. Historically, it has been about protection in the rural environment, but the future is urban. So I think denim is going to be dynamic – who knows, maybe you will only have one pair and that pair will adapt to the heat and the cold, maybe you will throw it in the dryer and it will change color. More and more you see different

characteristics being applied through the dryer. P&G are working on it, it's still experimental but yeah – you will be able to say: "Oh it's raining today, let me add a layer of rain protection."

What sounds like a gimmick now might come in pretty handy considering the unpredictable weather patterns that await us in the future courtesy of climate change. Surely more versatile and reliable clothing able to change its properties on command would be useful.

Wearable technology, in whatever shape or form, is coming whether we like it or not. From a sustainability point of view that is a tricky concept, unless the wearable tech follows the same circular schemes that we expect from regular fashion. Smart design needs to be easily updatable, unlike a smart phone you dispose of as soon as the latest version has arrived. WEAR Sustain, a project funded by the European Union, is looking at just that: how to make technology wearable and sustainable at the same time.

Perhaps the biggest mystery of future fashion is: What kind of fiber will take the lead in denim in particular? Can biotechnology help us save water and up cotton's reputation through clever – and safe – bio-engineering? Will we produce plant-based polyester with no harmful effects on the environment or on human life? Or will we grow new fiber in the lab, leaving room in agriculture to grow food?

For cotton, at least, the scenarios are as diverse as the industry itself. The sustainable cotton initiative Cotton 2040 from Forum of the Future has mapped out four possible scenarios for the year 2040 (Figure 8.1). The organization assumes that 9 billion people will inhabit planet earth in 2040. The scarcity of key resources such as water and oil will have "massive impacts" across the clothing supply chain, affecting the price of polyester, pesticides and fertilizers as well as transport. The initiative predicts that a rise of global temperature by 2°C by 2034, as assessed by the IPCC (Intergovernmental Panel on Climate Change), will negatively impact agriculture through droughts, decreased oil moisture, flooding and other extreme weather events. On the positive side, with the spread of information and communications technologies consumer calls for more transparency will become more prevalent and easier to implement. Consequently, the Forum for the Future has identified the following four scenarios.[9]

Slow is beautiful

In this scenario, sustainability has become mainstream. After decades of large-scale, cross-nation investments, prices of sustainable goods have fallen below prices of unsustainable ones. A single sustainability standard developed by Europe is launched globally, valuing organic virgin fiber as the most precious type of cotton. Overall, cotton production is down, but the quality is higher. Designers create smart, long-lasting garments suitable for deconstruction and recycling. Customers are willing to pay more for higher quality and consume

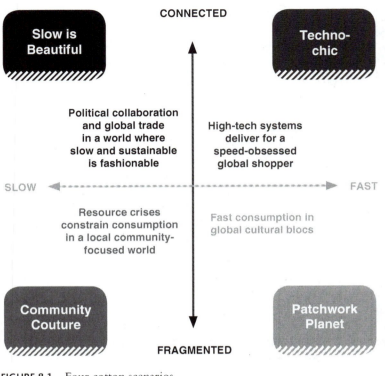

FIGURE 8.1 Four cotton scenarios
Source: Collison et al.

less. Consequently, the prices of garments are up, while retailers are content with higher margins. Interconnectivity and collaborations take center stage as the cotton industry works together with scientists, brands and retailers, which invest heavily in sustainable farming, including advanced crop rotations and condition-specific varieties, in fear of losing customers. Synthetic fibers like polyester have been phased out. International agreements produce fairer working conditions and enforce minimum wages. Cotton, a natural fiber, has finally become the most sustainable. Its main competitors are flex and hemp.

Community couture

The impacts of climate change and the lack of water cause serious disruptions to manufacturing. Communities strive to be more self-sufficient, while governments engage in protectionist measures to secure food and energy supplies. Cotton is still cultivated but on small, multi-purpose farms alternating between cotton and food crops while being run on renewable energies. High input costs for oil, water and labor drive the price of a cotton T-shirt to $100. As a result, "remanufactories" emerge, pushing the recycling of already existing cotton fibers in the market. Technological breakthroughs ensure that no thread of cotton goes to waste. The bulk of the crop is organic due to expensive chemicals. But finding good-quality seeds is tricky. Community-owned farms and factories are heavily guarded. Virgin cotton is still around, but it's become a luxury fiber and an important piece of investment. The second-hand market for cotton clothing is booming; so are leasing and repairing businesses, in which millions of environmental fugitives find work. Most people cannot afford washing machines and use community laundries instead. San Francisco opens the world's largest clothing library, in which the cotton section is the most popular.

Techno-chic

The world has gone high-tech. Clean technologies dominate the industry. R&D spending is massive. Who has invested early is the winner. Technology is believed to have offset the negatives of overconsumption. A new generation of highly sophisticated synthetic fibers with a zero-carbon footprint is taking over fashion. Fashion weeks are virtual and reach every corner of the world at once. Cotton production is going down because of competition from new fibers, but achieves higher margins thanks to high-tech methods, including GM-seeds that make the crop drought- and flood-proof. The price of cotton goes up, as does its image. As a consequence, many small-holder farmers go out of business; larger farms are directly connected to the buyers and excel in transparency. Sweatshops belong to the past, as manufacturing is fully automated now. Governments ensure free trade and the exchange of know-how. Water savings are achieved through high-tech irrigation methods and self-cleaning coatings on clothing. Because cotton is expensive, no scrap ends up in landfill; the industry switches to a made-to-order business model. Customers choose patterns online, which are then 3D-printed or sent to a local manufacturer for production and delivered by drones. Big brands are growing even bigger thanks to the proliferation of high-tech synthetics. It's the non-believers in this brave new world that still wear cotton as a symbol of heritage, opting for fabrics that can clean air, let off nutrients and repair themselves. Every now and then, scandals involving synthetic fiber pollution flare up due to malfunctions in the closed-loop system.

Patchwork planet

The world is an unequal place, split into cultural blocs. Conflicts over natural resources and technology dominate the news. Free trade has been replaced by high tariffs and tight quotas. The WTO is no longer in place. There is no coordinated response to climate change, which causes the cotton industry to collapse in some regions such as South-East Asia, while other geographies adapt. Cotton crops are protected by the military. Seed spies attempt to get hold of the latest innovations in technology. China bets on GM, India on specialized plant breeding. Climate change migration is in full swing, leaving whole regions, including factories, deserted. Consumers demand fast fashion but with a local flavor, regardless of green factors. Technology is mainly being developed to maximize yields. Cheap DIY sets turn consumers into fashion designers who make their own clothing with locally available fibers. Big brands are still around but are broken up into regional entities with regional supply chains and marketing strategies. Global fashion trends have fallen out of favor.

Asked which of the four scenarios is most likely, Charlene Collison, who heads Cotton 2040, said it keeps changing, according to world politics and the brands' own initiatives.

> Had you asked me two years ago, I would say I see fewer signs of the scenario in which global trading blocks get more and more separated. It was unlikely that globalization decreases and that fashion becomes more regional, but especially since Brexit and the election of Donald Trump in the U.S. we are seeing the trade barriers come up again in certain places. At the moment fast fashion just continues to get faster, and though we are seeing some improvement in companies that work with circularity, a lot of it gets eaten up by having even faster cycles and that is a bit of a paradox.

Whatever the future, says Collison, she wants "to see the fashion industry take big steps forward and move from being a really unsustainable, polluting and wasteful industry to one that works within planetary boundaries."

Some of the technology suggested by Cotton 2040 is already in place and is even going further. In the future, expect your blue jeans to be delivered by a drone. Amazon is so confident it can make it happen, it already teases "Prime Air" on its website. The futuristic delivery system can drop off parcels within 30 minutes of the customer placing the order.

Self-cleaning textiles are already a reality. Water-repellent and waterproof clothing mimicking nature's lotus effect have been around for a while. But removing dirt and stains is a different story altogether. Scientists at the Royal Melbourne Institute of Technology,[10] for instance, are convinced all you will need in the future is the sun. They have grown copper- and silver-based nanostructures capable of degrading organic matter when exposed to light. The structures, which are less than a billionth of a meter, are woven directly onto the cotton fabric. As they absorb the light, their electrons get excited; they start producing heat and with the released energy spontaneously break down food stains within minutes. Given that most water consumption throughout the life of a pair of jeans is on the consumer side, sun-cleaned fabrics could result in substantial water savings.

And imagine if the researchers managed to apply the concept to synthetic fibers, as well; they could also solve the problem of microplastics.

The smart technology was among the finalists of the INDEX – Design to Improve Life Award, but eventually lost to the world's first commercial drone delivery system designed to drop off critical medical supplies such as blood and vaccines in remote areas.

Fabrics not only can clean what's on them, but also what is around them. Kassim, a Pakistani denim mill, developed a denim that can eliminate air pollution by using natural sunlight. The fabric, dubbed "The Invisible," is coated with nanocomposites that can bind air particles; it scooped the HighTex Award at the Munich Fabric Start in 2017.

"When you are walking down the street, the sun is out, and air hits the surface of the denim, it eliminates the pollution right away," says Ahmed Quasim, head of branding at Kassim, who noted that the mill is currently testing how much of the toxins swirling around a pair of jeans can actually be eliminated. "We are basically filling the room with air pollution, sending people in there and measuring the level of pollution before and after." The difference such jeans could make would be significant, considering that "7 million people died because of air pollution in 2016 compared to 6 million who died of smoking," says Quasim, adding: "When you live in a city like Paris you lose 6 months of your life expectancy every year."

Some bio-engineers advocate the idea of genetically manipulating and mass-planting trees that could absorb large quantities of carbon dioxide – perhaps jeans could do the trick instead?

The next step will be to connect living systems with non-living materials, which is something MIT is after. Once again, mimicking nature, where plants are known for their self-healing powers, the researchers coaxed *E. coli* bacteria to build bio-films that could be modified to capture non-organic surfaces. The bacteria were engineered in a way so that they were able to communicate with each other and self-assemble. This could be the starting formula for smart, self-repairing fabrics, MIT says.[11]

Microbes in general can be used to grow new materials in the lab. Bacteria, yeast, fungi and algae can already produce bacterial cellulose through fermentation in a vat of liquid. Having started a small project called Biocouture in her London studio, Suzanne Lee produced an astonishingly handsome array of garments, including bomber jackets, wedged shoes and laser-cut skirts – all out of bacteria. They looked deceivingly like leather, a concept Lee is pushing further as now chief creative officer with Modern Meadow Inc., a US biofabrication company. Lee thinks that not only could living organisms make materials and then die, so that the material exists like any other, but also that in the future the material itself would be alive while it's on you, creating a direct relationship to your body and "perhaps diagnosing and treating, nourishing in some way the body surface so becoming part of your wellbeing."[12]

For denim specifically, Lee has other ideas. Two technologies already in practice could truly revolutionize denim as a fabric, and thus its performance, she says. One is the work of Israeli scientist Oded Shoseyov, who is looking at a natural protein that enables cat fleas to jump 100 times their height. That's "the equivalent of a person standing in the middle of Liberty Island in New York, and in a single jump, going to the top of the Statue of Liberty," says Shoseyov.[13] The protein is called resilin and is billed as the most elastic rubber in the world. After finally catching a flea, the team managed to clone it into a less-jumpy organism like a plant. Shoseyov and his team are engineering it for the use in the biomedical field. Lee says: "It's a naturally stretchy substance. It is possible to imagine a stretch, natural protein material based on resilin, though it's still very much science fiction for fashion." In any case, Shoseyov already found a way to produce it from plants, though still at an extremely high cost, which for now is only acceptable in the biomedical field, where there is a market for it. "Now imagine," says Lee,

> having spider silk jeans mixed with stretch from resilin. Maybe a company like Bolt Threads could even engineer resilin and mix it with its fiber, so that it's part silk, part resilin. That's how I imagine the future: fashion meets bio-tech. When you mix properties of one natural protein with another natural protein – that's where it becomes really cool.

With profound societal and lifestyle changes coming our way, the one question that remains is: If by mid-century "we should all be living in a mixture of real and virtual reality," as Kaku predicts, will we still care about the exact shade of our blue jeans? And since we will be spending half of our time in the virtual world, where we can wear what we want without depleting any natural resources other than the energy needed to operate a computer, which by then will be run by renewable energies, will we still want to horde more and more clothing in our closets instead of living the dream online, where we will chat with friends about fashion and present our impeccable selves to colleagues via virtual imagery? Clothes, after all, get boring after a while. So why not change them often in the virtual space and stick to a set of essentials that are meant to last in the real world – both aesthetically and physically?

Dio Kurazawa's guess is that we will still buy fabric, but PFD, or prepared for dyeing, which basically means blank.

> I think it will be like a screen. We will definitely program our lives and our physical appearance through our mobile devices. We will be walking down the street looking at the world through our sunglasses or contact lenses and see what we programed to see. But it might take a while, because everyone would have to be on the same page, so that no one thinks you're crazy walking around in off-white.

If robotic expert systems will indeed be part of our daily lives by mid-century, they could perhaps help us put together a pair of jeans in our own four walls via the expertise and knowledge encoded in them through A.I. technology. Steve Zades argues that some of these databases are coming faster than you think, at least on an industrial level.

Q&A STEVE ZADES, GLOBAL VICE PRESIDENT OF TRANSFORMATIONAL INNOVATION VF CORP

Q: How can A.I. be useful to denim?

A: Think of the A.I. as a whole team of designers and scientists who are hugely knowledgeable about the fiber, yarn and its properties, and sensitive to what you are trying to achieve. Let's say, you want to make your denim super light-weight, breathable, but really durable. Many of these things are contradictory, but the A.I. and designer can work together. The A.I. will suggest possibilities for new designs that will go directly to the factory and be ready to be made.

The A.I. will suggest [the] right percentage of the components, the degree of sustainability and renewability you want to hit, and where to source it. Let's say that you have discovered kapok and its properties, and I can make that for you very efficiently, with the flares that you like or a boyfriend cut and a particular wash. That will become your favorite pair of jeans and if that is your favorite pair of jeans, you will be very loyal to it, and you will tell that story to your friends, you will wear it more than any other jeans.

And you won't need to make a billion of yards of a fabric any more. Now warehouses are full of unwanted inventory which goes to T.J.Maxx or some other discounter, which is the way most of the industry works. With A.I. and designers coming together, it will be about smart customization.

Q: How quickly is this coming our way?

A: The technology to build up these databases is coming really fast.

One of the other reasons why some of the stuff I'm describing used to be really hard and therefore expensive is computing power. Now we can plug and play. Ten years ago, this stuff we are talking about was impossible. The industry was in a status quo. But in the last five years the technology in apparel has exploded, and it is moving at an exponential rate. Once Gen Z, which is a generation of makers gets hold of these technologies, it's unbelievable what is going to happen. Maybe everybody wearing jeans in the city will purify the diesel. Why not? The possibilities are very good.

Q: What advice do you have for denim brands?

A: We need companies that are willing to take risks and pioneer these new spaces that are unknown. I'm one of the lucky ones, our CEO is keenly interested in what we are doing. In the next five years you should be seeing the future of denim on the shelf. And I want to be the first to bring them to the market. Example stretch: consumers love stretch. If you are shopping at high street you will be hard-pressed to find anything without stretch, so if you could find more sustainable ways to make stretch you would have a real breakthrough.

Q: You head up the cognitive sciences and design lab for VF Corp. What else can you do?

A: The area that I head up is called transformational innovation. There is vision science, evolutionary psychology, multisensory cognition and artificial intelligence. Thanks to vision science we have created Body Optix for Lee Jeans. That's a line of figure-enhancing looks where we place flattering patterns on the denim that are derived from an algorithm.

Evolutionary psychology has to do with the science of attraction, so why are we attracted to what we are attracted to? Sometimes we don't even know why, it's viscerally hardwired. Multisensory cognition is a huge field now, especially for companies like ours that have a lot of stores, and stores are like theaters – you have to consider why we even go there when the stores can come to you. It has to do with the sense of vision, with smells, touch, hearing, and how they work together, this creates a multisensory presentation to you. When it's congruent it will stick, you will remember. When it is incongruent, which is what most retail is these, senses cancel each other out and it just becomes clutter.

New is artificial intelligence, machine learning, predictive analytics and algorithms. It may sound a little out there, but this kind of science is teaching robots to see and cars to drive and computers to think like humans. That's interesting for us, because we have a lot of insight into behaviour and data and analytics. We can do a much better job serving our consumers.

Q: Any ideas on how to make sustainability sexy in the future?

A: The barriers to sustainability that were there before are disappearing. The world is changing around the consumer. Look at Tesla. Pretty much all you are hearing about these days is electric cars, particularly in big cities, which are banning diesel. Everywhere you turn, consumers are seeing sustainability in sexy forms. So maybe the average person didn't think he would be driving a lithium battery car. Well, now they probably will and probably a lot faster. So my guess is, when you see sustainability everywhere around you except in one category, you will start to wonder why not?

Q: Where do you see the future of denim?

A: Let's talk about the tyranny of buying denim – you have to pick out an x number of pairs, you go to the dressing room and 9 out of 10 don't fit. And then you walk away thinking: "It's me." And that's not right. In the future the A.I. will know you – it will know what you like, it will know your body, your physical and emotional state. And that tyranny will be over. And when a new finish is delivered, you will find out about it instantly. The blending of synthetics that bring technical capability such as cooling, warming, wicking, protection of all sorts, will create a fortress around you. When you are on the subway you won't have to worry about germs, denim will protect you in the urban environment. Historically, it has been about protection in the rural environment, but the future is urban. So I think denim is going to be dynamic – who knows, maybe you will only have one pair and that pair will adapt to the heat and the cold, maybe you will throw it in the dryer and it will change color. More and more you see different characteristics being applied through the dryer. P&G are working on it – it's still experimental but yeah, you will be able to say: "Oh it's raining today, let me add a layer of rain protection." My idea is you are going to love the denim of the future, you will love shopping for it, and love wearing it, because all of the things that are holding you back today, are being solved.

Notes

1 Kaku, Michio. *Physics of The Future: The Inventions That Will Transform Our Lives.* London: Penguin, 2012, p. 214.
2 Ibid., p. 137.
3 Ibid., p. 181.
4 Ibid., p. 275.
5 Ibid., p. 24.
6 *The Internet of Clothes.* https://netofclothes.com/
7 Woolam Cotton Gin Certified as First U.S. Organic Textile Processor Utilizing Applied DNA Organic Cotton Traceability System. *Applied DNA Sciences*, August 24, 2017. http://adnas.com/2017/08/24/woolam-cotton-gin-certified-first-u-s-organic-textile-processor-utilizing-applied-dna-organic-cotton-traceability-system/
8 DiPietro, Ben. Q&A with Sourcemap CEO [Wall Street Journal Risk & Compliance Report]. *Sourcemap*, December 12, 2014. http://www.sourcemap.com/blog/qa-leonardo-bonanni-ceo-sourcemap-wall-street-journal-risk-and-compliance-report
9 Collison, Charlene, Gazibara, Ivana, Schubert, Alexa & Goodman, James. *Cotton 2040: The Scenarios.* Forum for the Future, n.d. https://www.forumforthefuture.org/sites/default/files/Cotton%202040%20The%20Scenarios.pdf
10 Kaszubska, Gosia. *No more washing: nano-enhanced textiles clean themselves with light.* RMIT News. April 1, 2016. www.rmit.edu.au/news/all-news/2016/april/nanoenhanced-textiles-clean-themselves-with-light
11 Trafton, Anne. Engineers Design "Living Materials." *MIT News*, March 23, 2014.
12 Fairs, Marcus. Microbes Are the "Factories of the Future." *Dezeen*, February 14, 2014.
13 Shoseyov.

CONCLUSION

Sustainable fashion does not mean the end of fashion. It means opportunities for businesses, designers and consumers. It will transform the current system as we know it, but it will also clean the air – literally and figuratively – in an industry that is suffocating under its own weight.

The new code to work by is simple.

Consumers, consume smarter. It doesn't mean that you need to stop wearing denim. On the contrary, quality jeans are among the most durable garments in our everyday wardrobes. And durability equals sustainability. But we own too much, and what we own we know doesn't always fit, causing dissatisfaction. Consuming smarter means buying less, but buying better. We live in an era of fast communication and ruthless information. Tracking denim that is both green and gorgeous should be our goal.

Brands and retailers, innovate. Fashion is about change: The Industrial Revolution, which took us out of the manufacturing Dark Ages but brought us overconsumption, started with textiles. There is no reason why apparel can't be once again at the forefront of another revolution: the green revolution. Sustainability has the ability to bring new jobs, new business opportunities and new types of raw materials that would not only save costs but create new revenue through novelty. We know sustainability requires initial investment, but it can and will pay for itself in the long run. What it takes is will.

Designers, play. Creativity is fashion's greatest gift to society. More than ever, sustainability is in need of creative solutions that will make it look cool and desirable – surely this is something fashion can manage.

We are looking at a strange proliferation of fashion. New brands are sprouting from the ground like mushrooms, and the young designers they are helmed by beam with enthusiasm. They are rigorous in designing mood boards and describing the inspirations behind their collections. But instead of looking to the future, almost exclusively these young creatives are looking to the past for styling influences, quoting Coco Chanel or Yves Saint Laurent as their heroes. The reason why everybody remembers these icons' names is because they were directional and in touch with the zeitgeist. They changed the course of fashion by picking up on the societal changes going on around them. "Chanel gave women freedom. Yves Saint Laurent gave them power,"[1] Pierre Bergé, the latter's business and life partner, once noted. Today, the lines between the sexes are getting blurry. Yes, more work remains to be done for true gender equality to become reality, but the world of today is facing a new challenge, and that's the relentless overconsumption we have engaged in while exhausting the planet.

If you desire to be the next Coco Chanel or Yves Saint Laurent, this is where you start.

Finally, as fashion media, we should celebrate design that is responsible and support those designers that work to make it happen, instead of judging fashion based on purely aesthetic criteria.

Clothes are not just clothes anymore.

Note

1 Groves, Ellen. *Year in Fashion : Au Revoir Yves*. WWD, December 15, 2008. http://wwd.com/fashion-news/designer-luxury/au-revoir-yves-1892770/

INDEX